THE
ESSENTIAL
WOODTURNER

Classic Projects & Smart Techniques
Every Turner Needs to Know

Publisher: Paul McGahren
Editorial Director: Matthew Teague
Editor: Tim Snyder
Design: Lindsay Hess
Layout: Michael Douglas
Book Editor: Kerri Grzybicki

Spring House Press
3613 Brush Hill Court
Nashville, TN 37216

ISBN: 978-1-940611-47-1
Library of Congress Control Number: 2016955203
Printed in the United States of America
First Printing: July 2017

The information in this book is presented in good faith; however, no
warranty is given, nor are results guaranteed. Woodworking is inherently
dangerous. Your safety is your responsibility. Neither Spring House Press
nor the author assume any responsibility for any injuries or accidents.

The following list contains names used in *The Essential Woodturner*
that may be registered with the United States Copyright Office:
3M (8884 Stretchable Tape); Anchorseal; Beall; Behlen Master Woodturner's
Finish; Berkshire Traveller Press; BioShield Stain/Finish; Boos Block
Board Cream; Briwax; Crown Tools Skewchigouge; Deft Clear Wood
Finish; Delta; DeWalt; Easy Wood Tools (ci2; ci3; Detailer; Rougher; R2);
eBay; Forrest Woodworker I; General Finishes (Salad Bowl Finish; Water-
Based Wood Turner's Finish); HUT (Crystal Coat; Gloss Wax; Satin Wax;
Ultra Gloss Plastic); Jet; Loctite; Micro-Mesh; Milescraft; Mirka Abranet;
Mylands High Build Friction Polish; National Institute for Occupational
Safety and Health; Old Masters; Oneway (Stronghold; Termite); Plasti Dip;
Robert Sorby Spiraling/Texturing Tool; Satellite; *Shop Drawings of Shaker
Furniture: Volume 1;* SpectraPly; Stick Fast CA Wood Finishing Kit; System
Three Quick Cure 5; Teknatool SUPERNOVA²; Titebond (III; Instant Bond);
TruStone; United States Croquet Association; WATCO (Butcher Block Oil;
Danish Oil); Waterlox; Whiteside; Williams-Sonoma; WoodRiver

To learn more about Spring House Press books, or to find
a retailer near you, email info@springhousepress.com
or visit us at: www.springhousepress.com.

THE
ESSENTIAL
WOODTURNER

Classic Projects & Smart Techniques
Every Turner Needs to Know

EDITED BY
TIM SNYDER

SPRING HOUSE PRESS

CONTENTS

Small Projects & Gifts

PAGE 24

Bowls

PAGE 50

Furniture & Home

PAGE 90

Kitchen

Sports & Outdoors

Tools & Shop

PEN TURNING 101

An overview of the right tools, materials, and techniques

BY JOE HURST-WAJSZCZUK

In this day of text-messaging and emails, one might assume that handwritten notes are a thing of the past, yet custom pens are more popular than ever, and they're super easy to make. With a lathe, a few scraps of wood, and a pen kit, any woodworker possessing basic turning skills can create a writing implement that's useful and unique. With a little practice, you'll soon be turning out pens in less time than it takes to read this article.

In the next few pages, I'll show you what you'll need to get started, walk you through the pen-making process, and then suggest a few products that can save time, stock, and frustration for beginner and experienced turners alike.

For this exercise, I used an attractive, inexpensive, and easy-to-turn olivewood blank. I paired it with a pen-turning kit designed specifically for ball point pens— you can find several similar options online or at your local woodworking store. The same techniques can be applied to any of the other styles, but you may need to purchase additional drill bits, mills, and bushings to match the kit.

Pen Anatomy

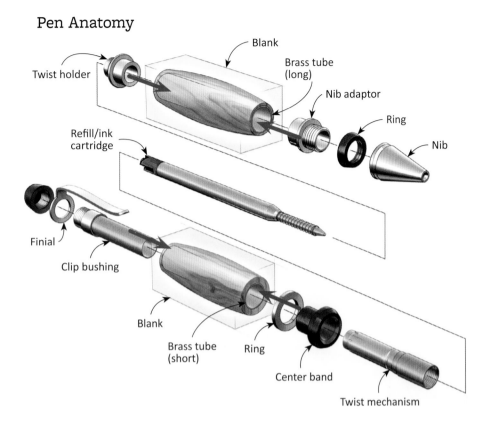

Getting started

As the figure above illustrates, pen turning boils down to turning a cylinder. The body, consisting of one or more blanks, is bored and fitted with a brass cylinder, mounted to a lathe, and then turned, finished, and assembled. A particular pen kit may have more or fewer parts than those shown here. The instructions included with the kit will explain the exact assembly sequence.

Tooling up

Entire catalogs are dedicated to pen-making accessories, but if you own a lathe and a few turning tools, you won't need to spend a lot of money to start. Check your arsenal against the Pen Turner's Start-Up Kit, shown on page 8. A few of these items don't need any introduction; you may have some of them sitting around your shop. A few of the specialty items deserve explanation.

Pen blanks: You can buy ready-made blanks, or saw your own. Advanced turners can make pens out of plastic, metal, and even bone, but when starting out, stick with less-exotic woods that are stable and easier to work, such as cherry, maple, or walnut.

Drill bits: The blanks must be drilled to fit the kit. You can use a good brad-point bit, but pen maker's bits are ground to drill straight, deep holes without clogging. Make sure your bit matches your pen kit. (For the cigar pen, you'll need a 10mm bit.)

Epoxy: You'll need a sure-fire means of attaching the brass to the blank. Epoxy isn't as quick-setting as cyanoacrylate glue (CA), but until you master the art of fitting the tube, you will appreciate a few extra minutes of working time.

Pen mill: This two-part cutter helps ensure easy-to-assemble barrels and gap-free pens. The shaft slides into the

Pen Turner's Start-Up Kit

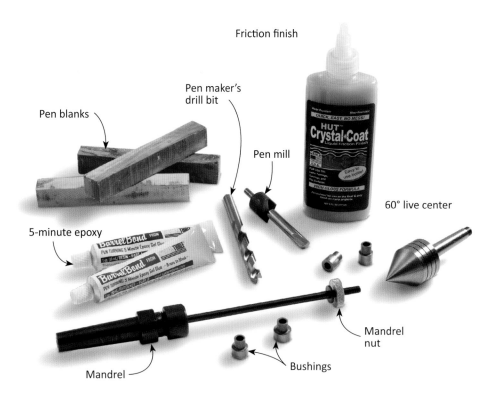

Friction finish

Pen maker's drill bit

Pen blanks

Pen mill

60° live center

5-minute epoxy

Mandrel nut

Mandrel

Bushings

brass tube and cleans the barrel while the trimmer head squares the ends for perfect-fitting parts. (For the cigar pen, you'll need a trimmer with a 10mm shaft.)

Mandrel and live center: These two items partner up to secure the blank to your lathe. Insert the mandrel into the headstock, slide the bushings and blank on the shaft, and then secure the assembly with the mandrel nut. The rod's free end is dimpled to fit the live center at the tailstock. Mandrels and live centers are available with #1 and #2 Morse tapers. Buy the size that fits your lathe.

Bushings: These metal rings are mounted on either end of your blank to provide an indication of when to stop turning. (For this project, you need a bushing set for cigar pens or pencils).

Friction finish. Finish your blank before it leaves the lathe. To create a glass-smooth finish, simply apply, let dry, and then buff.

Pen turning step-by-step

1 Draw a line along one face of your blank, and mark the cap end with an arrow to help you realign the parts. Using measurements from the kit's brass tubes, cut your blanks to rough length (about ⅛″ longer than the tubes).

Next, draw a pair of intersecting lines on the ends of both blanks from corner to corner to determine the center points. Check that your drill press table is perpendicular to the chuck, hold the blank in the clamp as shown, and drill completely through each blank. (To ensure that the blanks line up at the middle of the finished pen, start the holes from the inside ends.)

2 Scuff-sand the brass barrels with fine-grit sandpaper. Mix a small batch of 5-minute epoxy, and then coat the outside of the brass tube. To ensure good glue coverage, rotate the tube as you insert it into the blank. Make

Pen Turning Step-by-Step

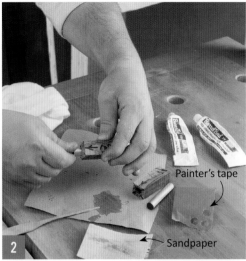

Painter's tape

Sandpaper

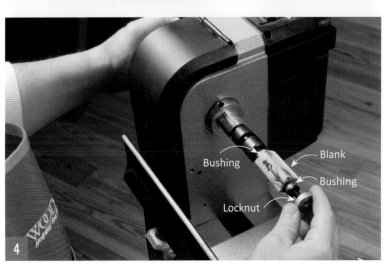

Bushing

Blank

Bushing

Locknut

sure that it fits completely in the blank. (To keep glue from clogging the tube, plug the end with a piece of painter's tape.)

3 After giving the epoxy time to cure, square both ends of both blanks. To do this, chuck a pen mill in a cordless drill. Secure the blank in a bench vise; then slide the shaft into the brass tube and trim any overhanging wood from the end of the brass tube. (The object is to touch—but not cut into—the tube. If you listen carefully, you'll hear when the trimmer touches the brass.)

4 Insert the mandrel into the headstock, and then sandwich the blank between two bushings, as shown. Secure the assembly with the locknut. Finally, slide the tailstock and live center against the mandrel's free end.

5 Adjust your tool rest parallel and as close as possible to your work. Rotate the blank by hand to make sure that it does not touch. Now set the lathe to 1,000 rpm, and round the blank with a roughing gouge. To do this, place the gouge perpendicular to the rest, touch the bevel against spinning blank, and then raise the handle until the tool starts to

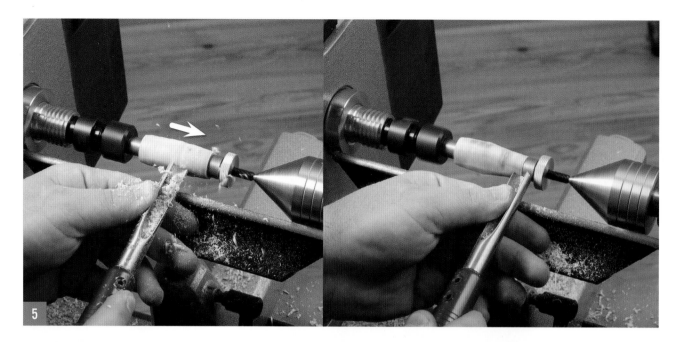

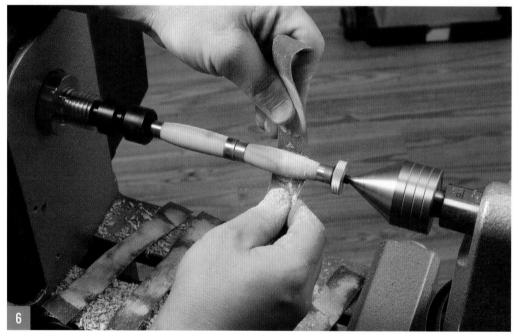

cut. Rotate the handle so that the flute faces in the direction of your cut.

Once you've turned a smooth cylinder, set the lathe to 1,500 to 2,000 rpm and continue shaping the blank. You have some leeway here, but be careful not to cut into the bushing or brass tubes. (Leave the ends of the blanks a hair larger than the bushings.) Repeat the turning process with the second blank.

6 Paying attention to the grain orientation of the finished pen, arrange both blanks onto the mandrel. Remove the tool rest and set the speed to 500 rpm. Starting with small strips of 150-grit sandpaper, remove tool marks and shape the ends of the blanks flush to the adjacent bushings. Continue sanding both blanks through 600 grit. (Pinch the strips of sandpaper, as shown, so that if the abrasive catches the work,

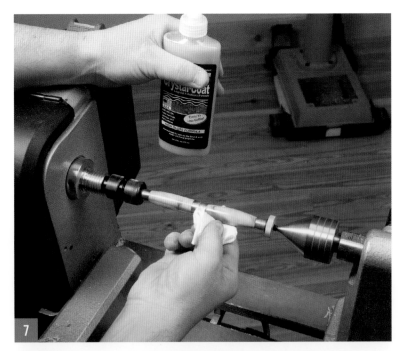

the paper will slip from your grip without pulling your fingers in.)

7 Turn the lathe off and apply a small amount of finish to a small piece of cloth or paper towel. Spread the polish onto the barrels. Now turn on the lathe and adjust the speed to 1,000 rpm. Working from beneath, apply even pressure with the still-damp pad. Move the applicator from side to side until the solvent evaporates and the surface begins to build a finish. Apply additional coats until you achieve the desired sheen.

8 Inspect the brass tubes to make certain that they're free from any clogs that might prevent assembly. Arrange the rings and bands as shown in the figure on page 7, or according to the instructions included with your kit. Now assemble your pen. To prevent cracks or splits when pressing parts together, apply smooth, steady pressure. (If using a metal-faced vise, attach wood or MDF pads to both faces to protect the pen's metal parts.)

Useful pen-making tools

As your hobby progresses from pastime to passion (or profession), you'll want to consider a few items that can help turn pen-making pains into pleasure. I've arranged the list in order of importance. Start with the ones at the beginning; save up for a few at the end.

Pen maker's bits

Don't run the risk of ruining blanks with run-of-the-mill bits. These specialized drill bits sport sharp points to cut quickly and accurately and deep flutes to clear chips. The six-piece set provides ample opportunity to experiment with different pen kits.

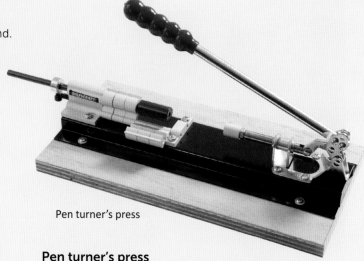

Pen turner's press

Pen maker's
bit set

Pen turner's press

Have a pen slip in the vise, or the wood split because the one part isn't perfectly square with its mate, and you'll appreciate the value of a dedicated press. The spring-loaded self-feeding mandrel holds the pen parts in place while the solid steel head provides the leverage needed to smoothly assemble pen after pen.

Pen mill set

The two-piece mill trims and cleans barrels, ensuring gap-free assemblies. You can buy the shafts individually, but if you plan on making a few different kinds of pens, it makes sense (and cents) to invest in the multi-shaft set right from the start.

Self-centering vise

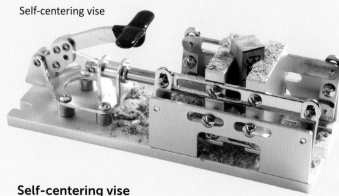

Pen mill set

Self-centering vise

A self-centering vise makes blank drilling a set-and-forget operation and eliminates the risk of blowing a bit out one side of your blank. The V-slotted jaws provide a solid grip on round and square blanks. In addition to pens, the vise proves useful for turning bottle stoppers, key chains, perfume vials, and more.

Carbide turning tools

Advanced turners step up to carbide-tipped tools because they require less sharpening, but many beginners start with them because they're easier to master. To use, simply advance the cutter slowly into the workpiece, and then sweep the tool from side to side.

Contrary to its name, the round-headed mini finisher is also well suited for rounding square blanks and general shaping. Equipped with the radiused R2 cutter (shown), the mini rougher tool is actually useful for finishing the blank right up to the edge of the bushing.

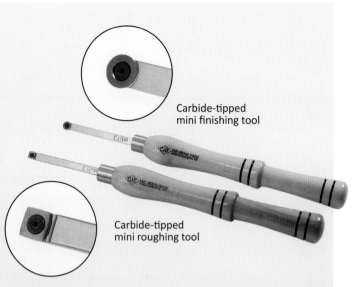

Carbide-tipped mini finishing tool

Carbide-tipped mini roughing tool

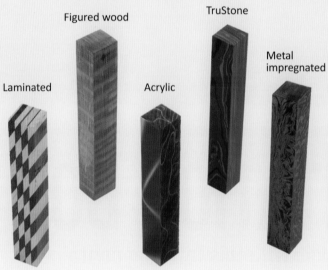

Figured wood

TruStone

Metal impregnated

Laminated

Acrylic

Better blanks

Exotic blanks offer experienced turners opportunities to try new materials that will produce one-of-a-kind pens and also test their technique. Laminated and figured woods require sharp tools and a light touch. Acrylic blanks come in countless color combinations and can be polished without finish. (Note: Composite materials containing stone or metal will make mincemeat of high-speed steel. You'll want to step up to carbide cutters.)

Finishes

Wax bars are great for beginners because they're simple to use and solvent-free. Simply press the stick against the spinning pen to polish out small scratches while melting material onto the wood to create a durable finish. Acrylic blanks don't require a finish, but you'll need super-fine abrasive papers and a plastic polish to build a shine. Experienced turners often use CA glue as pen finish. Apply a few drops to a paper towel, wipe down the blank, allow the glue to cure, and then buff.

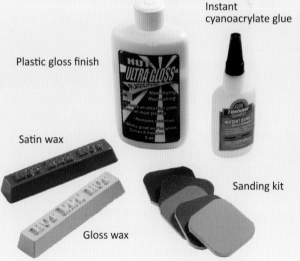

Instant cyanoacrylate glue

Plastic gloss finish

Satin wax

Sanding kit

Gloss wax

Overall Dimension: 7⅛"w × 1½"d × 1¼"h

PEN PRESENTATION BOX

Elevate the turned pens you give away with this fetching container

BY MARLEN KEMMET

A finely crafted turned pen deserves an equally impressive presentation box. This easy-to-build scrap project requires minimal stock but yields spectacular results. The key is to use a ⅝" core box bit and a pair of stops at the router table to form the pen-holding coves. For thick pens or those longer than 5½", see the note in figure 1 to make any needed adjustment.

Start with the box blank

1 Mill and cut a piece of straight-grained stock to 1⅜ × 1½ × 7¾".

(For safety when routing the coves, we started with a blank 1" extra in length. You'll crosscut it to final length after routing the coves.) Now, resaw a ¾"-thick piece from the blank for the box bottom (A) so that the grain in the box top (B) and bottom match nicely.

2 Fit your table-mounted router with a ⅝"-diameter core box bit. Raise it to full height. Position the back fence ⁷⁄₁₆" from the bit's cutter. Clamp a pair of stops on the fence at 3⁹⁄₁₆" from the bit's cutter with one on each side of the bit. The goal is to

End View

Figure 1: Pen Box Exploded View

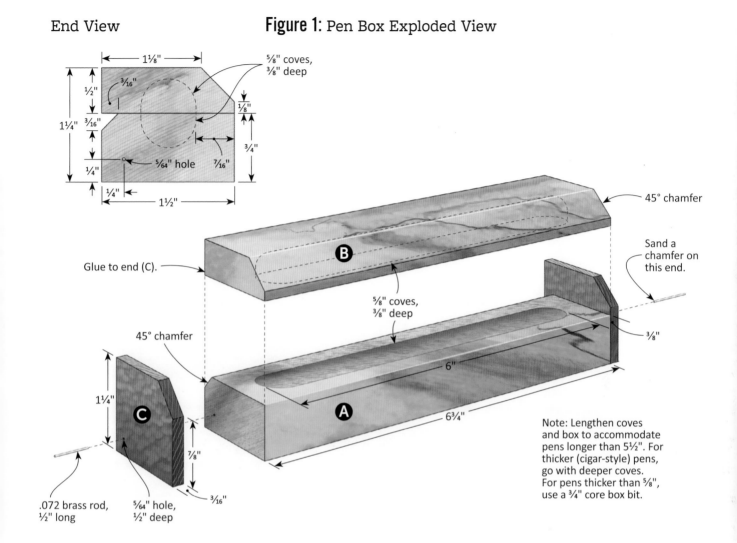

End View labels:
- 1⅛"
- ³⁄₁₆"
- ½"
- 1¼"
- ³⁄₁₆"
- ¼"
- ⅛"
- ¾"
- ⁷⁄₁₆"
- ⅝" coves, ⅜" deep
- ⁵⁄₆₄" hole
- ¼"
- 1½"

Exploded view labels:
- 45° chamfer
- Sand a chamfer on this end.
- ⅜"
- **B**
- Glue to end (C).
- ⅝" coves, ⅜" deep
- 45° chamfer
- 6"
- **A**
- 6¾"
- 1¼"
- **C**
- ⁷⁄₈"
- ³⁄₁₆"
- .072 brass rod, ½" long
- ⁵⁄₆₄" hole, ½" deep

Note: Lengthen coves and box to accommodate pens longer than 5½". For thicker (cigar-style) pens, go with deeper coves. For pens thicker than ⅝", use a ¾" core box bit.

A

Lower the workpiece onto the bit with a pullstick; use a pushstick or pushpad to advance it to the left-hand stop. After making the cut, stop the router and raise the workpiece with the pullstick.

cut identical coves in the bottom (A) and top (B). Clamp on a second fence to the table, making it parallel to the table fence. Its function is to keep the blanks over the bit and guarantee straight cove cuts. Allow just enough clearance to slide the blanks between the fences. Mark an "X" on one edge of each blank. For perfectly aligned coves in the bottom and top, keep the marked edge against the table fence for each pass. Lower the bit height to ¹⁄₁₆".

3 Rout mating ⅜"-deep coves in the box bottom (A) and top (B), raising the bit in ¹⁄₁₆" increments in hard woods or ⅛"

B

Use a pushblock to move the taped-together bottom and top pieces along the fence and through the blade.

increments in softer woods. Start with a blank against the right-hand stop. Then, lower the left end onto the spinning bit using a notched pullstick. Move the blank to the left, switching to a shoe-style pushstick or pushpad to apply downward pressure. Turn off the router after each pass and allow the bit to stop before lifting the blank with the pullstick from the router table, as shown in photo A.

4 Rip a chamfer along the back edge of the bottom (A), where shown in figure 1, end view. The chamfer creates clearance, allowing the top (B) to open and close.

5 Adhere the bottom (A) and top (B) together with double-faced tape. Rip a 45° chamfer across the top front edge of the box top, where shown in figure 1 and as shown in photo B. Clamp a stopblock in a mitersaw extension fence, and cut exactly ½" from each end of the assembly. Do not separate the pieces at this time.

6 Mill and plane a 12"-long piece of contrasting stock to ³⁄₁₆" thick. From it, cut a pair of slightly oversized ends (C) to the shape in figure 1. Tape them to the ends of the taped-together bottom (A) and top (B), making them flush with the back and bottom of the assembly.

7 Carefully mark and lightly indent the hole center points on each end of the taped-together assembly, where shown in figure 1. (Note: For a smooth opening and closing action, the holes must be perfectly aligned

C

Drill the hinge-pin holes in the ends of the taped-together box assembly, using a simple right-angle jig.

from end to end. The indentations keep the bit from wandering when drilling the hinge-pin holes.)

8 Using a right-angle jig on your drill press for alignment and the depth stop on your drill press, drill a $\frac{5}{64}$" hole $\frac{1}{2}$" deep through both ends (C) and into the bottom corners of the box, as shown in photo C. Remove all of the tape from the box assembly.

9 From a length of .072 solid brass rod, crosscut two pieces to $\frac{1}{2}$" long using a hacksaw. Sand a chamfer on one end of each piece for easier insertion through the ends (C) and into the box bottom (A). (I bought the brass rod at a local hobby store.)

10 Finish-sand the box bottom (A), top (B), and ends (C). Trim $\frac{1}{32}$" off one end of the box bottom so that the lid assembly (B/C) doesn't bind. Glue the ends to the box top only, wiping off any excess glue with a damp cloth. Let dry.

11 Tap the brass rods through the end pieces and just far enough into the box bottom to check the fit. Sand the proud edges of the ends (C) flush with the bottom (A) and top (B). Pull the pins and do any final sanding. Add finish to the disassembled box bottom (A) and lid assembly (B/C). (I used a wiping oil, but spray lacquer would also work.)

12 Fit the parts together, lightly tapping the brass pins in place with a small hammer to hinge the box lid assembly (B/C) to the bottom (A). The pins should be flush with the outside faces of the box ends (C). Sand, if necessary, and refinish.

Approximate overall dimensions: 2½" dia. × 4¼" h

SPIRAL TURNED BOX

A simple container with a twist

BY CHRIS POUNCY

It's not surprising that turners enjoy making wooden boxes just as much as people appreciate receiving them. This gem of a box can be used to package another gift, such as a piece of jewelry, or as a gift by itself. In addition, it's easy to make, letting you transform a few special pieces of scrap into a prized possession.

You'll find several turning lessons with this little box. First, you'll learn how to hollow end grain and form a lid that fits the container's base. You'll also find a primer in using the Robert Sorby Spiraling/Texturing Tool, a unique turning tool that adds

twists to bowls, hollow forms, and platters quickly and easily. The system includes an additional texturing cutter that can create striations, whorls, orange peel, and still other textures, but here we'll stick with spirals.

Note: For the cleanest spirals, select a tight-grained wood. For this example, I chose purpleheart, but maple and cherry are also good choices. Be sure to use a well-seasoned blank; otherwise future dimensional changes may result in a lid that doesn't fit the base.

Tool: ¾" roughing gouge
Speed: 1,500 rpm

Tool: ⅜" beading and parting tool
Speed: 1,800 rpm

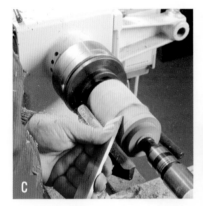

Tool: ¾" skew
Speed: 1,800 rpm

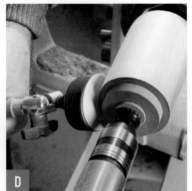

Tool: Rotary sander
Speed: 1,800 rpm

Figure 1:
Spiral Box Profile

⅜" rabbet,
⅜" deep

1¼" R

1¾"

1⅛"

⅜"

¼"

¼"

⅛"

2½"

Note: Except for the
lid dimensions, overall
dimensions for this box
are approximate.

Prepare the blank

1 Mount the 3 × 5″ blank between your headstock and tail centers. Set the tool rest just above the blank's centerline and clear of the spinning corners. Set the lathe to 1,500 rpm and then round the blank using a ¾″ roughing gouge. Work from the center towards the ends (photo A) rolling the gouge in the direction of the cut, so the wood doesn't catch the tool's top edge.

2 Adjust the tool rest close to the tailstock and set the speed at 1,800 rpm. Using a beading and parting tool, turn a ⅜″-long tenon (roughly the width of the tool) to fit your scroll chuck, as shown in photo B.

3 Adjust the rest slightly above the centerline of your blank and smooth the cylinder with a skew. Here, rest the tool's bevel against the blank with the skew's long end pointed up and move it across the surface as shown in photo C. Don't push the tool; just let the cutting edge slice the wood.

4 In order to maintain the crispness of the spiral beads, now's the time to finish-sand the cylinder. Using a rotary sander as shown in photo D, finish-sand the cylinder starting with 120 grit and working up to 400 grit.

Tool: Spiraling tool
Speed: 400 rpm

Do the twist

1 Adjust the lathe's tool rest so that when the spiraling tool is positioned horizontally on the rest, the cutter's bottom edge is level with the centerline of your work.

2 Set the lathe speed to 400 rpm. Next, hold the spiral cutter at a slight downward angle against the rest, and lightly press it against the blank until the cutter begins to spin. (Note: For right-hand spirals, start on the left side of the blank; for left-hand spirals, start on the right.)

3 Slowly raise the cutter, so that the top edges of the teeth engage the work at centerline height (photo E).

Don't move the cutter on the rest just yet. Simply hold it against the workpiece to create a few reference grooves. You'll use these grooves every time you set the spiraling tool on the work.

4 After stopping the lathe to inspect your grooves, turn the lathe on and reposition the cutter into the reference grooves. At this point the wheel is spinning, but not cutting. To start spiraling, raise the handle so that the top edge of the wheel begins to cut, and slowly feed the tool in the direction of the higher edge of the tilted head as shown in photo F.

After the cutter's first pass, the spiral may not be to full depth. If you like the look, stop here. For more texture, simply reference the cutter against the starting grooves and make another pass.

QUICK TIP

Regular sanding tends to over soften the turned spirals, but you can use a bronze bristle brush to remove loose fibers and to lightly burnish the surface.

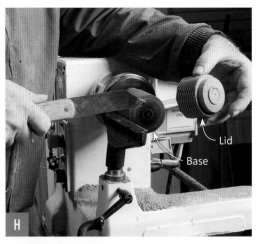

Tool: Thin-kerf parting tool
Speed: 1,500 rpm

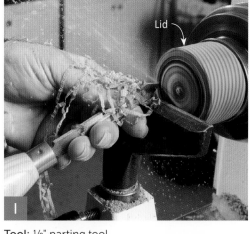

Tool: ⅛" parting tool
Speed: 1,700 rpm

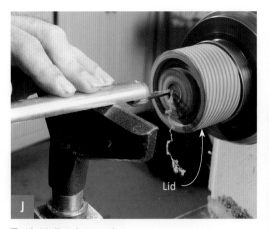

Tool: Hollowing tool
Speed: 1,700 rpm

5 With a pencil, lay out the lid at one end of the blank making it about 2″ long (photo G).

6 Adjust the lathe speed to 1,500 rpm. Using a thin-kerf parting tool, separate the lid from the base as shown in photo H, or part down to ½″, turn off the lathe, and separate the two with a saw. (The thin kerf helps maintain the continuity of the grain pattern where the lid meets the base.)

Turn the lid and fit the base

1 Mount the lid blank on your scroll chuck using the tenon cut earlier. True the face with a scraper. With a parting tool, make a ¼″-deep flange ¼″ in from the outside edge as shown in photo I and where shown in figure 1. When measuring wall thickness, be

sure to account for the depth of the spiral. Note that the flange should be straight or slightly taper out; if it tapers in, it won't accept the base.

2 With the tool rest set so that the tool sits above the center of the lid, remove the waste from the lid with a hollowing tool. As shown in photo J, ease the tool into the wood so that you get a thin shaving and then pull the tool toward you to gradually widen the cavity.

3 Use a depth gauge to obtain the depth of the cavity and transfer that measurement to the outside of the lid, as shown in photo K. Now part the lid above the line.

4 Mount and true the end of the base blank. Then turn the end to fit the lid. Using a dial

Base

Tool: ⅜" parting tool
Speed: 1,700 rpm

Tool: Hollowing tool
Speed: 1,700 rpm

Tool: ⅜" spindle gouge
Speed: 1,000 rpm

caliper, measure the inside dimension of the lid, and then flip the caliper to transfer the outside dimension to the base. Draw a line on the face of the base piece, as shown in photo L.

5 Adjust your tool rest to the side of your base. Using a parting tool, as shown in photo M, carefully cut through the spiral and up to your pencil line. Take light cuts and check the fit after each cut. Aim for a "suction cup fit"—tight enough to hold the lid in place, but loose enough to pull off. (Note: Tapering the tenon slightly inward will provide a little wiggle room, but still

provide a tight fit when the lid is installed on the base.)

Once you achieve a snug fit, adjust the rest parallel to the end of the base and use the parting tool to create a ⅛"-thick flange.

6 Hollow out the base in steps, as you did with the lid but to a depth of 2⅛" inches, as shown in photo N. (Note: If you have a drill chuck adaptor for your tailstock, you can use a ⅝"-diameter bit to drill out the base to finished depth. Mark the desired depth on the bit with a piece of tape.)

Tool: ¼" round skew
Speed: 1,000 rpm

Tool: ¾" oval skew
Speed: 1,000 rpm

Tool: ⅜" spindle gouge
Speed: 1,000 rpm

Finishing touches

1 Install the lid on the base and reinstall the tailstock. Employ the depth gauge to obtain the depth of the lid's cavity, and mark the location on the outside of your box to make sure that you don't cut into the lid. Now at 1,000 rpm, shape the top of the lid with a spindle gouge as shown in photo O.

2 Using a ¼" round skew chisel, make a shallow V-cut where the lid fits the base as shown in photo P. (This detail will help disguise a gap that may show up as the wood dries out.)

3 Turn off the lathe. Now hand-turn the box and flood its surface with a penetrating finish (photo Q), using a brush. Allow the finish to soak in for 10 to 20 minutes, and then wipe off the excess.

4 Using an oval skew chisel on edge as shown in photo R, remove the nib from the top of the box. Carve off the nib with a penknife, and hand-sand smooth.

5 Wrap the base's flange with masking tape for protection, and then mount the base into your scroll chuck. Using a spindle gouge, make the base slightly concave, carefully working up to the tailstock (photo S). Finally, remove the tailstock, adjust your rest, and trim off the remaining nib with a round skew chisel.

INSIDE-OUT ORNAMENT

Turn a profile into a picture

BY MIKE KEHS

Overall dimensions: 3" dia. × 7¾" high

The world of woodturning can produce some pretty tricky looking projects. Among them are "inside-out" turnings. These spindle-turned pieces feature a hollowed-out interior that's visible through shapely window silhouettes that are created by the edges of the interior profile.

As mystifying as an inside-out turning might appear, it's not all that difficult to make one. Basically, you bundle together four identically sized, squared lengths of stock, and mount them on the lathe between shop-made chucks that hold the unglued pieces tightly together. You then turn the bundle to a specific profile. Afterward, you remove the pieces, orient the turned surfaces inward, and glue the pieces together. This creates the windows that expose the shapely hollowed interior. If you like, you can then remount the assembly on the lathe, and turn the outside of the block to a complementary shape.

Here, I'll show you how to make a simple tree ornament with a turned exterior. Although it's too heavy to hang on a Christmas tree, you can suspend it from a

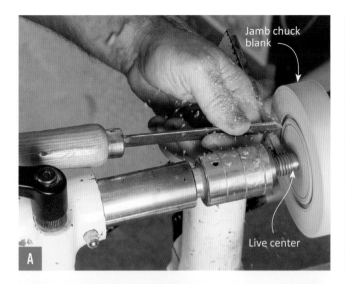

Jamb chuck blank

Live center

Four-jaw chuck

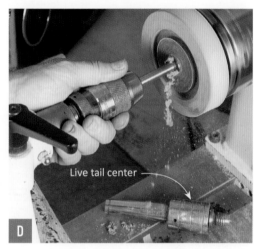

Live tail center

ceiling hook or curtain rod. It also makes a very nice standing table ornament. Just be prepared for someone to ask you, "Say, how did you do that?"

Make the tailstock jamb chuck

1 Turn a 1"-thick piece of MDF to about 5" in diameter. Press this jamb chuck blank between a four-jaw chuck and a live tail center, and turn a ¼"-deep groove that's wide enough to accept the jaws of your four-jaw chuck (photo A). Afterward, reinforce the tenon fibers by dripping thin CA glue onto the shoulders of the tenon.

2 Invert the jamb chuck, inserting the tenon you just turned into your four-jaw chuck. Touch a pencil to the spinning disc to determine its center point, and then use a compass on the stopped disc to lay out a precise 3"-diameter circle (photo B).

3 Turn a ¼"-deep recess within the circle (photo C). Then invert the blank again, mounting it by expanding the chuck jaws outward into the recess you just cut.

4 Drill a recess that will fit snugly onto the rotating section of your live tail center (photo D). This will allow the jamb chuck to remain securely in place on the tailstock when replacing and removing turning blanks.

5 Hold a drafting triangle precisely tangent to the circle's perimeter and lay out the corners for the square recess (photo E). Remount the jamb chuck, and enlarge the

diameter of the existing recess to 3½".
(This minimizes the amount of chiseling
necessary to square the recess.)

Turn the inner profile

1 Dress four pieces of hardwood to
1½" × 1½" × 8". Mount these as an
unglued bundle between your four-jaw
chuck and the jamb chuck you just made,
shimming the walls of the jamb chuck
recess if necessary to ensure a snug fit.

2 Referring to figure 1, lay out the 4"-long
center section to be turned, extending the
lines across two faces so they'll be visible
when spinning (photo F). Also, number
the quadrants of your chucks and turning
blanks for precisely balanced remounting
if necessary.

3 Using a small bowl gouge, round the
section between the layout lines almost to a
cylinder, leaving slight flats at the seams for
now. Taper inward from about 1" outside of
the layout lines to allow better gouge access
for subsequent cuts (photo G).

4 Referring to figure 1, lay out the lower
extent of the top bough by marking ⅝"
down from the layout line at the tailstock
end (photo H).

5 Make a parting cut to the left of your
layout line to turn a 2¾"-diameter groove.
To the right of the groove, part as deeply as
you think you can without cutting into what
will be the adjacent swooped section (see
figure 1, detail). Follow up by shaping the
swooped section of the bough using a ⅜"
spindle gouge with a fingernail grind.

6 Lay out the lower extent of the middle
bough, measuring down 1½" from the top of
the tree profile, where shown in figure 1.

7 Make the parting cut to the left of the
middle bough layout line. The easiest way
to determine its 2½"-diameter is to check

Figure 1: Inner Profile

Cutting Detail

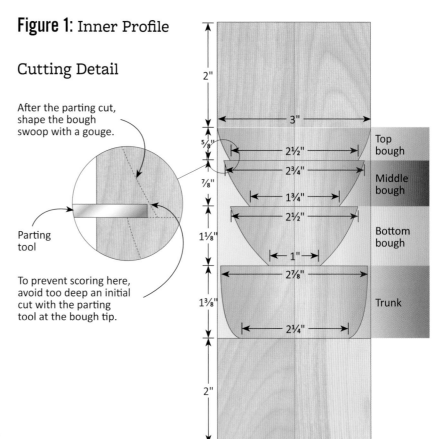

After the parting cut,
shape the bough
swoop with a gouge.

Parting
tool

To prevent scoring here,
avoid too deep an initial
cut with the parting
tool at the bough tip.

2"

3"

⅝" 2½" Top bough

2¾" Middle bough

⅞" 1¾"

2½" Bottom bough

1⅛" 1"

2⅞" Trunk

1⅜"

2¼"

2"

for a ¼″-deep groove, as measured from the seam at the flat unturned section (photo I).

8 Now make the parting cut to the right of the groove (photo J). As before, cut as deeply as possible without endangering what will be the surface of the swooped section to be cut next.

9 Use a ⅜″ spindle gouge with a fingernail grind to shape the swooped section of the bough (photo K).

10 Turn the remaining (bottom) bough and the trunk section in the same manner. Then sand the turned surfaces to 220 grit.

Glue up the blank

1 Dismount the bundle, and glue and clamp the pieces together in pairs to create two halves (photo L). Apply clamp pressure at the seams to perfectly align them. Also, make sure the pieces are flush at the ends.

2 After the glue dries, sand the two inner faces on a disc sander or on a piece of sandpaper fixed to a dead-flat surface. Then, glue the two halves together in the same fashion as before, with the turned profiles oriented toward the inside.

> **QUICK TIP**
>
> The best time to paint or decorate the interior faces (if you wish) is before they're glued together.

Turn the outer profile

1 Mount the blank on the lathe between a cup center on the headstock and a live cup center on the tailstock. Referring to figure 2, mark out the extents of the 1¾″-long squared area at the center (which retains the corners of the block). Carry your lines across two sides so that they will be evident when spinning.

2 Using a ½″ spindle gouge, rough out the upper section of the ornament, making sure to leave a flat area surrounding the entire tree cutout.

3 Mark out the extents of the crown, head, and collar details where shown in figure 1 and use a parting tool to cut just shy of their final diameters.

4 Use a ⅜″ spindle gouge with a fingernail grind to detail the crown and head (photo M). Then, shape the collar (photo N), and finally, the shoulder (photo O).

5 Moving to the lower section, begin by roughing out the ogee using a ½″ spindle gouge with a fingernail grind.

6 Turn the pedestal section to a 2½″-diameter cylinder.

7 Still using the ½″ spindle gouge, go back and finesse the ogee curve, cutting inward from each end downhill to the grain (photo P).

8 On the pedestal section, mark off the individual elements, and then use a parting tool to size them just slightly larger than their final diameters. At the same time, turn away as much as possible of the bottommost ⅛″ waste section to remove the marks left by the live center.

9 Round over the foot with a ⅜″ spindle gouge.

10 Round over the bead (photo Q), and turn the small cove between the bead and the foot, leaving the lower transitional shoulder.

Figure 2: Outer Profile

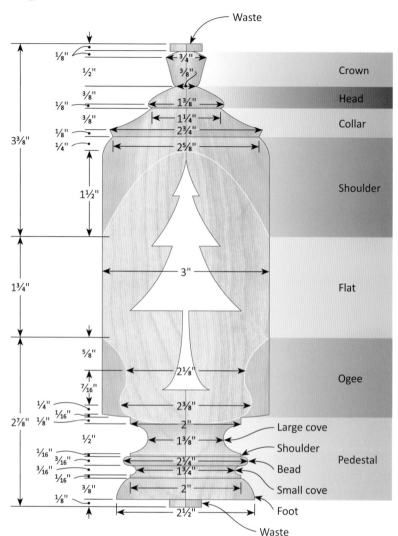

11 Turn the large cove with its small adjacent shoulders (photo R).

12 Use a ⅜″ spindle gouge to turn a shallow recess of about 1/16″ into the underside of the foot for stability.

13 Finally, use a spindle gouge or skew chisel to reduce the waste at the ends to about ⅜″ in diameter to minimize cleanup afterward.

Finishing up

1 Hand-sand through 220 grit, stopping the lathe to smooth the flat sections.

2 Dismount the piece, and cut and sand away the nubs.

3 Apply a finish. I usually brush on oil or spray on an aerosol lacquer or acrylic finish.

LADY'S PURSE MIRROR

Reflect your woodturning talents with these eye-candy creations

WRITTEN BY JIM HARROLD WITH WOODTURNER TOM SCHOTTLE

There's no end to the patterns you can assemble when you glue up contrasting wood scraps into pleasing blanks for these simply turned purse mirrors. They definitely put cheesy plastic compact mirrors to shame. See the "Three Colorful Blank Ideas" sidebar on page XX for glue-up blank considerations, or choose solid stock such as birds-eye or tiger maple, or fanciful exotics such as zebrawood, bocote, lacewood, or wenge.

Though we'll begin with a ¾"-thick blank, for a delicate look you'll want to achieve a final thickness of ⁵⁄₁₆" to ³⁄₈", with a ¼"-wide border around the mirror insert. Now let's get busy.

Note: Our expert, Tom Schottle, can complete a mirror in half an hour. Consider making a batch for quick and easy gift-giving.

Make and mount a glue block

1 Bandsaw a piece of 2"-thick scrap stock to a 2 ½" diameter disc and mount it to your chuck. Turn it down to a 2" diameter and form a tenon sized to fit your chuck as shown in the Glue Block Profile in figure 1. Unscrew the faceplate.

2 Mount your chuck on the lathe and insert the glue block you turned in step 1, tightening the jaws on the tenon. Turn on the lathe and flatten the face of the glue block with a parting tool.

Figure 1

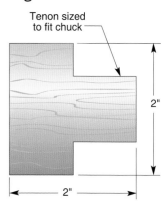

Tenon sized to fit chuck

2"

2"

QUICK TIP

You can make two purse mirrors from 1"-thick stock by resawing the blank into equal halves prior to turning.

Prepare and mount the mirror blank

1 Scribe a 4″ diameter circle on a ¾ x 4 x 4″ or larger glue-up or piece of figured stock as shown in photo A.

2 Bandsaw the mirror blank to size as shown in photo B. Sand the blank flat, then use a compass to mark a centered 2″ circle on one face as shown in photo C.

3 Spread CA (cyanoacrylate gap-filling) glue inside the alignment circle on the face of the mirror blank and spritz the glue block with accelerator. Then, using the alignment circle, center and adhere the mirror blank to the glue block as shown in photo D, holding the piece in place with the tailstock. Let the glue set up a few minutes before proceeding.

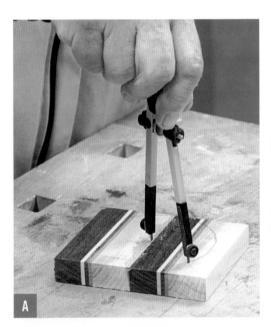

Three Colorful Blank Ideas

Using scrap stock to make exciting glue-ups for mirror blanks equals the fun you'll have turning the blanks. If you don't own a stash of contrasting woods, check out these ideas for guaranteed good looks.

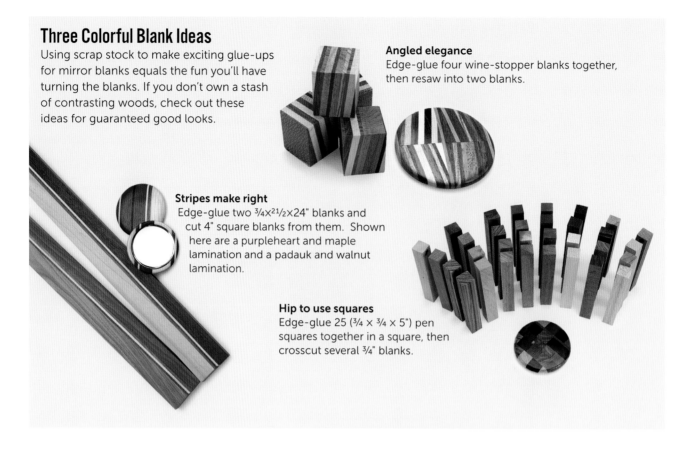

Angled elegance
Edge-glue four wine-stopper blanks together, then resaw into two blanks.

Stripes make right
Edge-glue two ¾x2½x24" blanks and cut 4" square blanks from them. Shown here are a purpleheart and maple lamination and a padauk and walnut lamination.

Hip to use squares
Edge-glue 25 (¾ × ¾ × 5") pen squares together in a square, then crosscut several ¾" blanks.

Turn the mirror blank front and edge

1 Bandsaw or scrollsaw the mirror recess jig in figure 2 from ¼" plywood. Mark the centerline where shown.

2 Using a ¼" gouge and maintaining a comfortable speed (from 750 to 1,000 rpm), rough the mirror blank face to just over 3½" in diameter and round over the front edge. You want the reveal or mirror border curving in toward the recess.

3 Stop the lathe and, holding the centerline of the jig to the center of the mirror blank, mark the perimeter of the mirror location as shown in photo E. Turn the lathe on and continue the mark with a pencil, establishing a perfect cut line circle.

4 With a parting tool held just above the workpiece center and 90° to the face, establish a recess depth equal to the thickness of the mirror at the cut line as shown in photo F. Switch to a ⅜" gouge

Figure 2

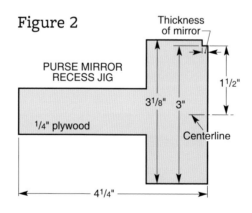

PURSE MIRROR RECESS JIG

¼" plywood

Thickness of mirror

3⅛"   3"

1½"

Centerline

4¼"

QUICK TIP

If turning several mirrors, use acrylic plastic or aluminum for a more permanent jig.

E

F

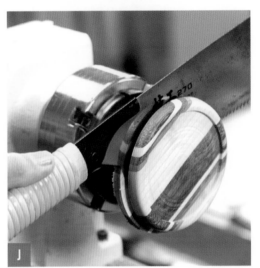

and remove the waste between this cut and the center of the recess, creating a flat or slightly concave surface. (Our mirrors required a depth of ³⁄₁₆″.)

5 Check the width and depth of the mirror recess using the jig as shown in photo G. Also, check the bottom of the recess for flatness. You do not want a hump in the middle as pressure on the edges may cause the mirror to break. At some point, you'll also want to test-fit the mirror in the recess. Be careful not to force the mirror into a snug-fitting recess. The mirror could prove difficult to remove, or worse, it could break.

6 When satisfied with the fit, continue rounding the front face and edge of the

mirror blank with a gouge. Remove any excess to achieve a 3½″ diameter.

7 Sand the face and rounded edges of the mirror blank, starting with 120 grit and working through a schedule of 150, 180, 220, and 320 (photo H). Shine light on the subject to ensure no sanding lines remain.

8 Aiming for a ³⁄₈″ blank thickness, mark the back edge with a pencil. Next, using a thin parting tool, make a parting cut at the line, creating a flat back to the mirror blank as shown in photo I. Work down to a ¼″ tenon. Finish the cut by turning the lathe off and freeing the blank with a fine-tooth handsaw as shown in photo J.

Shape the back and complete the purse mirror

1 Expand the chuck jaws to grip the inside edges of the mirror blank recess as shown in photo K. Avoid overtightening or you'll damage the wood rim.

2 With a ¼″ gouge and the tool rest ¼″ below the center, round the back edge of the mirror blank and form a straight or slightly convex back as desired and shown in photo L. Add any beads, grooves, or texture to the surface at this time if desired.

3 With the lathe on a low speed, sand the edges and back using the same grit schedule mentioned in the previous step 7.

4 Apply a lacquer or other finish, coating the blank 5 to 7 times and sanding between coats with super-fine grits. See "How to Apply a CA Finish."

5 Remove the mirror blank from the lathe. Mix up a small batch of 5-minute epoxy and dab it in the mirror recess, keeping it away from the edges, as shown in photo M. Next, insert the mirror and keep pressure on it until the epoxy sets up. Finally, if you haven't done so, take a second to determine the perfect recipient of your turning talent.

How to Apply a CA Finish

When you think of the abuse items in a woman's purse must endure, you might consider a finish that's up to the task. Turner Tom Schottle likes using a CA (cyanoacrylate) finish because it's fast, attractive, and super durable.

1) Wearing protective gloves, wipe on a thin coating of CA over the exposed surfaces of the mirror blank with a shop towel while it's still held in the chuck as shown. Quickly spray the surface with accelerator.

2) Repeat step 1 8 to 10 times to build up a coat of CA.

3) Sand the finished surface lightly, working through all the grits from 1,500 to 12,000. You don't want to sand through the coat of CA you just put on; you want to smooth it and bring out the shine.

K

L

M

Cap

End

Globe

End

Icicle

TREE ORNAMENT

Try your hand at polychromatic turning with a beautiful holiday project

BY DON RUSSELL

From the first time I started to turn wood in high school shop class, I've been fascinated with polychromatic turning. Instead of turning a blank cut from a single log, my preference is to glue up a variety of geometric shapes, using different wood species and strips of veneer. The result is a multicolored blank that can be turned into an object of unique beauty.

A good way to learn about polychromatic turning is to make tree ornaments like the ones shown here. These ornate turnings make excellent gifts and craft sale items. Although every ornament I make is unique, they all share the same basic anatomy, and are usually assembled from three parts that are turned separately: a top cap, an icicle, and a polychromatic globe that contains two end caps. I don't use patterns when turning the parts. In fact (as you'll see on the pages ahead), turning is the easy part of the project. Once you learn how to cut and assemble a polychromatic blank, you'll be able to apply these techniques when making other polychromatic projects like bowls, urns, and plates.

Cut tiny wedges to create a multicolored blank

The globe of the turned ornament I'm making here contains 48 pieces: 24 wedge-shaped pieces (12 padauk, 12 yellowheart) and 24 pieces of green veneer that go between the wedges. Wedges are identical in size, and each one contains two 7½° angles. To arrive at this cutting angle, you divide 360° by the desired number of wedges (360 / 24 = 15), then divide the result in half.

Though I prefer to use my radial-arm saw to cut tiny parts (see sidebar), the same job can be done on the tablesaw or chopsaw. Whatever tool you use, plan to spend some time getting the wedge angle exactly right. Otherwise, your blank won't have the tight joints required for a good-looking globe.

Get set for perfect cuts. With the blade tilted 7½°, I cut an angled stop block and clamp it to the radial arm saw's fence to establish wedge size. Note that the bottom of the stopblock is cut back to provide clearance for sawdust. Once you've cut one 7½° end, simply flip the workpiece to make the next cut and create a new wedge. I make sure to remove each wedge carefully.

Why I Love My Radial-Arm Saw

I've got a fine tablesaw in my shop, but I prefer using my 1960s-era DeWalt radial-arm saw (RAS) for many crosscutting operations. The absence of a blade guard demands close attention to hand position when cutting. But if you pay attention to safety, you'll come to appreciate these vintage machines for a number of reasons, just like I have.

- **No problems with tiny parts.** A RAS offers the same benefits as a power mitersaw or a tablesaw with a sliding table. Small parts can't jam between the blade and the fence, or be pulled into the throat plate opening.
- **Compound angles are easy.** The adjustability of the DeWalt's turret and carriage assembly provides excellent compound angle cutting capability for parts of all sizes. Dadoes in wide boards can also be cut easily.
- **Excellent build quality.** Over 50 years of use have done little to diminish the accuracy of the DeWalt saws in my shop. I get mirror-smooth cuts with a Forrest Woodworker I blade. I also find it amazing that spare parts for these antique machines are still available online. I can't think of a better example of a quality-built, American-made product.

Test and adjust as necessary. Cut enough test wedges to form a quarter circle (6 wedges in this case), then see how the assembled wedges fit against a square. A gap like the one visible here indicates that the saw's bevel angle is too steep. Keep testing and adjusting until no gaps appear.

Place the parts. Use the legs of a square to keep parts aligned as you press them onto masking tape.

Glue up the globe & tape it twice

When I've got all the wedges and green veneer strips to create my blank, I lay down a wide strip of masking tape on a flat work surface and along one leg of a plastic square (a metal square works just as well). With the sticky side of the tape facing up, you can place your wedges and veneer strips in a continuous line, ready for glue-up. The clear, stretchy "clamping" tape I use is made by 3M; it's called 8884 Stretchable Tape—great for clamping when regular clamps won't work.

Glue & assemble. After spreading glue in every opening and on the exposed ends, bend the parts into a cylinder and secure the assembly with masking tape.

Flatten as needed. If wedges have shifted out of alignment, apply hammer persuasion.

A tree for tiny turnings

I turned a tree-type display to show off some of my ornaments at craft shows. Once you get the hang of cutting tiny parts and assembling them in different geometric arrangements, there's no end to the variety of ornaments you can create.

Clamp with stretchy tape. Wrapping the cylinder with 3M's special tape provides more clamping pressure than you can achieve with masking tape alone.

Flatten & hollow the globe, then add top pieces

I use a SUPERNOVA² chuck to grip the cylindrical blank for the rough shaping that needs to be done at this stage. The goal here is to flatten both ends of the blank and then hollow out the interior so the ornament won't be so heavy. I also need to create a 45° bevel joint for attaching the two end pieces. The beveled connection will create a cleaner line than a butt joint when the globe's final shape is turned.

Cut a dovetail. After flattening one end of the globe blank with a ½" gouge, I use a scraper to dovetail the end, as shown above. The dovetail can be grabbed solidly in the chuck when I flatten the opposite end of the blank.

Hollow it out. A side-cutting, roundnose scraper makes quick work of hollowing the globe to make it lighter. I aim for a wall thickness of ³⁄₈" to ½".

Match the bevels. By pressing the globe's bevelled opening against the bevelled end piece while it's spinning in the lathe, I can tell when bevels match to make a good glue joint. A dark burn mark indicates good contact. Before removing each end, bore a centered hole with a tailstock-mounted bit. The bit's diameter should match that of the mandrel you'll use to turn the completed blank.

Glue with a screw. The centered holes in the end pieces make it easy to glue these parts to the globe body using a long, ¼" machine bolt. Use washers and a wing nut to apply even pressure.

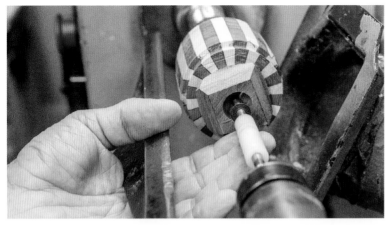

Turn the globe, then sand & finish

The globe blank is ready for its transformation, but mounting it on the lathe is a little tricky. The ends are already drilled to fit over a pen-turning mandrel, but I also counterbore each end, drilling ½" deep with a ¾"-diameter bit. This makes it easer to turn the ends down to their shallow profiles. Plastic bushings forced tight against the workpiece hold it fast, while also providing clearance for turning tools.

Set up for a spin. A pen-turning mandrel extends through the blank, held in the headstock and in a ball bearing tailstock. Plastic bushings and a pair of rubber washers grip the workpiece so that it doesn't rotate on the mandrel.

No pattern required. I use a ½" gouge with a standard fingernail grind to rough out the globe's shape. I aim for a pleasing form, judging by eye rather than relying on a pattern. To smooth the globe, I use a scraper.

Sand with an air assist. The globe needs to be sanded, but dark sawdust can get into the pores of the globe's light-toned wood. To avoid contamination, I blow compressed air over the workpiece while sanding at 180 grit.

Start to finish with sanding sealer. Four light coats prevent dark resin and dust from bleeding into the lighter wood. I go over each coat lightly with a fine scouring pad, then apply two light coats of spray lacquer. The final touch: a buffed coat of suntan lotion to prevent UV damage.

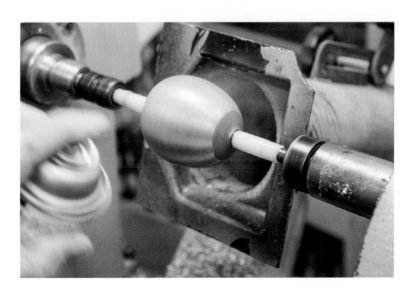

Turn the icicle & cap

I like to use ebony for the icicle and cap because the dark wood contrasts nicely with the globe colors. Whatever wood you use for these small parts, make sure it has ebony-like characteristics—clear, dense, and strong. Since I've done so many of these ornaments, I don't need a pattern to create a pleasing icicle or cap shape. If you're new to a project like this, you might want to create a pattern. Remember to turn a tenon on these two parts so they can fit in the holes bored in the ends of the globe.

Work back from the tip. The point of the icicle isn't supported by the tailstock, so it needs to be shaped first. I use my ½" gouge for this work.

The ¼" tenon comes last. An open-end wrench that matches the diameter of globe holes is the perfect measuring device as I turn the tenon with a parting tool.

Sanding = finishing. Thanks to ebony's resinous makeup and tight grain, it can gain a polished appearance simply by sanding with 220-grit sandpaper. I fold the paper to get into contoured sections of the profile.

Finish up with hook & line

Completing the ornament calls for a couple of unusual ingredients: some monofilament fishing line and a medium-size fish hook. The small eye in the hook is just the right size to hold the plastic line used to hang the ornament. With a pair of wire nippers, I snip off the curved section of the hook so the straight length can extend through a hole drilled in the cap. Bending the end of the metal over holds it in place.

Fine work. When the cap piece has been fitted with its string and steel hanger, you can glue the cap and icicle to the globe.

PEN TURNING MADE EASY

A step-by-step guide to success

BY TOM HINTZ

If you own a woodturning lathe, you have the right one for turning pens. Any lathe from a benchtop mini to the biggest floor model will do nicely. Also, turning tools that handle spindle work will at least get you started with turning pens. Most turners do not feel they need special or miniature tools to make any except highly specialized pens.

Most woodworkers have lots of pen blanks languishing in the scrap bin. Because pen blanks are usually ¾" square and under 3" long, many cutoffs can cheaply and easily be cut into blanks (fig. 1).

When cutting your own pen blanks, keep in mind that the grain should run along the long axis. This makes turning the blank easier and reduces its tendency to split.

Pen-sized blanks, precut from exotic woods, are available at most outlets that handle pen supplies. Because pens are so small, using exotic woods is surprisingly affordable.

The hardware

You can set up your shop to turn pens with a small investment if you buy all of the associated tools used in pen turning. (You can spend even less by improvising or building your own.) You can use the same tools to make other projects like letter openers, magnifying glasses, mechanical pencils, perfume atomizers, and more.

The one piece of hardware you will have to buy is a pen mandrel. You will choose between fixed- and adjustable-length models. The main advantage of the adjustable version is not having to hunt down and add or remove spacers when you vary the lengths of your pen barrels.

A mandrel mounts in the lathe spindle with a Morse taper. The other end of the mandrel shaft has a cone-shaped recess that accepts the point of the tailstock live center. Supported on both ends, the mandrel runs steadily even at higher speeds (fig. 2).

All of the metal parts for building a pen come in a kit, including the ink refill. The kits include two (usually) brass tubes to which the wood blanks are glued. The remaining metal parts are pressed into the tubes during final assembly (fig. 3).

Equally complete parts kits are available for all of the projects that can be produced with pen-making tools.

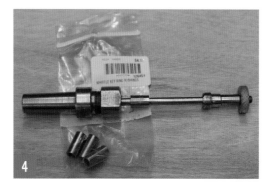

The key to turning a wooden barrel that matches the diameter of a pen kit's metal parts is using a bushing set designed for that pen style. These metal sleeves have a common inside diameter that fits the mandrel, and the outside dimensions are designed to match the metal parts for specific pen kits. Most bushing kits have three pieces, one for either end and another that is mounted between the barrels on the mandrel (fig. 4). Some bushing kits also have a ring that floats on the center bushing to be used for sizing a tenon cut in the upper barrel for a decorative ring.

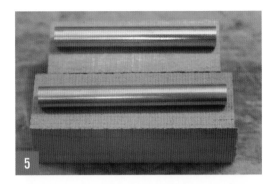

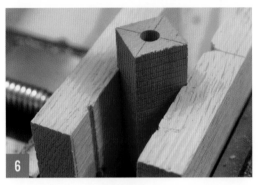

Bushing kits can be used to make dozens of pens. The biggest problem is keeping track of which bushings go with what pen style. Wise pen turners label their bushing kits with the names or numbers of corresponding pen kits.

For this article, I built a Euro-style pen (twist action) using the European bushing kit, both from my local woodworking store. This makes a good "learning" pen, as it employs a set of techniques that are common to making many other styles.

Preparing the blanks

An essential first step is getting the wood even with and square to the brass tubes. Cutting the wood blanks approximately ¼" longer than the brass tube leaves enough material for cleaning up with a barrel trimmer, ensuring that the ends are perfectly flat and square to the tubes (fig. 5).

To drill the hole through the center, you need a way to hold the wooden blanks on end, square to the drill bit. Vises for doing just that are available, but I decided to make my own from a standard drill press vise. I removed the metal jaw inserts and used them as templates to drill mounting holes in a pair of 4 x 2½ x ¾" hardwood replacements. After attaching the wooden jaws to the vise, I closed the jaws and used an ⅛" brad-point bit (in the drill press) to drill a 2" deep hole, centered on the seam between the faces. This produces a shallow groove on each jaw face that is perfectly square to my drill press.

Clamp the pen blank with opposite corners in the drilled grooves (fig. 6). Mark the center of the blank and carefully drill completely through it. I have found that a good quality brad-point bit ensures a clean, straight hole. Follow the directions in your kit for sizing. My Euro-style pen kit called for a 7mm diameter.

Because blanks are often sliced from scrap, they may be less than perfectly square, and the hole can exit the blank a bit off-line. With a ¾"-square blank, plenty of material remains to round it out unless the hole is too far off center.

Installing the tubes

To ensure a good bond between the brass tubes and wooden blanks, roughing up the outer surface of the tube is necessary. Wrap coarse sandpaper (80- or 100-grit) around the tube and twist it to make scratches that run around the tube's diameter, not along its length (fig. 7).

Pen makers use all sorts of glue to secure the tubes in the blanks, from epoxy to polyurethane and my favorite, thick CA. As long as the brass tubes are roughed up, any of these glues will work.

Before applying glue, make sure the tubes and blanks are correctly paired. Many pen kits have two different tube lengths, the longer usually used for the bottom barrel.

I add a drop or two of thick CA into the hole from one end of the blank, insert the tube in the other end just enough to hold it, apply a few drops of CA to the outer surface of the tube and then push it in, giving it a twist as it goes. A piece of wood scrap can be used to seat the tube within the hole so it is roughly centered between the blank's ends. A special tube-insertion tool that makes this step even easier is available.

Allow the glue to dry completely before moving on to the next step.

True the blanks

I have tried many ways of squaring the ends of pen barrels but only one, a purpose-designed pen mill, actually works reliably. The pen mill has a pilot shaft that fits inside the brass tube, accurately aligning the cutter that trims the wood square to the centerline of the tube (fig. 8). Unless the ends of the pen barrels are flat and square, the metal parts cannot fit properly later.

In addition to guiding the cutter, the pilot shaft has a reaming cutter ground into its end that clears the inevitable glue buildup inside the tubes (fig. 9).

Pen mill kits include several pilot shafts to fit the common pen tube inside diameters 7mm, 8mm, ⅜″, and 10mm.

Turning the barrels

With the mandrel in the lathe, mount the barrel blanks and bushings on the shaft, making sure they are in the proper order (fig. 10). Instruction sheets that show this arrangement for each style of pen kit are available from the retailer, often online. I find it easiest to put the upper barrel to my left. This habit allows me to visualize the final shape of the pen and reduces the chance of turning the wrong shape on the wrong barrel.

Some center bushings have two different end sizes and must be installed on the mandrel facing the correct way. This is most common when the center bushing has a floating ring used to size a tenon for a decorative ring to be installed during final assembly, as does the set I used. The floating ring and the step in the bushing on which it rides must face the upper barrel.

After tightening the barrels and bushings on the mandrel, bring the tailstock up to the end of the mandrel. The point of the tailstock's live center fits into a recess in the end of the mandrel to support it. Lock the tailstock in position and apply just enough pressure against the end of the mandrel to support it (fig. 11). Excessive pressure can "bow" the mandrel and cause a dangerous vibration.

Start the lathe on its slowest speed and slowly increase the rpm to a comfortable rate that does not induce vibration. Round the blanks so both are smooth, shut the lathe off, and adjust the tool rest in to the new diameter.

In most cases, a considerable amount of wood must be removed during this step. I find it easiest to begin forming the final shape of the pen barrels as soon as they are rounded. This allows me to reduce the material close to the bushing diameters in increments, with less chance of removing too much wood.

Though experienced pen turners let their imaginations run free, save the wild shapes for after you gain familiarity with the process. Strive first to match the bushing diameters precisely.

Using a sharp gouge (I like a ½" spindle gouge) take light, smooth cuts to begin forming the shape of the barrel. The diameter of the wood should end up slightly larger than the bushings to allow for final sanding. Naturally, the smoother your cuts, the less sanding you will be left with, but leave a little extra diameter on the first few pens—just in case.

Decorative ring tenon

The kit I used has a decorative ring fitted to the lower end of the upper barrel. The bushing set has a floating sizing ring on the center bushing that helps cut a properly sized tenon.

I use a sharp, ¼"-wide parting tool to cut this tenon because an ultra-smooth surface is not necessary (fig. 12). In fact, a little roughness enhances the bond between the ring and tenon.

The width of the tenon should also be accurate, so the barrel ends will not show where they meet. I usually cut the tenon about 1/16" narrower than the decorative ring to hide this junction.

Hold the decorative ring on the blank, mark the length of the tenon, and slowly reduce its diameter (fig. 13). Stop the lathe

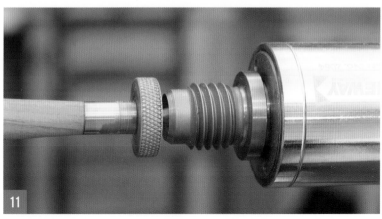

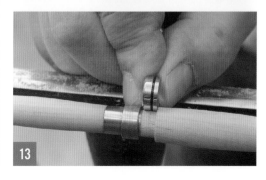

frequently to check your progress by trying to slide the sizing ring onto the tenon. Ideally, the sizing ring slips onto the tenon with just a little resistance.

Also, the upper barrel diameter next to the tenon should match the outer diameter of the sizing ring. Like the barrel ends, leave this slightly oversized so it can be sanded down to match the bushing diameter perfectly.

Sanding

First, remove or move the toolrest. Sanding a spinning object can be dangerous, particularly if the sandpaper is wrapped around the fingers. Hold a folded piece of sandpaper between your fingers so that if it should catch, it pulls out of your grasp rather than pulling your hand into the piece (fig. 14).

Until you become more comfortable with turning pens, sanding may be part of the final shaping and sizing process in addition to refining the surface for finishing. The good news is that such a small piece of wood can be turned at relatively high speeds, making sanding more effective and less time consuming. We also have to remember that we are sanding on a thin metal rod (the mandrel shaft), making it important to use light pressure to avoid distorting the mandrel.

In most cases, 220-grit paper is sufficiently coarse to begin the sanding process, even if some shaping is required. Gently refine the shape and diameter until the ends are nearly flush with the bushings. Some like to sand down to 600-grit or finer, and there is nothing wrong with that. I have had good luck with 320-grit paper applied lightly until the bare wood develops a dull sheen.

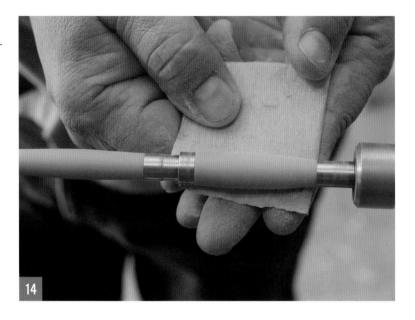

14

Finishing

Applying a finish to a spinning piece is an accepted part of turning, but the same cautions I mentioned for sanding apply. Use small pieces of cloth to polish the finishes and never wrap the material around your fingers. Fold it into a pad and hold it between the fingers so if it should catch, it is pulled away from your hand.

Finishing is one of the more mysterious aspects of pen turning. The problem is developing a glossy finish with the durability to withstand handling by human fingers and the natural oils and acids common to them. Over the years, I have turned lots of pens, finishing few of them the same way as the last. In this search for a perpetually shiny finish, I tried a broad range of finishing techniques, materials, and sequences of application. In the end, they all succumbed to the wear and tear of human fingers to some degree.

For your first few pens, keep finishing simple. These will probably reside on your desk or in the shop anyway. Using one of the "burn-on" wax sticks or friction liquids is easy and yields good initial results. Probably the most popular sticks and liquid finishes are manufactured by Hut.

The key to using these finishes is to apply small amounts and then "burn them in" with a clean, soft rag. Burning in is simply creating enough heat to melt the finish material so it flows into the wood. To do this the speed of the lathe is increased and the cloth is held against the wood and moved over the surface slowly enough to maintain the heat developed by friction. As with sanding, we need not apply heavy pressure. The speed of the wood rubbing against the cloth will generate more than enough heat to spread the wax-based finishes.

A common mistake when applying finishes is using too much, which can make it just as difficult to achieve a nice shine as using too little. Changing spots on the polishing cloth will show how much of the finish material is transferring to it. When the transfer of finish material to the cloth begins to disappear, the amount on the wood is close to perfect.

Many pen turners use thin CA glue in the finishing process, building multiple coats of CA and polishing them to a high luster. With the lathe set at its slowest speed, the CA is dribbled onto the wood and spread with a finger shielded behind a plastic bag. You have to be reasonably quick and

spread the CA in one pass over the wood before allowing it to dry (fig. 15). Let the CA harden fully before sanding with very fine paper (320- to 600-grit) to level it out; then repeat the process.

I have had limited success using CA as a stand-alone finish system but do use it regularly as a base for my (current) favorite pen finishing method. With the barrels sanded, I apply one coat of CA glue to the surface and allow it to dry. I smooth that surface with fine sandpaper, usually a worn-out piece of 320-grit, and remove the barrel segments from the mandrel.

After finishing on the mandrel, go back to the pen mill and lightly touch up the ends of the barrels to be sure there is no buildup of finish or glue that might cause problems when the metal parts are installed.

After the CA glue, the only finish I apply is carnauba wax, regarded by most as the hardest wax available. I use the Beall buff system, going through both abrasive wheel stages, followed by the carnauba wax buffed on last (fig. 16). This system has produced good results that appear to be lasting—at least as long as anything I have tried so far.

Assembly

I initially resisted spending the money to buy a pen press. Instead, I used my bench

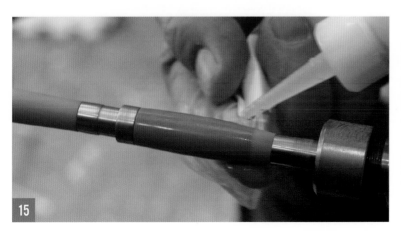

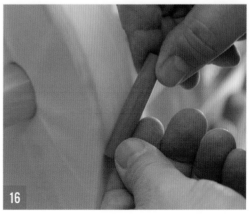

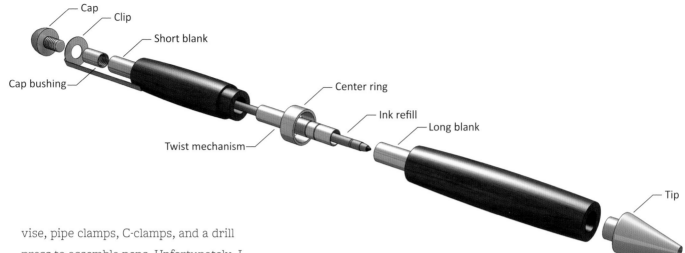

Cap

Clip

Short blank

Cap bushing

Center ring

Ink refill

Long blank

Twist mechanism

Tip

vise, pipe clamps, C-clamps, and a drill press to assemble pens. Unfortunately, I managed to destroy pen kits with each of them before realizing the combined cost of those ruined kits was quickly approaching the price of the press. I cut my losses and purchased the pen press used here (fig. 17).

Identify the ends of the barrels to be sure the parts are pressed into the correct ends. They will fit in either end but the diameters often differ.

Start assembly by pressing the pocket clip retainer into the top of the upper barrel, just enough to seat it. In most cases, the end of this assembly unscrews to install the clip itself. While this can be pressed in fully assembled, adding the clip afterward reduces the chance of scratching the barrel (fig. 18).

Apply one or two drops of thick CA glue to the tenon and slide the decorative ring on, giving it a twist to spread the glue. Make sure the rounded edge of the ring (if it has one) faces the end of the barrel (fig. 19).

Push the nosepiece into the bottom barrel (fig. 20). Before installing the twist mechanism, read the instructions carefully for suggestions on its installed depth. This is the easiest way to mess up your pen on the press, because the depth is critical and the margin for error is small.

Press the twist mechanism into the barrel, with the brass tip going into the tube first. This is what actually secures the action in the tube. In most cases, there is a crimped ring around the mechanism that is used as a landmark during installation. I usually press the mechanism in just enough to hide that crimped ring, screw the refill in place, and then operate the mechanism to check how close the writing tip is to the end of the nose. Go slowly when adjusting this

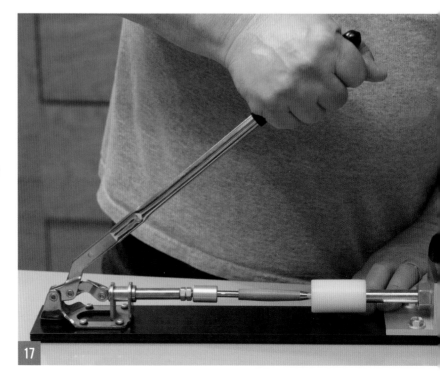

17

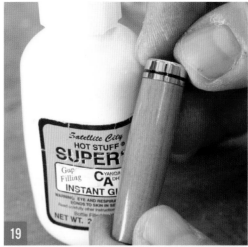

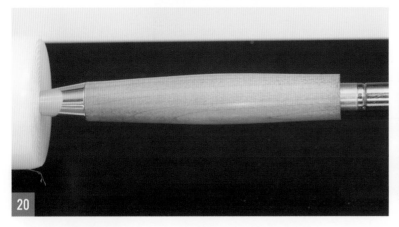

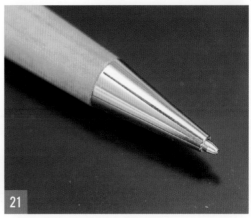

position because if you go too far, moving the mechanism back out without damage is very difficult.

When the mechanism is twisted, the goal is to have the writing tip fully exposed through the nose but retracting completely when twisted back the other way (fig. 21).

With the ink refill installed, press the upper barrel onto the exposed part of the operating mechanism by hand. This is not a tight fit and is meant to be taken apart to replace the refill. Since the upper barrel is not keyed to the lower portion, you can align it as desired to create the most attractive grain lines.

Check the operation of the mechanism one final time, and your pen is complete.

Once you become familiar with turning and assembling a basic pen, there are many pen styles, mechanical pencils, and an ever-growing array of other small projects you can make with your pen-making equipment. As is usually the case in woodturning, you are only limited by the bounds of your imagination.

STYLISH SALAD BOWL SET

For everyday use or to give as a gift

DESIGNERS/TURNERS/WRITERS: REX BURNINGHAM & KIP CHRISTENSEN

We asked expert turners Rex Burningham and Kip Christensen of Utah to give us a blow-by-blow account on creating an eye-pleasing maple salad bowl set from green wood, and, boy, did they ever. Save bucks by using green wood from your own backyard, or save time by going with air-dried blanks. This latter option lets you complete the bowls in a day or two. You will need 5 × 12"-diameter green or air-dried wood blanks for the large serving bowl, and four 2 ½ × 7"-diameter green or air-dried wood blanks for the smaller side bowls. We'll begin turning the large serving bowl from green wood. If working with air-dried wood, you can skip the rough-turning and storing steps (required when using green wood) and turn the blanks into finished bowls in the same day.

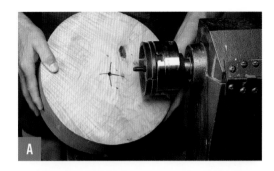

Stage one: Rough-turning a green blank

Controlling wood movement plays a huge role in forming a successful salad bowl set. Though working with dried stock is ideal, you'll more than likely use green bowl blanks. That means rough-turning the blanks and setting them aside for drying prior to completion. Here's the first stage of this two-stage process.

1 Drill a mounting hole into the top of the bowl blank that is equal to the root diameter of the lathe screw shown in photo A and slightly longer than the screw. Mount the blank onto the lathe screw center secured in the jaws of a four-jawed chuck for initial turning.

2 True up both the side and the face of the blank with a ½"-deep fluted gouge before shaping the bowl. With the tailstock providing support, use a push cut (push the gouge toward the chuck) with the bevel rubbing to clean up the side as shown in photo B. Next, move the tailstock out of the way, readjust the tool rest parallel to the blank face, and use a pull cut (start from the center and pull the gouge to you) to true up the face as shown in photo C.

Tool: ½" bowl gouge
Lathe Speed: 400 to 500 rpm

3 Lay out the diameter of the bowl's foot as shown in photo D. See also figure 1 for reference. For the bowl to be functionally stable without looking bottom-heavy the foot should be approximately one-third the diameter of the rim. In this case the foot will be approximately 4" in diameter.

QUICK TIP

Make inside and outside rough and finish cardboard cutouts of the two bowl shapes in figure 1 and use them as templates to shape a matching set of bowls like those shown here. Hold these profiles against the turnings frequently to check your work.

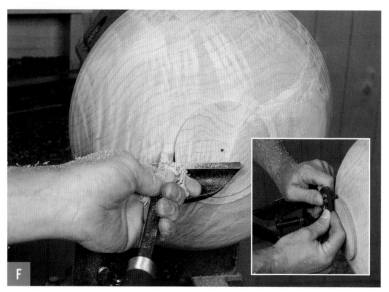

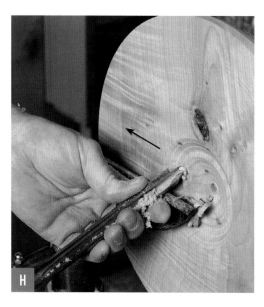

4 Shape the outside of the bowl by removing the bottom corner and then rounding the bottom of the bowl between the foot and the rim as shown in photo E. These "roughing" cuts can be fairly aggressive. Note that the bevel of the ½″ gouge rubs on the wood just behind the cut to help control the depth of the cut.

Tool: ½" bowl gouge
Speed: 600 to 700 rpm

5 Using a skew, turn a spigot that will allow the chuck to grip the blank in the next step. Lay a skew flat on the tool rest and cut with a scraping motion. Shape a spigot (figure 1) that measures between ¼″ and ⅜″ deep, maintaining a crisp and clean bottom corner as shown in photo F. Notice the straight shoulder at the bottom of the spigot that the jaws will contact. Photo F's inset shows how the jaws of the chuck will grip that spigot. The spigot should be shorter than the depth of the jaws so it does not bottom out at the base of the jaws.

Tool: ½" oval skew
Speed: 600 to 700 rpm

6 Remove the blank from the screw center and secure the spigot in the chuck jaws. Bring the tailstock into position to support the wood while truing up the face of the blank. To do this, make a light scraping cut, working from the center of the bowl toward the rim as shown in photo G.

Tool: ½" bowl gouge
Speed: 500 to 600 rpm

7 Back off the tailstock and hollow out the bowl, beginning at the center and progressing toward the outer rim using a ½″ bowl gouge as shown in photo H. Make the opening larger in diameter and deeper with each pass. To keep the bevel rubbing on the wood just behind the cut, swing the tool handle in a large arc as shown

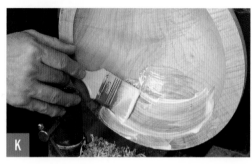

in photo I to advance the gouge's cutting edge toward the bowl bottom. When the opening in the bowl gets sufficiently large, adjust the tool rest so it angles in toward the bowl bottom as shown in photo J. This prevents the gouge from extending too far out beyond the tool rest. Regularly check the bowl wall shape with the template and the wall thickness with a double-ended caliper. When the wall approximates 1¼″-thick, prepare the rough-turned bowl for drying.

Tool: ½" bowl gouge
Speed: 700 to 800 rpm

8 Brush the green-wood bowl with a generous coat of wood sealer, such as Anchorseal, as shown in photo K to prevent it from cracking as it dries. Drying time varies depending on several factors and is increased considerably by the application of wood sealer. Expect the large salad bowl to take from 3 to 6 months to dry before it is ready to be remounted and turned into a finished bowl. The bowl blank is dry when it measures less than 10% moisture content with a moisture meter or when it goes several days without losing weight through moisture loss.

Stage two: Finish-turn the dried bowl

1 Remount your dry bowl blank securely in the chuck jaws and bring the tailstock into position for support. Now true up the rim, using a light scraping cut as shown in photo L.

Tool: ½" bowl gouge
Speed: 400 to 500 rpm

2 Next, true up the outside of the bowl. Direct push cuts from the rim to the base as well as pull cuts from the base to the rim. You'll achieve the cleanest cuts when moving from the base toward the rim because the tool is not cutting directly into end grain. Note in photos M and N how the tool contacts the wood to make the cut and the adjustment in the tool rest. Model your stance after the one in photo O, which shows the tool handle supported by your body. Control the tool by slowly leaning with your body as you make the cut. Your guide hand should follow the curve of the bowl along the tool rest. The combination of hands and body working together as one will produce a smooth and flowing cut.

Tool: ½" bowl gouge
Speed: 400 to 500 rpm

3 Now remove the tailstock, reposition the tool rest to the inside of the bowl, and true up the inside. Use the bevel to control the depth and accuracy of the cut.

Tool: ½" bowl gouge
Speed: 600 to 700 rpm

4 Determine the wall thickness at the rim and define the rim while there is still a mass of wood toward the bowl bottom. Note in figure 1 how the rim curves slightly and slopes gently toward the center of the bowl. Continue to turn to the final wall thickness by working from the rim downward as shown in photo P.

Tool: ½" bowl gouge
Speed: 700 to 800 rpm

Scrape zone

5 Occasionally turn off the lathe and check the wall thickness with double-ended calipers as shown in photo Q.

6 Use a large half-round scraper to reach the inside bottom of the bowl. Adjust the height and angle of the tool rest so the scraper can easily contact the center height of the bowl. Now, working out from the bowl center, begin to cut, keeping the tool handle slightly higher than the cutting edge, and the flat bottom of the scraper held flat to the tool rest as shown in photo R. Work outward just far enough to complete the curve and meet the previous cut made with the bowl gouge. Avoid scraping up the side of the bowl toward the rim.

Tool: Half-round scraper
Speed: 700 to 800 rpm

7 Power-sand the completed bowl both inside and out with a portable drill and attachment that uses a 2″ sanding disc applied to a foam holder. Angle the drill upward slightly into the bowl at about the nine o'clock position as shown in photo S. (Power-sanding is most aggressive when the rotation of the disc is opposite that of the bowl.) Begin with 100-grit abrasive and progress to 320-grit.

Tool: 2″ bowl sanding kit
Speed: 700 to 800 rpm

8 Add a decorative detail on the bowl's outside by first laying a skew flat on the tool rest and cutting two pairs of V-grooves ⅝″ and 1″ down from the rim using the tool's point. Now, wire-burn the grooves to make them stand out as shown in photo T and figure 1. The wire burner shown here makes fast work of this task. To employ this tool, hold the ball handles of the wire burner securely in your hands, rest one hand on the tool rest, and bring the wire into the V-groove. Friction from the wire against the

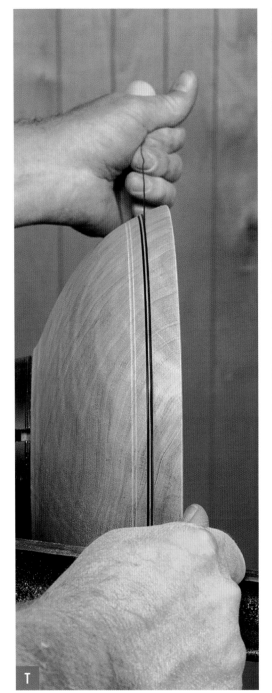

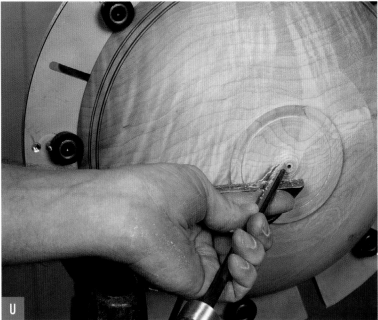

rotating wood creates the black detail lines.
Remove any burn residue by sanding lightly
with 320-grit abrasive.

Tool: Wire burner
Speed: 700 to 800 rpm

9 Remove the bowl from the chuck, and
replace the standard jaws with jumbo jaws.
Mount the bowl in the jumbo jaws and
apply light pressure with the tailstock.

Using light cuts with the ⅜″ spindle gouge,
remove the spigot and shape the foot as
desired. Turn as much as possible with
the tailstock in position, then remove the
tailstock and complete the turning as shown
in photo U. Then, power-sand the bottom of
the bowl.

Tools: ⅜" spindle gouge, 2" bowl sanding kit
Speed: 500 to 600 rpm

Figure 1: Full-Sized Bowl Templates

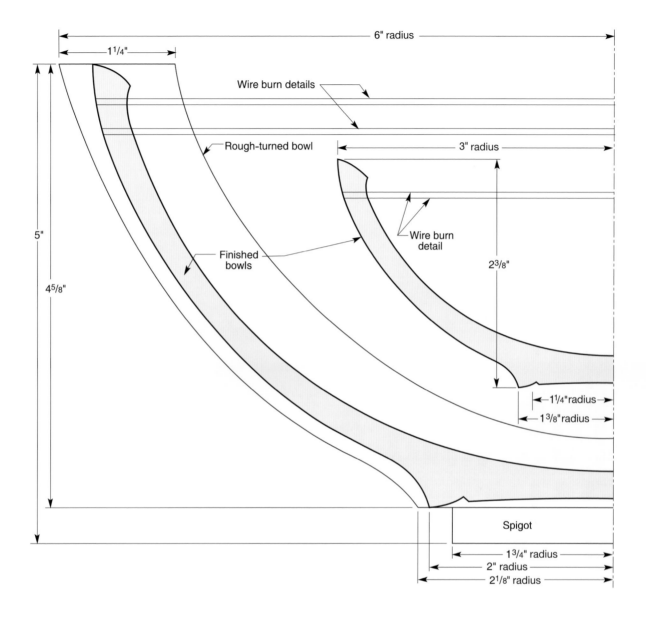

6" radius

1¹/₄"

Wire burn details

Rough-turned bowl

3" radius

Wire burn detail

5"

4⁵/₈"

2³/₈"

Finished bowls

1¹/₄" radius

1³/₈" radius

Spigot

1³/₄" radius

2" radius

2¹/₈" radius

10 Finally, apply a finish to your salad bowl as shown in photo V. We rubbed in a generous amount of wax. After 15 minutes, wipe off the excess wax, and your salad bowl is ready for use. Clean the bowl by wiping it with a damp cloth and then drying it immediately. Restore periodically by applying an additional coat of wax when needed.

Turn a matching set of side bowls

To turn the side bowls for your salad bowl set, follow the same procedure used for the large salad bowl with a few exceptions. Go with a ⅜" rather than a ½" bowl gouge, and use smaller (no. 2) jaws in the chuck. Use the smaller templates found in figure 1, and the smaller 2½ × 7"-diameter bowl blanks.

TURNING A CALABASH BOWL

Master the tricks for working green wood

BY MIKE MAHONEY

Many people ask me if the wood I make bowls from is green wood. The answer is always "yes." However, there's more to the story. In order to make large bowls, you have to start with a green piece of wood. That's because it would be rare to find a dry piece, say, 5″ thick × 12″ wide that does not have a crack in it. (Such cracks in salad bowls make them filler for the rubbish bin.) So the trick is to take the green blank, rough it into a bowl shape that is 10% as thick as the diameter, seal it with an appropriate sealer, and store it away for slow drying. Later, after the rough bowl has fully seasoned, you turn it to final shape and wall thickness. The downside here is the painfully long wait; rough-turned bowls take from months to over a year of drying time.

However, there's another way to work with green wood and make very

Figure 1: Log Sawing Sequence

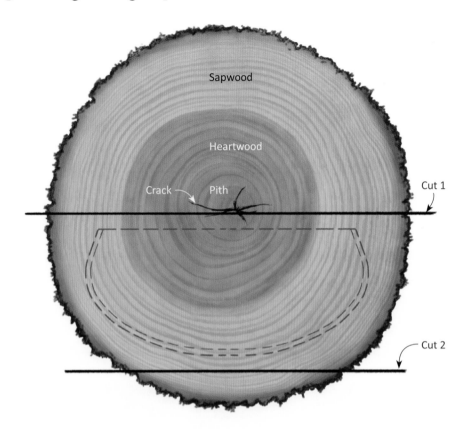

handsome bowls without going through the interminable drying process. That is to turn what I loosely call a "calabash bowl." This is a Polynesian term for a gourd. It is essentially a baseless bowl carefully extracted or cut from the log to create a visual balance after the bowl has dried. In my opinion, bowls generally do not need bases to be functional. Another reason: if you make a traditional based bowl from green wood, it usually will not sit flat after it dries. So, let's make a calabash and explore the joy and secrets of green wood turning.

Note: For my green wood calabash, I chose a variety of white oak (Quercus lobata), known as a California valley oak. Oak is a good choice since you can find it throughout North America. Plus, due to its difficulty in drying, the woodturning community shies away from it for their seasoned turnings. For me, white oak for bowls (especially a calabash) is underrated. Its medullary rays can look stunning!

Creating the blank

1 Start with a fresh round log about 14″ in diameter and at least 14″ long. (I'm using one I cut from a windfall tree on a vineyard near my farm.) Select a cylinder-shaped log that doesn't have knots or other defects. Now, study both ends of the log, noting the pith and any radiating cracks that may affect the bowl blank. Avoid including the pith (the log's center) in the bowl. Mark a cutline with a black marker on the log's end so its annual rings and sapwood will be balanced evenly in the finished piece. (See figure 1, cut 1.) This also helps in the drying process.

Template

Nail

2 Chainsaw the log almost in half where marked (photo A), splitting it through the pith. That way, the log still sits firmly on the ground for cut 2. If uncomfortable using a chainsaw, split the log at a bandsaw using a right-angle sled.

3 Cut a flat on the bottom of the log (cut 2) so the blank will sit flat on the bandsaw (photo B). Finish cutting the log in half.

4 Make a round hardboard or plywood template the diameter of the desired bowl. (While every bowl blank will be a different size, this one is 6″ high and 14″ across). Mark the template's center and the center of the half log's top face. Secure the template by driving a nail through its center and into the log's center.

5 Rest the log half on the bandsaw table and cut out the blank, running the blade along the edge of the template as you rotate the blank (photo C). Note: For the best results, I use a ½″ × 3 TPI (teeth/inch) blade.

6 Remove the template, and, using a drill, bore a ⅜″ hole 1¾″ deep into the blank's nail hole to accept a screw center (photo D). Work to keep the bit at a right angle to the blank's face.

Mount the blank & turn the outside

1 Install a four-jaw chuck onto your lathe's headstock, and tighten a screw center into it. Install a live cup center into the tailstock. Now, screw the blank onto the screw center, and bring up the tailstock to secure the blank.

Figure 2: Hollowing the Calabash

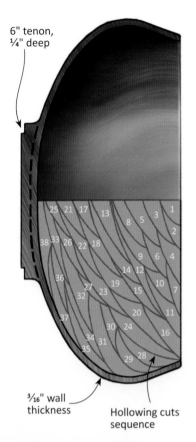

6" tenon, ¼" deep

25 21 17 13 8 5 3 1
38 33 26 22 18 9 6 4 2
36 14 12 10
27 19 15 7
32 23 20 11
37 30 24 16
34 31 29 28
35

³⁄₁₆" wall thickness

Hollowing cuts sequence

2 Now, with the lathe running at 800 rpm, use a ½" bowl gouge with a fingernail grind to round the blank (photo E). Move the tool back and forth on the tool rest while riding the bevel. Note that when turning fresh green wood there will be water spraying from the blank as it spins. This is part of the fun. The moisture keeps your tool cool and is not as abrasive on the tool's edge as seasoned wood. For safety, I stand forward of the turning as shown.

3 Next, angle the tool rest and begin shaping the bottom of the bowl by removing the waste wood, using a ½" bowl gouge (photo F).

4 Form a ¼" tenon on the bowl's bottom to fit in your four-jaw chuck (photo G). To perform this step safely, make the tenon around 40% of the diameter of the bowl blank if possible. Here, the tenon is about 6" for the best possible grip. If using a smaller chuck jaw opening, make

sure that the blank size is one you can safely handle. I turn the tenon with a ⅜" fingernail spindle gouge. Its deep grind makes it suitable for detail work. I shape the tenon so it is at a right angle to the bowl bottom, which is flat at this point. This lets the face of the chuck fit snugly against the flat bottom.

5 With the bowl blank held firmly in the chuck and the tailstock still in place, true up to the finished calabash shape (see figure 2), using a series of shear scrapes. I try to make a typical calabash shape that is slightly enclosed to create a pleasing look after it dries.

Turn the inside

1 Remove the tailstock and fit the tenon in the four-jaw chuck on the headstock. Locate the tool rest so that it is parallel to the top face of the bowl blank and just below center. Now, flatten the face with a ½" bowl gouge. Then, begin to hollow the

½" fingernail gouge

E

F

G

SAFETY TIP

There is a lathe speed formula by the late Utah turning teacher Dale Nish that he used to help students turn safely; I recommend it here. It goes like this: The diameter [of the turning] x rpm should equal between 6,000 to 9,000. For instance, if you have a 10"-diameter piece and your lathe is spinning at 1,000 rpm, you are at 10,000, and over the safety limits for that project.

interior of the bowl with the gouge (photo H). Start near the center of the blank, and take a series of cuts, working from left to right in the order in figure 2. Make deeper and deeper cuts until most of the bulk is removed. I carefully leave more bulk at the bottom of my piece so I can make cuts on the upper portion of the bowl without losing structure to make those cuts.

2 Note: At this point, you want to establish the wall thickness. Since this is a green-finished bowl, aim to cut the walls evenly and relatively thin to help with the drying process. Uneven walls and thick wood invites cracking during the drying process.

Using a ⅜″ bowl gouge, establish a wall thickness of ³⁄₁₆″ as shown in photo I. To do this, I cut down from the rim one third of the depth of my bowl and stop. Now, make sure you are cutting the wood evenly and cleanly. If you like what you see, cut the next one third down until you blend that with the first third. Proceed to blend in the bottom one third. I'll use a ½″ bowl gouge that has been traditionally ground to finish this task. That's because the grain direction changes from the sides to the more end-grain-like wood at the center, which the traditional grind handles better than a fingernail grind.

3 Remain very conscious of the depth of the bottom. I make that judgment by eying the outside shape and determining where the outside bottom will be. Since I am shooting for a ³⁄₁₆″ wall thickness, I make the inside ³⁄₁₆″ from my perceived exterior's bottom. I also want a continuous flowing curve on the inside that mimics the exterior shape. This takes patience and thoughtful measuring with a caliper throughout the process (photo J).

Sand and complete the calabash

1 With the tool work done for now, it's time to sand your calabash. I use 3″-diameter Mirka Abranet mesh sanding discs attached to a 3″ foam pad accessory for a portable drill. (I prefer Abranet over traditional sandpapers because the mesh abrades green wood faster and smoother.) I also protect myself from sanding dust with a respirator.

2 Before sanding and with the piece stationary, carefully examine the surface areas that have torn grain or tool marks. Then, with the lathe running at 500 rpm, sand the bowl's inside surface, as shown in photo K. Once you smooth out the troubled areas, spin the piece and sand over the entire surface inside and out. I start with 120 grit and sand through 400, going over the inside and outside surfaces within reach. Carefully clean the bowl with compressed air between sanding with each grit. Don't overheat the wood during this process. Green wood can create heat-checking, which can ruin your project. Apply the sanding mesh lightly to the wood, and replace the discs as soon as they lose their cutting/sanding ability.

3 Next, remove the finely sanded calabash from the lathe and make a jamb chuck from a piece of scrapwood that you screw on to a faceplate (photo L). Using a ⅜″ spindle gouge, cut a ⅜″-long tapered tenon on the jamb chuck that fits snugly inside the rim of the completed bowl. Test-fit the bowl to get the size just right.

4 Further secure the bowl by holding it in place with the tailstock and live cup center. Then, finish shaping the bottom of the bowl (photo M). Sand as before. Remove the tailstock and take some delicate cuts to trim off the last bit of wood at the center. Sand the area. This approach will let you give your baseless bowl better balance when it rests on the table.

Dry the calabash and apply a finish

Note: While you dodge months of drying by turning a calabash, a little careful drying is still critical. And, since oak is particularly hard to dry, you need to slow the process down at this point.

1 Place the bowl in a thick paper sack from the grocery store and leave it in a cool dark place for a few days to a week. Since the piece is thin-walled, it should be dry by then. If you have a sensitive scale, one way to know is to weigh the bowl after a day or two and keep weighing it until it stops losing weight. You could also use a moisture meter, provided you don't mar the surface.

2 Finish the calabash once it is dry. Notice how the dried calabash has warped. It has moved into an organic shape that is very pleasing to the eye. To finish the piece, first determine how you see it being used and the wood's color. If I am making a decorative calabash, I go with a tung oil or shellac. If the wood is a light color, I avoid these finishes since they may go yellow over time. Gloss polyurethane works well on a lighter wood. I see the bowl I turned here as a utility item and will therefore use a penetrating oil finish like walnut oil. Penetrating oils are better for utility items since there is no film to harm while cleaning. Also, penetrating oils require no skill to apply and can be restored by anyone. Once the finish dries completely, put your calabash to work.

Jamb chuck

Tapered tenon

LIVE-EDGE BOWLS

Turning to the natural look

BY MIKE KEHS

There's something particularly satisfying about turning a "natural-" or "live-edge" bowl. First of all, the scalloped lip and the elongated grain on the bottom of the bowl give it a pleasing oval appearance, and the intact bark on the edge imparts a distinct character not seen on typical bowls. Secondly, there's a real joy in creating a bowl completely from its inception—beginning with selecting the log and "finding" the bowl within it, to bandsawing the blank and turning it into an object of beauty.

Many novice turners are mystified as to how the unusual shape is created, but there's no magic involved. It's really all in how the bowl blank is cut from the log (see fig. 1) and how it's oriented on the lathe. There's nothing particularly difficult to the technique, but there are a few tricks involved that I'll explain, including how to select and cut an appropriate turning blank and how to best orient it to maximize aesthetics. No special tools are needed—just a four-prong drive center, a four-jaw chuck, a cup center, and a few typical turning tools.

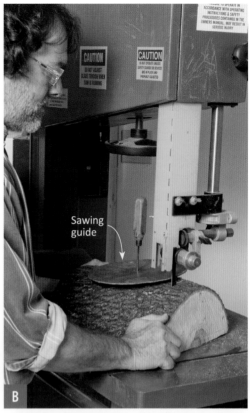

Select, prepare, and mount the blank

1 Select wood such as cherry, ash, oak, or box elder with an attractive bark. To ensure intact bark, harvest the log during late autumn through early winter, before the new cambium layer starts forming.

Figure 1: Alive in the Log

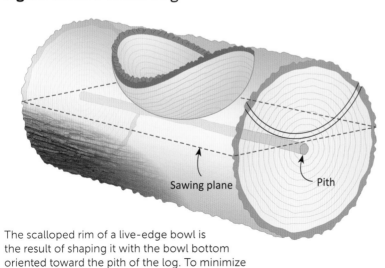

The scalloped rim of a live-edge bowl is the result of shaping it with the bowl bottom oriented toward the pith of the log. To minimize or eliminate cracking, avoid the log's pith.

2 For a symmetrical bowl, select a section of the log that includes a broad surface that approaches a true arc. Then crosscut that section to a length slightly more than the diameter of your desired bowl. Next, rip the desired section of the bowl blank from the log, supporting it between wedged chocks, as shown in photo A. It can help to first mark out the rough profile of the bowl on the end of the log and to strike a chalk line across the bark to guide your cut.

3 Rough-out the blank's circular shape on the bandsaw. I guide the cut using a hardboard template centered on the half-round log. I use an awl to pin the template in place, sawing just outside its perimeter (photo B).

4 Use a Forstner or multi-spur bit to drill a shallow blind hole through the bark at the former location of the awl to allow your four-prong drive center to bite into solid wood.

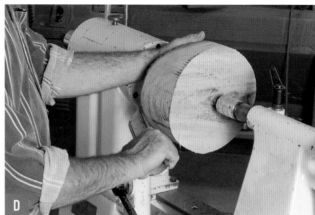

5 Mount the blank by placing the drive center into the blind hole, center-balancing the blank, and pressing the tailstock against the blank's sawn face using a live center. Use the locked tool rest as a reference for center-balancing the blank. With the tailstock pressed lightly enough against the blank to allow adjustment, begin by setting the opposing "low" walls of the bowl equidistant from the tool rest (photo C). Follow up by adjusting the "high" walls in the same manner (photo D). Then fully engage the tailstock center, and lock it in place. Check the balance of the mounting by running the lathe at a low rpm.

Turn the outside

Note: All of the shaping—inside and out—on this bowl was done with a ½″ bowl gouge, except where noted in the text.

1 With the lathe spinning at a speed appropriate to the size of the blank, waste away much of the lower outside of the bowl (photo E). (For this 11″-diameter bowl, I began with a speed of 500 rpm.) Once the bowl is mostly concentric, you can increase your lathe speed.

2 Flatten the bottom of the bowl, and turn a tenon to suit your four-jaw chuck (photo F). Make the length of the tenon equal to the depth of your chuck recess minus about 1/16″, refining the shape with a ½″ spindle gouge.

3 Begin refining the outside shape of the bowl, working from the center outward (photo G). When you reach the lip of the bowl, keep a very firm grip on the tool, as its tip will be suspended in midair during some of the bowl's rotation (photo H). Keep

QUICK TIP

Before taking the final outside cleanup cuts, carefully apply CA glue to the side (but not the top) edges of the bark to solidify it.

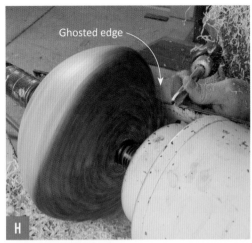

Ghosted edge

Tape as depth gauge

an eye on the spinning ghosted form to monitor your tool travel.

Turn the inside

1 Remount the bowl, inverting it and securing the tenon in a four-jaw chuck. Hold a long drill bit up against the "high" side of the bowl, with the tool's tip about ½″ away from the intended bottom of the bowl. Wrap tape around the shank of the bit at the highest point of the bowl to serve as a depth gauge. Then drill a hole to that depth using a drill chuck on the lathe (photo I).

2 Begin shaping the inside of the bowl, moving inward toward the center in a series of successively wider passes (photo J).

3 While removing most of the interior mass, leave the wall relatively thick. Then begin taking it down in sections to a final thickness of about ¼″ (photo K). The

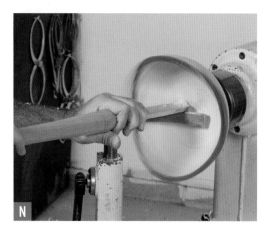

the measurement with calipers (photo L). Then refine the cut as necessary to bring the whole section to a consistent thickness.

5 Now move down into the bottom of the bowl in the same manner, bringing the wall to its final thickness (photo M). Angle your tool rest as deeply as possible into the bowl to provide good tool support as you turn. When you've finished the wall as well as you can with the gouge, switch to a scraper to clean up (photo N).

6 Finish-sand both the inside and outside of the walls through 220 grit (I use a foam-backed disc mounted in a drill). You can sand the spinning bowl up to the lip section, at which point you'll need to stop the lathe and sand the projecting sections of the lip individually (photo O).

reason for taking it down in sections is that the uncut mass toward the bottom of the bowl helps support the projecting thin section of the wall as it is being finessed. Taking the wall down all at once would invite flutter and rough cuts.

4 As you approach the final thickness of the first section, stop the lathe, and check

Twice-Turned Bowls

A bowl made of wet wood can either be turned to completion at once (and left to dry in finished form), or it can be turned oversized, left to season, and then re-turned afterward. Finishing a bowl in one shot is faster, but the piece is almost certain to warp some afterward, which may or may not make it more attractive. On the other hand, a "twice-turned" bowl is roughed out to expedite drying, then set aside wrapped in newspaper to slowly season before performing the final shaping, at which point the piece will retain its concentricity.

Jamb chuck

Turn the foot

1 Dismount the bowl, and make a jamb chuck like the one in photo P. It's nothing more than a turned concave cylinder covered with thin rubber. (I cut the rubber away here for a better view of the turned section.) In general, the diameter of a jamb chuck like this should be about half the diameter of the bowl.

2 With the jamb chuck mounted in your four-jaw chuck, mount the bowl bottom-side-out, bringing a tailstock cup center against the residual divot in the bowl bottom.

3 Using a ¼" bowl gouge, reduce the tenon to the diameter of the cup center, creating a slightly concave "foot" in the process (photo Q). Sand the freshly turned area with the lathe spinning.

4 Dismount the bowl, chisel off the remaining tenon waste, and sand any nub smooth.

5 Apply the finish of your choice. I wiped on two coats of Danish oil, buffing afterward to create a low-luster sheen.

Dimensions: 5" dia. × 6¾"h

BOWLS

HOLLOW TURNED VESSEL

An uncompromising cheat makes a tricky job easy

BY MIKE KEHS

A hollow turned vessel can be a real piece of art. Well executed, it's not only a visual treat, but a wonder of workmanship since many people can't imagine how you can excavate a thin-walled piece through a small hole at one end. But that is how it's usually done, using special long-shank offset turning tools and a deft touch. The biggest challenge with this approach lies in maintaining the control of cut while reaching deeply into a blind hole. To help students ease into the techniques involved, I've developed a sort of "cheat" that simplifies the process.

In a nutshell, my technique involves first hollowing out just the top section of a vessel using an offset scraper. I then part off that section, which allows easy access for hollowing the remainder of the vessel with regular gouges and scrapers. Afterward,

Figure 1: Hollow Turned Vessel

Basic Shaping Sequence
1) Turn tenon.
2) Turn upper 5½" to shape, and remainder to a cylinder.
3) Hollow out top section.
4) After parting off lid, hollow middle section.
5) Refine exterior 5" down from joint.
6) Complete hollowing.
7) Complete exterior shaping.

I reattach the top and add a decorative bead to conceal the joint line (see fig. 1). The "split-top" is a great way to get started at turning hollow vessels, while producing a piece that will wow your friends and family.

Tools, Centers, and Chucks

You'll need a basic complement of turning tools, many of which you may already have (photo A). The three less common tools shown here include the straight-bodied scraper (Ci3 Easy Finisher), offset scraper (Ci3 Easy Hollower), and ¹⁄₁₆" parting tool. You don't necessarily need all these specific tools, and I'll note when you can use an alternative.

For this project, you'll also need a four-jaw chuck, a cup, or safety center, and a cone

center. If you don't have a commercial cone center, it's easy to make one for this job, as shown in figure 2. (Note: Unless you have another lathe, you'll need to make the cone center before beginning work on the vessel.)

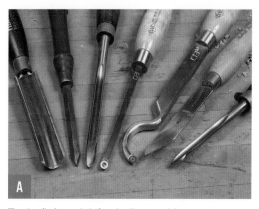

Tools: (left to right) spindle roughing gouge, standard parting tool, ½" bowl gouge, Ci3 Easy Finisher, Ci3 Easy Hollower, ¹⁄₁₆" parting tool, and detail spindle gouge.

Figure 2: Shop-Made Cone Center

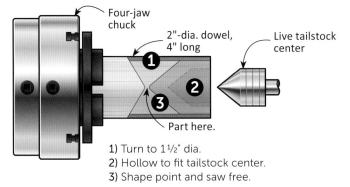

Four-jaw chuck

2"-dia. dowel, 4" long

Live tailstock center

Part here.

1) Turn to 1½" dia.
2) Hollow to fit tailstock center.
3) Shape point and saw free.

Shape the vessel's outside

1 Bandsaw the turning blank to a rough 5¼"-dia. cylinder (photo B), and then locate the center point on each end. (Note: The 9¾"-long blank shown here provides enough excess length to allow working at a safe distance from the chuck. If you're comfortable turning adjacent to a spinning chuck, you can begin with a blank as short as 8".)

2 Mount the blank on your lathe between a cup, or safety, center in the headstock and a live center in the tailstock. Turn the blank to a true cylinder using a spindle roughing gouge or bowl gouge. Then use a standard parting tool to turn a ⁷⁄₁₆"-long × 2½"-diameter tenon on the tailstock end (photo C).

3 Switch out your cup center with a four-jaw chuck, and remount the blank with its tenon clamped into the chuck.

4 Referring to figure 1, turn the uppermost 5½" of the outside of the vessel to its finished shape with a bowl gouge. Turn the lowermost section to a cylinder for now. (The extra mass will provide stability when hollowing out the interior.) Undercut the area at the joint line by about ⅛", using a detail spindle gouge (photo D). Now rough out the edge of the bead at the top to a 1 ⅝"-diameter, but don't undercut it yet.

5 Still using the detail gouge, turn a flat on the top end of the vessel (photo E) for better bit registration when drilling the hole.

Shop-made thickness gauge

Use drill extension to catch freed top section.

Hollow and remove the top section

1 Outfit your tailstock with a drill chuck. Attach an extension to a 1"-diameter Forstner or multi-spur bit, and mount it in the chuck. With the blank spinning at about 500 rpm, advance the tailstock to drill a 6⅜"-deep hole (photo F). (If your extension isn't long enough, just drill as far as you can for now, and complete the job after removing the top section.)

2 Begin to hollow out the top section, accessing what you can with a straight scraper or the Ci3 Easy Finisher. Then move to the Ci3 Easy Hollower to turn the corner (photo G). Hollow out the section to a bit below the joint line. As shown in figure 1, remove material by "scooping" it out in successively deeper passes. Use a ruler and

a thick wire with inward-turned ends set 1" apart to gauge your progress (photo H). Aim for a ¼" wall thickness in the area just below the joint. Leave the area above the joint about ⅜" thick, tapering to ¼" at the top of the vessel, as shown in figure 1.

3 In preparation for parting off the top, first draw reference lines across the joint area for grain reorientation during reattachment later. Also, insert your drill extension rod into the hole to catch the lid once it's freed. Then part away the top section with a ¹⁄₁₆" parting tool, holding it at 45° to the vessel axis (photo I). (Using a thicker parting tool would cause the top section to sit too deep in the main body when reattached later.) Remove the drill extension rod and top section.

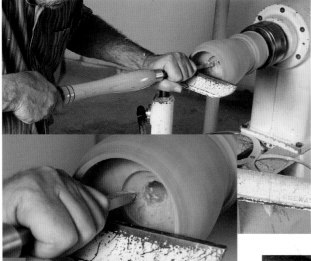

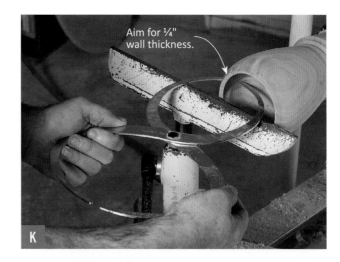

4 Refine the top edge of the body with a
detail spindle gouge for a complementary fit
with the edge of the top section. Make the
surfaces mate as well as possible to ensure
a good glue joint. Test and fit as you work,
sighting for gaps on the exterior and feeling
for them on the interior.

Hollow and refine the interior

1 Hollow out the middle section of the
vessel (photo J with inset). You can use a
bowl gouge for the roughing, followed by
cleanup with a scraper, but I find that the
Ci3 Easy Finisher cuts quickly and with
enough finesse to do the whole job. As
before, take a series of progressively deeper
scoops, working from the center outward, to
remove the material. Use a caliper to check
your wall thickness as you progress (photo
K), again shooting for ¼"-thick walls.

2 Turn the outside of the bottom section
to final shape, working down to about 5"
from the joint line. Now finish hollowing the
interior, gauging the ¼" wall thickness from
the exterior walls and stopping when you've
reached a depth that meets the bottom of the
drilled hole. (You won't be able to gauge the
bottommost ¾" or so of wall thickness yet.)

3 Use a commercial cone center mounted
on your tailstock (or the shop-made version
slipped over a live center, as shown in
figure 2) to hold the inverted top section
against the top of the vessel. Center it
carefully, and then use a detail spindle
gouge held in scraping position to refine its
underside surface (which will be the target
for many exploring fingers), as shown in
photo L.

4 Back up the tailstock, apply yellow glue
to the mating edges of the top and body,
and glue them together using the cone
center on the tailstock to apply clamping
pressure (photo M). Use the reference lines
drawn earlier to align the top as originally
oriented, with its edges projecting evenly
all the way around.

Grain-matching reference lines

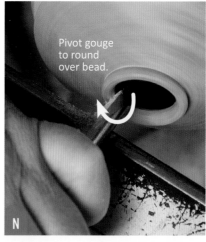

Pivot gouge to round over bead.

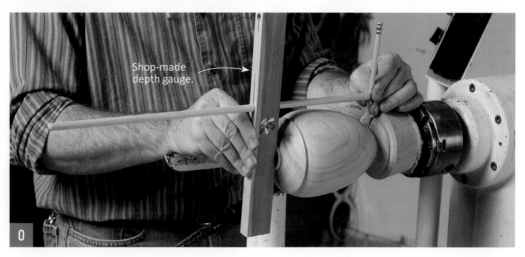

Shop-made depth gauge.

QUICK TIP

When hollowing the lower half of the interior, angle your tool rest as far as possible into the opening for tool stability.

Refine the reassembled exterior

1 With the vessel still attached to the four-jaw chuck, refine the exterior surfaces using the detail spindle gouge. Clean up at the joint line to remove glue and to ensure that the areas adjacent to the joint are truly concentric. Use the offset scraper to smooth the interior at the joint line. Turn down the outside edge of the bead to its final diameter, and undercut its outside edge. To do the final rounding, insert the gouge into the hole and pivot it around to the outside (photo N).

2 The next step is to double-check the depth of the interior, add ¼" to that measurement, and then mark off that length at the bottom of the vessel. To do the job, I use the simple depth-gauge jig shown in photo O. It's just a stick with a hole drilled through the center

to accept a ⅜"-dia. dowel. A bolt and wing nut squeeze together a slot bandsawn inward from one face and intersecting the hole to pinch the dowel in place.

To use the jig, first place the stick across the vessel opening, bottom out the dowel inside the vessel, and then lock the dowel in position. Next, place the dowel alongside the vessel, with a pencil held against its end, and mark that location at the bottom of the vessel (again, as shown in photo O). Accounting for the pencil tip offset, calculate a ¼" distance outward from the interior vessel depth. After scribing a line completely around the vessel at that location, part in enough to leave 1"-diameter of material remaining. This establishes the vessel bottom.

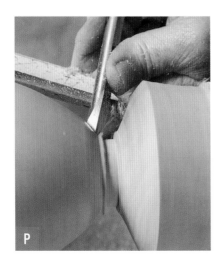

Jamb chuck

3 Using a detail spindle gouge, finish refining the exterior down to the parted line (photo P). Then sand the vessel through 320 grit, and remove it from the lathe.

4 Dismount the vessel to make the jamb chuck for finishing the foot. Begin with a 10″-long piece of 2″-square hardwood, squarely crosscut at its ends. Mount it in the four-jaw chuck, with its opposite end supported by a tailstock center. Turn down the outermost 8″ of the piece to a hair less than 1″ in diameter.

Slip the vessel completely onto the chuck to check the fit. If it rattles at the opening, wrap masking tape around the chuck to build it out for a snug fit. Also attach a 1″-diameter disc of 100-grit sandpaper to the turned end of the chuck, using spray adhesive or double-faced tape for a better purchase on the vessel.

5 Slide the vessel onto the jamb chuck again, and bring the tailstock up against the end of the turning blank, ensuring that the tailstock center sits in the existing divot. Use a spindle detail gouge to turn a shallow recess in the vessel bottom (photo Q). Then finish-sand the recess.

6 Dismount the vessel and use a small handsaw to cut away as much as possible of the tenon without scarring the base. Chisel away the remaining nub, and then sand the surface.

Finishing up

Apply your preferred finish. I wiped on two coats of Danish oil, followed by a thorough buffing to bring up the shine.

CLASSIC CANDLESTICK

Three custom jigs make this splendid little candlestick well suited to large production runs

BY JON HUTCHINSON

Traditionally I make small holiday gifts for employees and family members. This year I thought it would be unique to give hand-crafted candleholders designed with a yesteryear flair. My objective was to design a candleholder that could be actually used or just set out as decoration. It also should be fairly easy to make since my production run would be about 20 units.

I turned two prototypes from which I was able to design and construct a couple of jigs that made the process much easier, more accurate and less time-consuming. This project covers the candleholders themselves and the jigs I used to make them.

I chose mahogany for its color and workability, but any wood will do. My prototypes were turned from hard maple.

The basic holder consists of three pieces: a base, a stick, and a handle. The base begins as a 6"-square x 1"-thick piece. The

stick is a 2″-square x 4½″-long piece. And the handle starts life as a ½″-thick piece whose finished size is 1¼″ in diameter (only three sides are rounded). The finished holder stands 5½″ tall, and the base diameter is 5⅜″. The base is tapered on the underside and dished on the face. The design of the stick includes tapers, a bird's beak, and beads.

Prepare the stock

Once the base and stick stock are dimensioned, flattened, and squared, find the center on both sides of the base and both ends of the stick (photo A). The handle can be laid out and finished later. Using a compass, draw a 5⅜″ circle on one side of the base; this will be the "up" side. Use an awl to dimple the centers on both sides of the base and both ends of the stick.

A ⅜″ piece of dowel centers and holds the base to the stick when gluing up (photo B). Chuck a ⅜″ bit in the drill press and drill a center hole on the base about ¾″ deep. Then

cut it circular, keeping the blade just to the outside of the circle you marked.

Now drill one end of the stick ¾″ to 1″ deep (photo C). To make turning easier, cut the corners off the stick to form an octagon before gluing up the base and the stick. At 4½″ long, this piece is a little small for running through the tablesaw. And it's awkward to run through a bandsaw with the table tilted to 45°. I used a sled on the bandsaw to cut the corners. Taking the time to build a sled to cut the corners off is well worth the effort.

I already had a sled since I turn quite a few bottle stoppers that are cut to an octagonal shape before mounting on the lathe. For my sled I used some scrap 1″-thick walnut that had already been cut on a 45° angle. The two pieces were only 3″ wide, but would work to cut blanks as long as 5″. If you make a sled from two pieces of wood, cut a base from ¼″ hardboard that's longer than the distance from the blade to the miter slot and as wide as the wood you're using. Glue the two pieces to the hardboard base so the 45° angles form a V. Once dry, measure ¹¹⁄₁₆″ from the center of the V and cut off the excess on the tablesaw. Place this edge against the bandsaw blade and put a mark on the other end where it crosses the miter slot (the side of the slot closest to the blade). Then cut off the excess on the table saw.

Next, mill a piece of hardwood that's about 6″ long and at least 2″ wide to the thickness of your miter slot. Slide this into the miter slot. With the two pieces on the bandsaw (to ensure correct alignment) glue them together and use screws or brads to reinforce the joint. Glue a small piece of scrap to the back of the block with the V as a stop, and you're in business (photo D). The square stock rides on a 45º angle through the blade. Just keep flipping the block until all four corners are cut (photo E).

Secure the base in the lathe

With the stick cut into an octagon, glue it to the base using a piece of dowel. While this is drying is a good time to fabricate a special faceplate to hold the base in the lathe. The tailstock holds the end of the stick. My custom faceplate started with an aluminum 3″ plate (photo F). I screwed a piece of 1″-thick hard maple that had been cut to a 3¼″ circle to it and turned it down to just over 3″ in diameter next to the metal plate

and just under 3″ on the other end.

Drill a ³⁄₁₆″ hole in the center while the faceplate is still mounted on the headstock. Cut a piece of ³⁄₁₆″-diameter steel rod to about 1½″. Chuck it in the drill press and file or grind the tip to a very sharp point while the rod is spinning. Epoxy this rod in the hole in the faceplate so that only ⅛″ to ⁵⁄₃₂″ of the point is proud of the surface.

The metal plate I used has two sets of mounting holes. I used the outer holes to screw the plate to the wood face. I drilled holes through the wood face through the inner set of mounting holes. Then I ran 1¼″-long pan head screws through these holes so that the points of the screws protruded ³⁄₃₂″ or less beyond the surface of the wood face (photo G). If your screws are too long, use washers to adjust them so that very little of the point shows. The center rod, which should protrude farther than the screws, and these four screws act much like a spur center.

It takes a little pounding with a mallet to

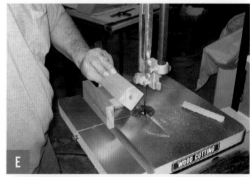

mount the blank to the faceplate. But you don't want to pound directly on the metal plate; you'll want to use a piece of scrap to protect it. I drilled a 1¼" hole in a small scrap of 8/4 stock 1" deep for this purpose. Set the blank with the stick end down on your workbench and align the pointed center rod with the awl dimple in the base of the blank. Slip the scrap over the metal plate and give it a couple of good whacks with a mallet to seat the faceplate to the blank. The pressure from the mallet is distributed on the back of the metal plate and the pan head screws, not on the threaded collar.

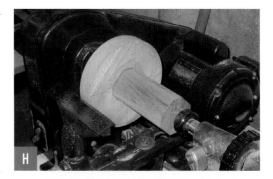

Start shaping the candlestick

Mount the whole assembly on the lathe and run the tailstock up into the dimple on the end of the stick.

Start the process by turning the base down to the 5 ⅜" mark you made earlier on the face of the base (photo H). Then turn the stick round to just over 1½" (photo I). With the lathe turning (I like to turn these at around 1,500 rpm), put three marks on the stick: one at the bottom of the candle cup, one at the top of the lower bead, and one at the bottom of the lower bead (photo J).

Turn the space between the bottom of the candle cup and the top of the lower bead down to 1" in diameter (photo K). Then use your parting tool to turn a groove below the lower bead down to 1" also (photo L). Next, turn the lower bead area down to 1¼".

Now turn your attention (and your tool rest) back to the base. With the piece spinning, mark a line on the edge of the base ⁵⁄₁₆" from the face (photo M). The base is tapered on the underside from this mark down to the faceplate (photo N), leaving a lip that's about ¹⁄₁₆" high (photo O).

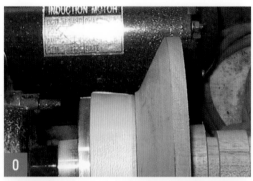

Next, reposition the tool rest parallel with the face of the base and start roughing out the dish profile (photo P). My favorite tool for this is the Skewchigouge by Crown Tools, which can work as both a skew chisel and a gouge.

The profile should start ¼″ from the edge and the deepest point of the dish should be ⅜″, about 1 ⁷⁄₁₆″ from the outer edge. The bottom of the stick completes the dish, so moving back and forth from base to stick is necessary to get the right profile (photo Q).

Before leaving the base, round over the edge. The underside roundover is quite shallow because of the taper. The topside roundover should be a pleasant profile that ends in a point on the face where the dish profile began.

Move back to the stick and turn a rough profile of the candle cup, then use a parting tool to turn the ¼″ bead area below the cup to ¾″ in diameter (photo R). Now mark the center of the bird's beak and turn the underside, tapering it to the lower bead. Again, I used my Skewchigouge for this. Then finish turning the profile.

The top of the candleholder need not be flat. I used a parting tool to sneak in around

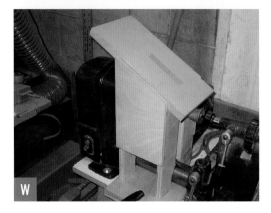

the live center on the tailstock and taper it from about ¹⁄₁₆″ from the edge to as close as I could get to the live center without running metal against metal. The taper I put on the top is very slight, starting about ¹⁄₁₆″ from the edge, about ¹⁄₁₆″ deep at ³⁄₈″ from the edge. This leaves a flat lip on the top the same size as the flat part on the side of the candle cup at the very top edge.

Sand your candleholder and burnish it with wood shavings while it's turning. Then apply your favorite finish while it's still mounted on the lathe. I used Behlen Master Woodturner's Finish (photo S).

Build a jig for cutting the handle slot

The next step is to cut a slot in the base for the handle. For this, you'll need to build another jig. The taper on the bottom of the base is pretty close to 28°. Our jig will have a 28° slope and will be wide enough to accommodate the base of a router. It also must straddle the candleholder (photo T).

My lathe has a tube rail, so this jig is designed to fit over the rail and index to a baseplate that is clamped to the table on which my lathe is mounted (photo U). Different lathes will require a different design for this jig, but the common elements are that the top of the jig has to slope 28° and the slot in the top of the jig has to be in the exact center and must be sized to accommodate a guide bushing on the router baseplate (photo V).

This jig is made of plywood, both ½″ and ¾″, and ¾″ MDF for the top. I chose MDF because the slot in which the guide bushing

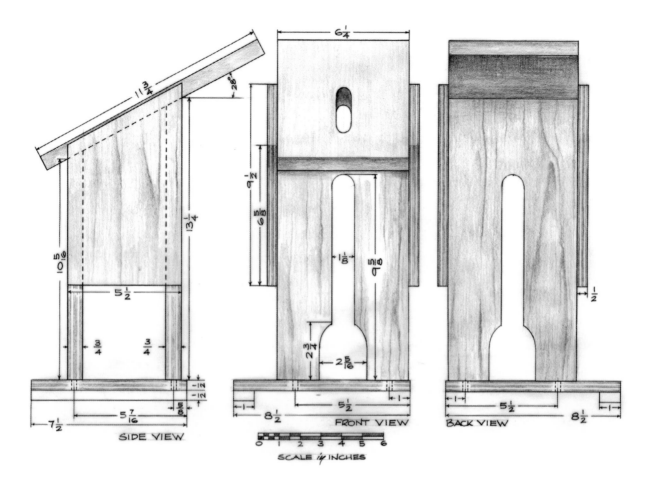

SIDE VIEW

FRONT VIEW

BACK VIEW

SCALE in INCHES

runs is smoother than it would be if cut through plywood. The jig is basically a box with slots cut into the front and back so it slips down over the turned candleholder. The front of the jig faces the headstock and slips over the faceplate collar so it is behind the faceplate. The back of the jig slips over the candleholder below the candle cup. The sloped top is higher at the front (photo W).

However you build this jig to fit your lathe setup, it is imperative that it not move. And there must be about 1/8″ clearance between the top of the jig and the base of the candleholder. Mine is a two-piece jig: the box and a baseplate. The baseplate slips beneath the lathe tube and has four 1/4″ holes drilled in it. These holes are aligned with dowels that are glued into the bottoms

of the four "legs" of the box. First I slide the base under the tube to the cleat that is glued to the bottom of the base and then slide the box over the workpiece. Next I align the holes in the base with the dowels in the box and set both pieces together, then clamp the base to the table. Nothing moves.

Before you set your jig over the workpiece, lock the headstock. You don't want your nicely finished candleholder turning wildly when you introduce your router into the base.

To cut the slot where the handle will be mounted, set your router up with a 1/2″ straight bit and a 3/4″ guide bushing. You'll have to do some measuring to get the depth of your cut just right. The cut should not be deeper than the point that you established

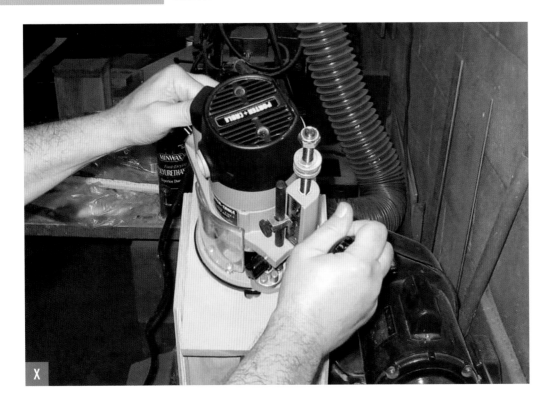

on the face of the base when you rounded over the edge where it meets the beginning of the dish profile. Now make one pass from the high part of the top of the jig to the lower part of the top (photo X). Going in the other direction could cause the jig to tip out of the index holes in the base.

The handle is attached to the base of the candleholder with a dowel. The next step is to drill a hole in the center of the cut you just made in the base to accommodate a short length of dowel. Make a drill guide for this procedure. All that's needed is a ¾" square of hardwood and another piece of hardwood that's 1" wide x ⅝" thick. Both should be between 2½" and 3" long. I made mine 2¾", a comfortable size to work with. Glue the two pieces together with the top piece overlapping the bottom by ⅛" on each side. Then drill a ¼" hole exactly in the center. What you've got now is a T-shaped guide with the ¼" hole running through the top of the T.

This drill guide fits into the slot on the top of the jig you built for routing a slot in the base of the candleholder. With the jig still in place, mark the center of the slot you routed in the base. Measure for the center very carefully (because there's not much material on the top and bottom of the base at the edge) and use an awl to punch a hole in the center mark. Place a ¼" brad-point bit in a drill and slide the drill guide up onto the bit. Put the brad point in the center mark and slide the guide down the bit and into the slot on the top of the jig. Drill a hole about ½" deep.

Smooth the underside with another jig

Whew! The lathe work is over. Remove the jig and take the candleholder out of the lathe. Now turn it over, and what do you see? Five holes in the bottom of the base; an unsightly mess. You've got a few options to deal with the holes. You can leave them; you can glue felt to the bottom to hide them (hmmmm); or you can construct another very simple jig

to eliminate them. I'll take door number 3; I prefer a more finished look even on surfaces that will seldom, if ever, be seen.

Again, using sheet goods (¾" MDF was my choice because it would not mar the finished edge of the base), I cut a piece that was 12 x 15". I also cut a piece of ¼" hardboard to the same size and glued them together. My router table insert is 12" wide, so making the jig 12" wide makes it easy to index it to the exact center of the table. The jig should be 1" thick since the base of the candleholder is 1" thick, although the part of the base that will ride against this jig is only around ⅞" high. Two pieces of ½" material will also work if you don't have a 1"-thick piece of sheet goods.

The size of this jig was determined by the size of my router table and the position of the miter slot in the table. Yours may differ. I cut a dado the same width as my miter slot 1¼" from one end (the hardboard is on the underside). Then I milled a piece of walnut ½" high and sized to slide in the miter slot.

The sheet material will have a large hole cut into it, centered over the router bit. To find the center, insert the walnut strip into the dado on the sheet goods and slip it into the miter slot. Slide the assembly over so the edge is bisecting the bit hole in your router table. Mark the center of the hole on the edge of the sheet goods and transfer this mark across the width of the sheet goods. Using a compass, draw a 7¼" circle.

Remove the walnut strip and cut out the hole with a jigsaw or a scroll saw. Sand the hole smooth and up to the circle that you drew. An oscillating drum sander works best. When you're satisfied that the hole is smooth and round, glue the walnut strip in the dado. If you made this jig the width of your router table insert, all you need to do is set it down into the miter slot, position it over the insert and clamp it to the table (photo Y). The hole is now centered over the router.

Chuck a ¾" straight bit in your router and set it for a ³⁄₃₂"-deep cut. Then turn it on.

Hold on to the candleholder tight and set it down in the middle (photo Z). Without turning the candleholder, make clockwise turns inside the jig until the edge of the base is rubbing on the jig, then make a couple more passes to ensure all the material you want to remove has been removed.

All that should remain is a very small hole where the center rod penetrated the wood. And that's not unsightly at all. If all went well, you have a hollowed-out bottom with about a ¼″ flat surface between the hollow and the taper that will sit nicely on any surface (photo AA). Now you can put some finish on the bare wood.

Only one step remains before getting to the handle: drilling a hole for the candle. The size of the hole will be determined by the kind of candle you intend to use. My choice was an 8″ Federal candle, which is straight. I chucked a ¹³⁄₁₆″ bit in the drill press and drilled to a depth of ¾″ (photo BB).

Make the handle

Finally, it's time to make the handle. The handle is ½″ thick to fit the groove that was routed in the edge of the base. It is 1¼″ round (on three sides) and has a ⅞″ hole in it. Since the edges of the hole need to be rounded over I started with a piece of mahogany that was 2¾″ wide and 12″ long. I laid out the outer diameter at a square corner and marked the center of the handle. First drill the ⅞″ hole. Then, using a ⅛″ roundover bit with a bearing guide in your router that's mounted in a router table, ease the edges of the hole on both sides.

On the tablesaw, crosscut the piece of wood at about 1½″. On the long-grain end of the square corner, put a mark on the edge that corresponds with the center of the hole you drilled in the base. With a ¼″

bit in the drill press and a fence to steady the thin piece of wood, drill a hole ¼″ deep. Now cut the handle out on the bandsaw. Remember only three corners get rounded; the fourth corner with the hole in the long grain remains square. Sand it smooth and ease the edges, leaving them square where the handle and the base intersect.

Put a finish on the handle, but not on the area where you'll glue it to the base. Cut a piece of ¼″ dowel to length and glue the handle to the base.

While this whole process seems like it may take weeks to finish given the special jigs and faceplate needed, it can actually be accomplished in a weekend. And once the jigs are built to fit your equipment, making candleholders by the dozen will be quick and enjoyable.

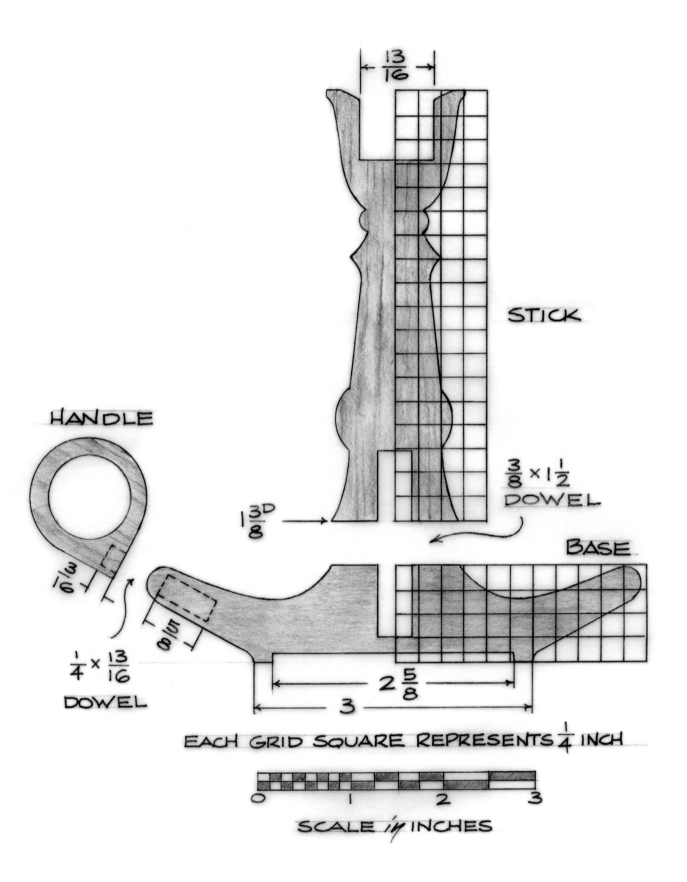

$\frac{13}{16}$

STICK

HANDLE

$\frac{3}{8} \times 1\frac{1}{2}$
DOWEL

$1\frac{3D}{8}$

BASE

$\frac{3}{16}$

$\frac{5}{8}$

$\frac{1}{4} \times \frac{13}{16}$

DOWEL

$2\frac{5}{8}$

3

EACH GRID SQUARE REPRESENTS $\frac{1}{4}$ INCH

0   1   2   3

SCALE *in* INCHES

SHOP-MADE SHAKER KNOBS

Simple and safe techniques for handsome handles

BY JIM HARROLD

Often taken for granted, well-crafted handles (knobs and pulls) say a lot about a piece of furniture or cabinet, especially handles that both please the eye as an accent and serve their function effectively. Ergonomically, their size and shape for the average drawer must accommodate a child's small hands, and those of an adult, providing comfort and plenty of purchase. Mechanically, a good knob or pull should open a drawer without separating from it, no matter how much ballast a pack rat has hoarded within. It should never come loose or spin on the door or drawer. And while it takes more time to

design and create stylish custom handles, the good news is that shop-made ones give you something unique compared to ho-hum store-bought offerings.

I've worked through the safe machining of a round Shaker knob. As shown here, you can attach them using tenons, wedged tenons, dowels, and screws. I'll also touch on two quick scaling methods.

Turned Shaker knobs

Shaker knobs appear in many understated furniture pieces and cabinets. Generally, 1¼″ to 2″ are common diameters. I like that I can turn a pair of knobs with tenons from one piece between centers. For a better hold, wedge the tenons in place during installation.

1 Cut a 6″-long blank from 1½″ dowel or turning stock and mount it between centers. At 1,500 rpm, round the blank to 1⅜″ diameter using a roughing gouge.

2 Mark the locations of beads, coves, and tenons shown in figure 1. Now, use a parting tool (or bedan) to establish the finished diameters.

3 With a roundnose scraper, form the coves (photo A), ensuring that the profiles match. Now reduce the waste diameter between

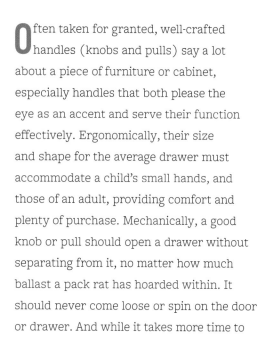

Scaling Handles to Match

While the handles here replicate store-bought sizes for cabinets and furniture pieces, you can scale them to any size you need with either of these easy solutions. Solution 1: Draw the desired handle on graph paper to full size. Reduce this image to the needed size at a copy machine by lowering the percentage from, say, 100% to 80%. Pick off measurements from the reduced copy for the desired handle size. Solution 2: Use a construction calculator that lets you multiply fractions by percentages.

Figure 1: Shaker Knob

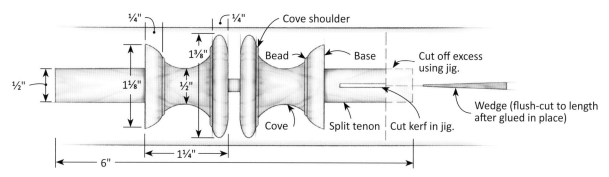

- Cove shoulder
- Bead
- Base
- Cut off excess using jig.
- Wedge (flush-cut to length after glued in place)
- Cove
- Split tenon
- Cut kerf in jig.

¼" ¼" 1⅜" ½" 1⅛" ½" 1¼" 6"

Kerfing Jig

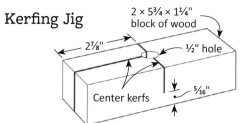

2 × 5¾ × 1¼" block of wood

2⅞" ½" hole

Center kerfs 5/16"

A With the tool rest above center, move the scraper in from the outside edges to form the cove.

B Form the rounded end profile of the knob by working from the center out and taking small cuts.

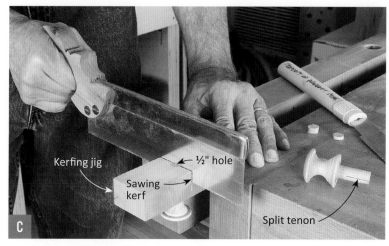

- Kerfing jig
- Sawing kerf
- ½" hole
- Split tenon

C Insert the knob's tenon in the jig and clamp the jig's kerfed end to secure the knob. Then flush-cut the tenon, and split it with a backsaw.

the pulls to around ⅛". Stop the lathe and finish separating the pulls with a handsaw.

4 Install a scroll chuck. Secure the tenon for one knob in the chuck. Position the tool rest at an angle to the knob's end and, with a spindle gouge, form the end profile (photo B). Shape the edges and base. Sand through 220 grit. Repeat for the other knob.

5 To split the tenons for the wedges, make the kerfing jig above. Flush-cut the tenons to rough length and kerf them (photo C). Cut tapered wedges that match the tenon's diameter.

TURN A SHOWY FINIAL

If you build classical furniture, you need this skill

DESIGNER/TURNER: CRAIG BENTZLEY
WRITER: JIM HARROLD

Common among the traditional furniture styles stemming from the classical revival, turned wood finials serve as a crowning ornament for many furniture pieces. While some are only turned, others take shape from both turning and carving as shown here. You've likely seen finials embellish grandfather clocks, china cabinets, and other classic case workpieces. Here, we focus on a turned vase and flame design and walk you through the essential steps from beginning to end.

From blank to rough-turned cylinder

1 Make a copy of the full-sized classic finial pattern on page 93 and pin it behind your lathe work area for reference. Consider sizing the finial as needed to suit a project you may be working on and add key diameter dimensions.

2 Mount the blank in a chuck (I prefer a Oneway Stronghold chuck with #2 jaws). Secure the opposite end of the blank with a bearing cup center in the tailstock. Using a 1¼″ roughing gouge, round the one end of the blank as shown in photo A at the

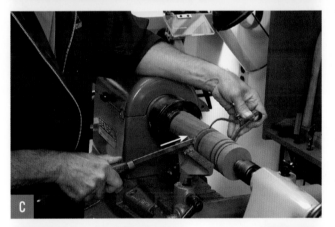

recommended speed indicated below. Stop the lathe, change the blank end-for-end, and complete turning the cylinder.

Tool: 1¼" roughing gouge
Speed: 300 to 500 rpm

3 Mark the locations (with the lathe running) of the various elements on the cylinder (tenon, coves, beads, etc.) with a pencil and 12" steel rule as shown in photo B. Use the dimensioned pattern as a guide.

4 Establish the diameters of the various elements on the cylinder by cutting to depth with a parting tool gauged by a set of calipers. Hold the tool at a slight angle at first and then level the tip as shown in photo C. Again, use the pattern for reference.

Tool: ³⁄₁₆" parting tool
Speed: 1,500 rpm

Now for the shapely vase

1 Remove the waste of the vase and tenon portion with a 1¼" roughing gouge. Use the parting tool to establish right-angle shoulders and handle any profiles without curves (such as the tenon). Create the vase shape with a ¾" gouge as shown in photo D. Move the tip from high to low, and keep the tip at a slight upward angle with the tool rest just below center.

Tools: 1¼" roughing gouge
³⁄₁₆" parting tool, ¾" gouge
Speed: 1,200 to 1,500 rpm

2 Turn down the flame portion to a cylinder of the finished outside diameter with a roughing gouge. Do this before forming the top of the vase. Lay a ¾" skew flat on the tool rest that's adjusted slightly below center and work the tool's angled cutting edge from the vase top to the side, shaping a curved edge as shown in photo E.

Tool: ¾" skew
Speed: 1,200 to 1,500 rpm

3 Shape the large cove between the vase and base/tenon using a ½″ round-nose scraper, laying the tool flat on the tool rest for control as shown in photo F. Again, keep the tool rest just below center. Arc the tip from right to left. Turn the smaller cove between the flame and the vase with a ¼″ round-nose scraper or a ¼″ spindle gouge. (If you use a ¼″ gouge, stay alert because small gouges are prone to catch your workpiece.)

Tools: ½" round-nose scraper
　　　　 ¼" round-nose scraper
Speed: 1,200 to 1,500 rpm

4 Create the bead between the flame cylinder and the vase with a beading tool as shown in photo G or with a ½″ oval skew. Using the beading tool, rotate the rodlike shaft counterclockwise and into the wood as you finely shave off the waste. At the same time, move the handle from left to right. Using the tools and methods above,

similarly turn the remaining elements below the flame to their final shape and diameter, referring to the pattern.

Tool: Beading tool or ½" oval skew
Speed: 1,200 to 1,500 rpm

Form the flame, sand, and finish

1 Carefully shape the flame, working from wider to narrower widths, using a 1¼″ gouge as shown in photo H. Stop the lathe as you near the finished tip and reverse the turning, securing the finial tenon in the chuck.

Tool: 1¼" roughing gouge
Speed: 1,200 to 1,500 rpm

2 Cut or part away the waste at the tip of the flame, and then sand the finial, working from 120- through 220-grit sandpaper as shown in photo I to remove sharp edges. Stain and/or finish as desired.

Tool: 120- to 220-grit sandpaper
Speed: 1,200 to 1,500 rpm

QUICK TIP

To shape the finial without vibration and for smoother results, turn the narrowest diameters last.

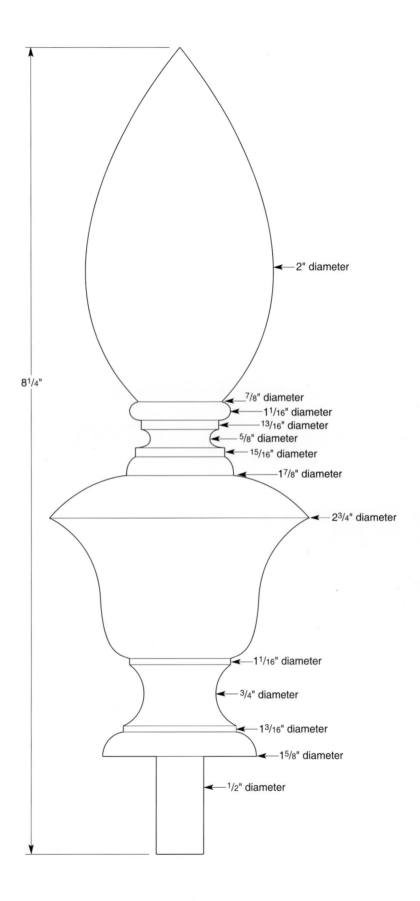

8¹/₄"

2" diameter

⁷/₈" diameter
1¹/₁₆" diameter
1³/₁₆" diameter
⁵/₈" diameter
1⁵/₁₆" diameter
1⁷/₈" diameter

2³/₄" diameter

1¹/₁₆" diameter

³/₄" diameter

1³/₁₆" diameter

1⁵/₈" diameter

¹/₂" diameter

TURN & WEAVE A SHAKER STOOL

A one-weekend introduction to Shaker chairmaking

BY KERRY PIERCE

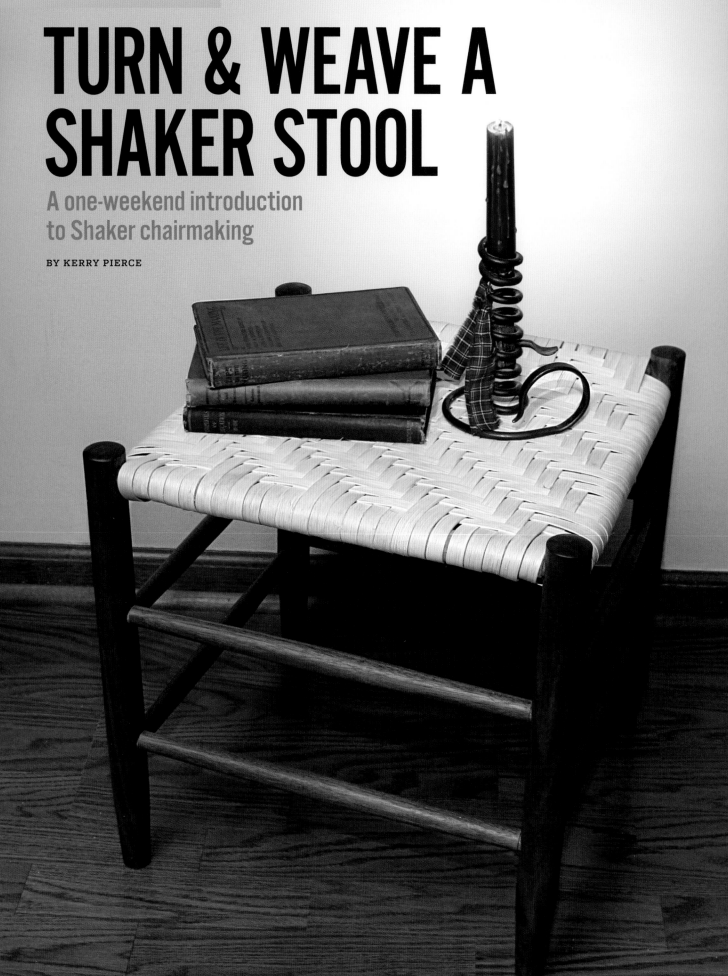

The little stool in this article is one of several that appear in *Shop Drawings of Shaker Furniture: Volume 1* by Ejner Handberg, published by Berkshire Traveller Press. I selected a stool high enough for seating, because we needed such a stool in our bathroom. There are, however, two others in that same book which are of a better height for use as footstools, and the construction methods I demonstrate here apply to those forms as well.

The original stool Handberg drew was likely made of hard maple, since that was the wood of choice in most Shaker chairmaking shops for several very good reasons. Hard maple is widely available. It's strong, and it's dense enough to work well under edge tools. Its only drawback is a rather plain appearance, a shortcoming the Shakers often addressed by dipping the frame in a vat of stain before applying a finish.

I chose walnut for mine, however, simply because I like the wood and hadn't worked with it for a good while. Ash, oak, or hickory would be solid choices, too, particularly for a stool likely to see heavy use. The stool could also be made of cherry or figured maple, although these are much less tough than hard maple, ash, or even walnut.

Working at the lathe

I have a set of story sticks for each of the many types of Shaker chairs and stools I build in my shop. Each set contains all the information I need to construct a particular piece, and although you can build this stool working from a drawing rather than a set of sticks, I recommend that you take the time to make the sticks before you start work on the stool, since they really do simplify the construction process. (You can see one of the story sticks being used in fig. 1.) This stool requires only a pair of story sticks: one cut to the length of the rungs with tenon lengths marked; and another cut to the length of the post with side-rung mortise placements marked on one side, and front- and back-rung mortise placements marked on the other side.

After your story sticks are made, you're ready to rip out the turning stock. Rung stock should be 4/4 (1″) on a side, and post stock should be 6/4 (1½″) on a side. Rip out a bit more than you expect to use—inevitably some parts will need to be discarded because of material flaws or because a tenon is turned a bit undersize.

Most Shaker chair parts can be turned with a very minimal tool kit. To create this particular piece of seating furniture, I needed only four lathe tools: a 1¼″ roughing gouge, a 1¼″ skew, a ½″ fingernail gouge, and a 1¼″ butt chisel I've reground for the purpose of turning rung tenons.

Begin by creating the stool's four posts. With your lathe set on a slow speed, use a roughing gouge to knock the corners off of a 6/4 turning blank, making frequent checks of the post's diameter. If the stock is accurately centered and reasonably straight, you should have a cylinder by the time the blank has been reduced to about 1⁷⁄₁₆″. Next select a faster lathe speed and use the roughing gouge to cut a taper at the bottom of the post. Then with your skew, cut about 50 percent of the rounded crown at the top of the post, but no more—if you cut more than that off the rounded crown while the work is in the lathe, you run a risk of having the piece break off while you're working it.

If you feel confident enough to skew plane, use the tool to reduce the post to its finished diameter of about 1⅜″. If you're insecure about your skew work, use the

skew as a scraper, then go back and finish the post with sandpaper. Once the post is finished, mark rung locations with your story stick (photo A).

The rungs are a bit more challenging to turn. They should finish out at a diameter of nearly 1″ in the middle, tapering to about $^{11}/_{16}$″ at the shoulder beside each tenon. Take your time with this critical process—tenons that are even a tiny bit oversized make the stool impossible to assemble, and tenons that are more than a few thousandths undersized will be too sloppy to give the stool the kind of strength you'll want it to have.

After reducing a rung blank to a 1″ cylinder, mark the tenon shoulder on each end by standing your skew on edge and using it to score the blank (photo B). Then switch to your ½″ fingernail gouge to hollow out the tenon, working cautiously until the smallest diameter of the tenon is just over the ⅝″ finished measurement (photo C).

At that point, I use my specially ground butt chisel to create the length of the tenon, laying the tool bevel-side down on my rest and engaging it with the work until the full length of the tenon is the same diameter as that section I hollowed out with my fingernail gouge (photo D). I then complete

the tenon by cutting a $^{1}/_{16}$″ taper on the end of it with my skew. If you don't have such a tool, a wide scraper will do the trick, as will a skew laid on its side acting as a scraper.

Although you can't see this detail in the finished stool, there are two different types of rungs used in the construction (photo E). The "show" rungs (top) taper from a 1″ midpoint to an $^{11}/_{16}$″ shoulder on each end. The seat rungs, on the other hand, maintain as much of their thickness as possible throughout their entire length. These two different shapes can be seen in photo I.

While you can sand each part as you turn it, I find it easier to do all my turning first. I then jack up the lathe speed, put on my dust mask, turn on my air cleaner, and sand all the turned parts in a single session, working my way up through the grits from 100, through 150, and ending with 220.

Marking the posts

There are two ways to mark the rung mortises on your posts. The method I use requires a lathe with an indexing head, which is simply a metal disk centered on the lathe's axis of rotation. This disk has holes drilled at regular intervals along its circumference, allowing the operator to divide turned forms into equal segments.

The indexing head on my lathe has 36 evenly spaced holes that divide anything on my lathe into 10° segments.

To draw a line on the outside diameter of the post parallel to its axis of rotation, I lock the indexing head into a position that places the post's most attractive figure and grain where it will be most visible. I then use the marking gauge shown in photo F to draw the line along which the rung mortises on one face of the post will be located. I next place my story stick on this line and mark rung mortises.

I then count off nine stops on the lathe's indexing head, relock it, and draw a second line 90° from the first line, then mark the rung mortise locations for the adjacent face of the stool on this second line.

If your lathe doesn't have an indexing head, here's another method of marking rung mortises: On your bandsaw or jigsaw, carefully slice a carpenter's pencil lengthwise so that the full length of the pencil lead is exposed. Lay a pair of stool posts on your bench side by side. Then run the sliced pencil along the posts so that the sliced lead engages the surface of both posts. This will result in a pencil line on the outside diameter of each post that is approximately parallel to the axis of each post. Then with your story stick as your guide, mark rung mortises along each of these lines.

Then rotate the posts approximately 90° and rub a second pair of lines onto their outside diameters with the split pencil.

Mark the rung mortises for the adjacent face of each post along each of these lines.

Don't worry if the second sets of lines aren't exactly 90° from the first sets of lines. The precise placement of the side-rung mortises will be achieved later through the use of the side-rung mortise jig.

Drilling the mortises and assembling the stool

To drill the first set of mortises on each post, press the post against a drill press fence set so that the lead point of a ⅝″ Forstner bit is a distance from the fence that is exactly half the finished diameter of the post. The fence in photo G is set to drill front and back ladder mortises in a post with a diameter of 1⅜″.

Slide the post along the fence under the bit until you've drilled each of the three mortises on that face of the post. These mortises should be ¹⁵⁄₁₆″ deep. This depth will accommodate the ⅞″ length of the tenon and leave a ¹⁄₁₆″ glue reservoir at the bottom of the mortise. Repeat on the three other posts (photo H).

After you've drilled the first set of mortises in each post, glue up your front and back ladders. (These are the ladders with the lower-rung mortise locations. The side-rung mortises are placed ⅝″ higher than the front and back mortise locations.)

Begin with a dry assembly of each ladder to ensure that all the tenons will fit into all the mortises. Then swab a little glue on each tenon and in each mortise. Tap the tenons

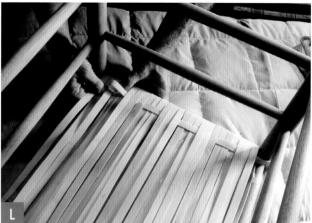

into place with a soft mallet. When both ends of all three rungs have been started into their mortises, press them into place with a pipe clamp working your way up and down the ladder (photo I).

Go slowly, because it's possible to crack a post with the pressure from your pipe clamp. Once they're assembled, check the squareness of each ladder with a framing square. Rack the ladder if necessary to bring it into the correct alignment. Clean up glue squeeze-out with a wet rag and a toothbrush.

Position the side-rung mortise jig—which is nothing more than a fence screwed to a sheet of plywood long enough to support the full width of the stool—to the drill press table so the fence is a distance from the lead point of your Forstner bit equal to half the diameter of the post.

Then slide the ladder along the fence under the bit and drill each of the side-rung mortises (photo J). These mortises, too, should be $^{15}\!/_{16}''$ deep.

Dry assemble the stool, but don't fully seat each tenon because some may get stuck in their mortises. When you're satisfied that all the parts will come together properly, swab glue on each tenon and in each mortise. Then press the tenons into place with your pipe clamp (photo K).

Before setting the stool aside to dry, check to ensure that all four legs make simultaneous contact with the surface of your bench. Rack the stool, if necessary, to bring it into alignment, then clean up glue squeeze-out as before.

Weaving the seat

The seat of this stool is nothing more than a basket woven in $\frac{1}{2}''$ rattan splint around the stool's seat rungs. I use rattan splint, also called "flat reed," because it's available in good quality from several American suppliers. The original stools were likely seated with ash splint, which is today much more expensive than rattan. Of course, you can make the seat with "Shaker tape," which is becoming harder to find at a reasonable price.

A single hank or coil of $\frac{1}{2}''$ splint is almost enough to weave this seat, but it's better to buy two hanks since it may be necessary to discard a few pieces of splint that may be too thin or too badly split. If you order three hanks, you'll have more than enough to seat two stools.

Prepare the splint by soaking it in a tub of warm water for a couple of hours. Then pull it out of the water and open the hank up on the floor.

I don't like to weave chair seats in my shop because I can never get the shop

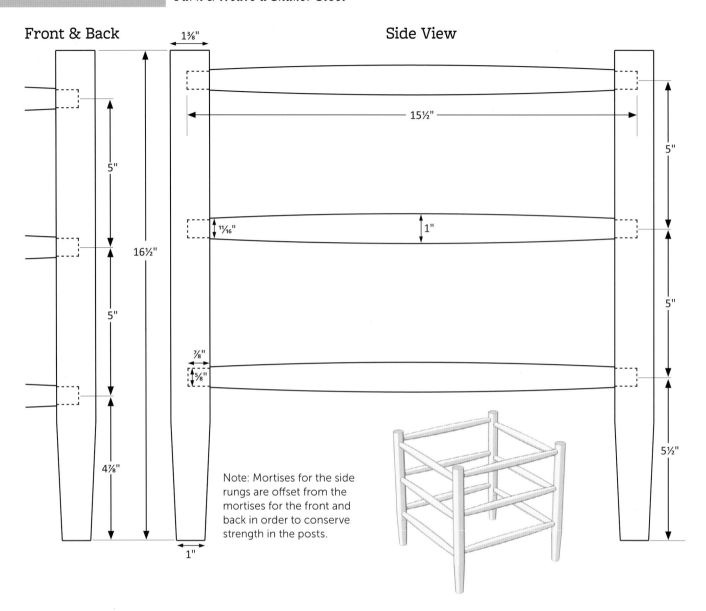

Front & Back

Side View

Note: Mortises for the side rungs are offset from the mortises for the front and back in order to conserve strength in the posts.

floor completely clean, and wet splint is an irresistible attractant to dust and dirt. Fortunately, I'm blessed with a very understanding wife, who never complains about the mess I make weaving chair seats in the house.

Select one of the longest strips of splint. (There should be a least a couple in each hank that measure 8′ to 10′.) Then tape one end of the long strip of splint to one of the side seat rungs with a wrap of masking tape.

Begin wrapping the splint around the front and back seat rungs. (These front-to-back strips are called the "warp." The side-to-side strips you'll add later are called

the "weave.") When you come to the end of the first strip, splice on another. You should do this on the bottom side of the seat where it won't be noticeable, even if that means wasting some of the strip. The splice is created by lapping the last 6″ to 8″ of the first strip over the first 6″ to 8″ of the second strip. Join the strips with three staples from a regular office stapler.

I know it sounds goofy. After all, those staples couldn't possibly support the weight of a person sitting on the seats. But the purpose of the staples is not to hold the weight of a person. The staples merely hold the strips together until the tightness of the

weave grips them and holds them in place. In fact, once the seat is finished, you can pull the staples out with a pair of needle-nosed pliers. I've been weaving seats in this manner for almost 20 years, without a single seat failure.

When the warp has completely filled the seat, tape the end of the last strip to the side seat rung, just as you did with the starting end of the first strip. You're now ready to begin the weave.

There are many different weave patterns from which to choose. My favorite is the herringbone pattern, which I used on this seat. This is a pattern in which the weaver—the single strip of splint that goes from side to side—is passed under three strips of warp, then over three strips, then under three and so on. Successive weavers are then staggered one strip before beginning the under-three-over-three pattern.

Begin the weaver on the bottom side of the stool, weaving across the full width of the bottom side of the seat (photo L). In this photo, note the masking tape holding the warp in place.

When you come to the opposite side of the seat bottom, turn the stool over so you're working on the top side. Then weave your way across the top side going over three strips of warp and under three strips of warp (photo M). When you reach the other side of the seat, invert the stool and weave your way across the bottom. Continue in this manner until you reach the end of your weaver. At that point, splice in a new piece by lapping the last 6″ to 8″ of the old over the first 6″ to 8″ of the new, as before (photo N).

Many craftsmen make these splices on the bottom side only. I splice on both the top and the bottom because the weaver splices are all but impossible to see, and they involve no unsightly staples.

As you work your way toward the front of the stool, you'll notice that the weave gets progressively tighter; at about three-quarters of the way to the front, you'll find yourself struggling to get the weavers inserted. I find that a butter knife inserted into the warp can help guide the weaver (photo O), and for the last couple of rows, a pair of needle-nosed pliers is very helpful in gripping and pulling the weaver through the warp. As the edges of the splint can be sharp, you may want to protect your fingertips when tugging on the weaver at this point. I simply wrap some masking tape around my fingers, but thin gloves would probably work just as well.

Final touches

If you choose to seat the stool with Shaker tape (you better have a fat wallet), you must apply the finish before you seat the stool. But if you seat the stool with splint, you can put off the finishing process until after the seat has been woven.

There are two reasons for doing this. First, the process of weaving a splint seat is very physical and finished parts can be scuffed as you muscle those last few rows of weavers into place. Second, the seat itself must be finished for both aesthetic reasons and to protect the splint from becoming soiled. A finished surface is much easier to wipe clean than is an unfinished surface. It makes sense then to hold off on the finishing process until you can finish the wood and the splint at the same time.

> ## MATERIALS
> Posts (4) 1⅜" x 16½"
> Rungs (12) 1" x 15½"
>
> Note: All wood is of a hardwood stock of your preference. Remember that these are all net measurements—extra length should be added to all turned parts to allow for centering in the lathe. Also, the gross (beginning) thicknesses should be a bit greater than the net thicknesses listed here to allow for stock removed during turning and sanding.
>
> ½" splint or flat reed
> Two hanks (coils)
>
> Connecticut Cane and Reed
> (800) 227-8498
> caneandreed.com
>
> 1" Shaker tape
> 28 yd. (one 20-yd. roll and one 10-yd. roll)
>
> ⅝" Shaker tape
> 42 yd. (two 20-yd. rolls and one 5-yd. roll)
>
> Shaker Workshops
> (800) 840-9121
> shakerworkshops.com

After the seat weaving is completed, let the splint dry for a couple of days before finish sanding. Begin with 220-grit paper, sanding all exposed wood very thoroughly, followed by 320-grit (photo P).

Next I apply a coat of finish (I like Waterlox) to both the wood parts and the splint, brushing it on liberally, then wiping it off with a clean, lint-free rag. (I find old T-shirts are best for this.) I let the piece dry overnight, then resand with 320 and refinish, again allowing the finish to dry overnight. At that point, give the piece a final sanding with 600-grit paper, followed by a good coat of paste wax to the wood parts only, rubbing it out vigorously when it's dry.

Overall dimensions: 3½" dia. × 2½" h (small lamp)
4¼" dia. × 2½" h (medium lamp) 5" dia. × 2½" h (large lamp)

GOLDEN-GLOW OIL LAMPS

Turn this trio and then ebonize the rim for a distinctive look

DESIGNERS/TURNERS/WRITERS: KIP CHRISTENSEN & REX BURNINGHAM

These complementary lamps make an attractive home accent, adding warmth to a romantic dinner or other occasion. We chose a 2 × 5 × 5″ blank of dry cherry to prevent cracking and/or warping. You can change the wood species and sizes if desired. The good news: you can turn the entire trio in an afternoon.

Note: Have the oil bottle in hand before turning the lamp. Bottles with wicks (for a confetti-style lamp) and lamp oil are available at craft stores. You can also size the recess to fit common tea light candles, but include a glass cup to protect the wood from the flame.

Turn the lamp blank

1 To mount the turning blank to minimize waste, drill a hole in a 2 × 3″-diameter bandsawn waste block and thread the block onto a screw center faceplate. Set your lathe speed at 1,000 rpm and turn the outside end of the waste block to 2″ diameter using a ½″ bowl gouge. Finally, turn the face so it's flat and smooth.

Now, attach double-faced tape to the face of the waste block and press the turning blank in position. Use the tailstock to center the blank and act as a clamp to help press the blank firmly against the block (photo A). The tailstock should remain in place whenever possible throughout the process. If it's necessary to turn without tailstock support, be sure to cut with only light pressure.

2 With the lathe set to 1,000 rpm, use a ½″ bowl gouge to true up the edge of the lamp blank. For a clean, controlled cut, ride the bevel on the wood behind the cutting edge as shown in photo B. Taking a light cut, push the gouge across the work.

3 With the flute facing the wood, take a light scraping cut to true up the face of the blank, pulling the gouge from the center of the blank to the outside edge (photo C).

4 To drill the hole for the oil bottle, secure a 1½″ Forstner bit in a Jacob's chuck and mount it in the tailstock. Using the oil bottle as a guide, mark the depth to be drilled on the bit using a felt-tip pen (photo D inset). Now slide the tailstock forward until the drill bit is near the wood and lock it into position.

Reduce the lathe speed to 300 rpm and turn the tailstock handwheel to advance the drill bit into the rotating wood (photo D). Stop when the bit has reached the depth marked on the drill bit.

5 Turn off the lathe and insert the oil bottle in the hole to check the hole depth. The hole

Figure 1: Lamp Full-Sized Profiles

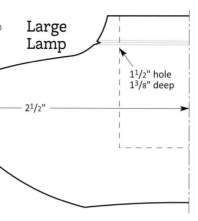

Large Lamp

1½" hole
1⅜" deep

2½"

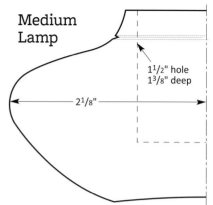

Medium Lamp

1½" hole
1⅜" deep

2⅛"

Small Lamp

1½" hole
1⅜" deep

1¾"

Cardboard Template

Note: To create turning templates, make copies of these full-sized profiles and spray-adhere them onto cardboard and cut to shape.

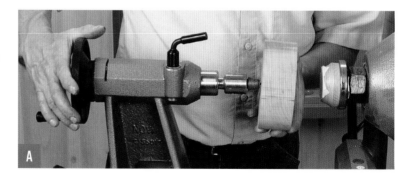

A

B

C

D

should be about ⅛" less than the height of the bottle below the neck. You can drill the hole deeper or turn a small amount of wood off the face of the blank to adjust the hole depth.

6 Reset the lathe back to 1,000 rpm. With a ½" bowl gouge, turn the rough shape of the oil lamp to within ⅛" of final dimension, using the profile in figure 1 as a guide. Photo E shows the top section of the lamp being turned, using a fairly aggressive pull cut with a scraping action and with the flute turned toward the wood.

7 Make final cleaning cuts to both halves with a ⅜" spindle gouge using a light shearing cut. The smaller gouge makes it easier to turn the small cove near the top (photo F). Hold the tool handle low to create the shearing angle.

Add an ebonized band

1 Reduce the lathe speed to 800 rpm and sand the turning inside and out (photo G). Begin with 120-grit sandpaper and progress to 180, 240, 320, and 400. (It is not necessary to sand the inside perfectly clean because it will be covered by the oil bottle.) Next, seal the wood inside the hole using two coats of sanding sealer. This reduces the possibility of dye bleeding through the pores from the inside of the hole to the outside surface of the lamp.

2 With the lathe set at 1,000 rpm and the skew lying flat on the tool rest in a scraping position, use the toe to create a small V-groove about ¼" down from the rim (photo H).

3 Next, turn the lathe speed up to 2,000 rpm and use a wire burner to create a

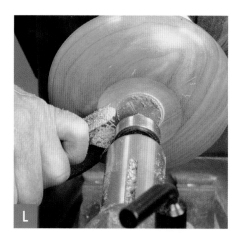

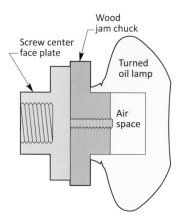

friction burn in the V-groove (photo I). The burn line provides a well-defined black groove that establishes a clean line when adding the dye.

4 To ebonize the rim, reduce the rpm to a slow speed (around 50 rpm) and use a black permanent marker or a cotton swab to apply black dye. A marker is easier to control on the outside (photo J). Use a cotton swab to apply dye inside the hole.

5 Spray a light coat of lacquer on the lamp, as shown in photo K. (A spray lacquer is recommended because wipe-ons can dissolve the dye and cause it to bleed across the burn line.) Use the slowest lathe speed (30 to 50 rpm) to reduce the possibility of the lacquer running. Let the lacquer dry, sand lightly with 600-grit abrasive or buff with 0000 steel wool, and then spray on a second coat. Repeat this process at least three times.

6 After the finish dries, remove the oil lamp from the waste block by applying firm constant pressure until the bond with the tape is released.

Turn the lamp bottom

1 To turn the bottom of the oil lamp you will need to mount the lamp on the headstock with the bottom face exposed. To do this, make a simple jamb chuck by turning a ½″ long by 1½″-diameter tenon on the face of a waste block (see fig. 2) using a ⅜″ spindle gouge and 1,000 rpm lathe speed. The tenon should fit tightly inside the drilled hole.

2 Fit the lamp over the tenon, bring the tail center with a cone point into position for support, and, using a ⅜″ spindle gouge, turn the bottom face to within ½″ of the tail center point. This surface should be slightly concave and produced with a shearing cut while rubbing the bevel on the wood (photo L).

Next, remove the tailstock and, using a light touch, turn off the remaining wood at the center. Finally, sand the bottom to match the top.

3 Using the same procedure followed earlier, apply lacquer to the bottom half of the lamp.

4 The oil lamp can now be removed from the tenon chuck and the oil bottle set in place.

Figure 2: Jamb Chuck

Screw center face plate

Wood jam chuck

Turned oil lamp

Air space

QUICK TIP

For a tighter fitting jamb chuck, shim the tenon with one or more layers of masking tape.

PENCIL-POST BOOKSHELF

Sharpen basic turning skills as you turn 2×4s into No. 2s

BY JOE HURST-WAJSZCZUK
DESIGN BY ANDY RAE

For those who think that pencil post furniture is too "period," here's a literal reinterpretation that fits perfectly in a child's playroom or bedroom.

Knowing how quickly kids outgrow furniture, designer Andy Rae created this bookshelf to be fun, easy to build, and inexpensive. You'll find the bulk of the materials at your home center: the posts are laminated 2×4s; the erasers are turned from a 4×4 cedar fence post; and the ferrules are 2½" thick-walled PVC conduit. (I used Baltic birch for the shelves, but you can save money by substituting hardwood plywood.) The connector nuts and cross dowels not only lock the shelves to the posts but also make it easy to disassemble the pieces and transport them to the grandkid's house.

Depending on your clamp collection, assembling the pencil posts may take a few glue-up sessions, but after that, the shelving unit can be finished in a weekend. Despite its simplicity, there are a few interesting twists and turns. You'll learn how to lay out a hexagon; practice turning cones, cylinders, and tenons; and discover a few

Figure 1: Pencil-Post Bookcase Exploded View

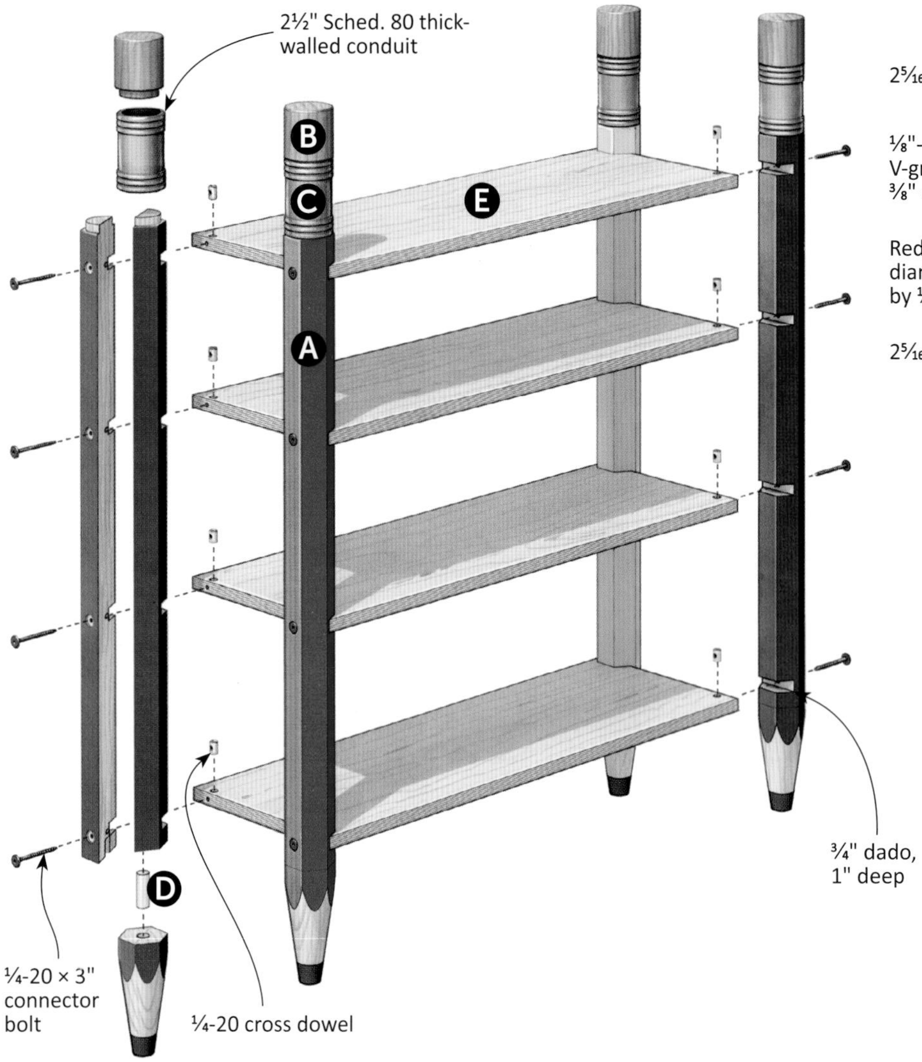

Leg Detail

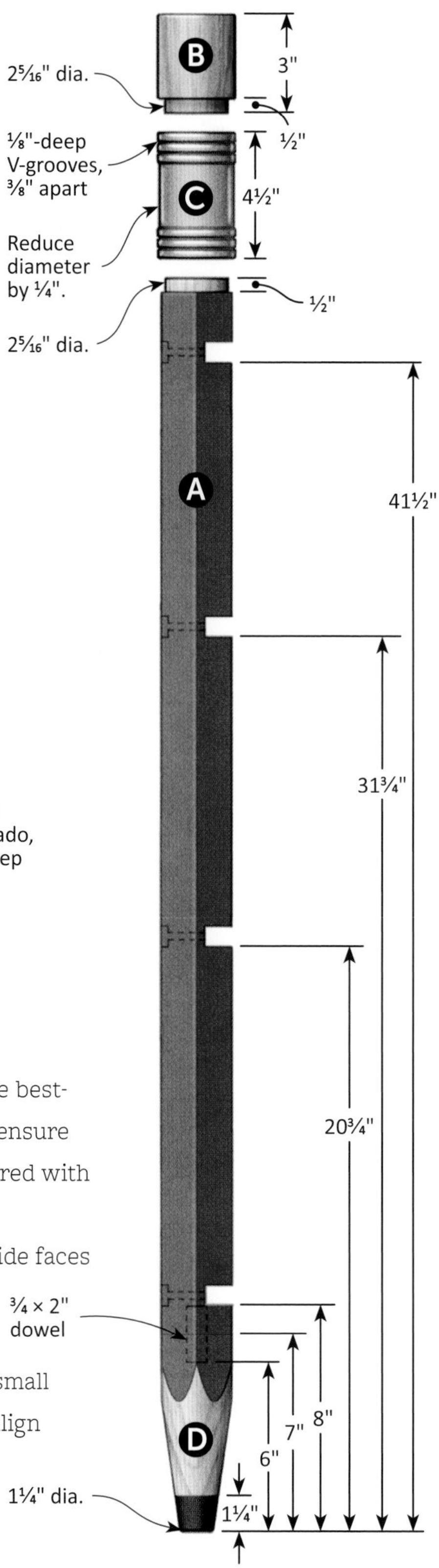

2½" Sched. 80 thick-walled conduit

B

C

E

A

¼-20 × 3" connector bolt

D

¼-20 cross dowel

¾" dado, 1" deep

2⁵⁄₁₆" dia. **B** 3"

⅛"-deep V-grooves, ⅜" apart **C** ½"

4½"

Reduce diameter by ¼".

2⁵⁄₁₆" dia. ½"

A 41½"

31¾"

20¾"

¾ × 2" dowel

D 8" 7" 6"

1¼" dia. 1¼"

tricks for negotiating long columns with a short-bed lathe.

(Note: Bright colors add a nice dose of whimsy, but painting the posts yellow or black—or leaving them bare—provide options that may work better with your home's decor.)

Make the legs

1 Select six 96″-long 2×4s to make the posts (A): one for each leg, one to test your setups, and an extra in case you make a mistake. (Note: Avoid loose knots and waney edges. The best 2×4s are sometimes sold as "select" or "prime" stock.)

2 Cut each 2×4 into two equal lengths and

arrange them side by side for the best-looking grain. Mark the ends to ensure that each half stays properly paired with its mate.

3 Using a jointer, flatten the inside faces and edges of each matching pair. Next, apply glue to the inside face of one half, attach a small clamp across the edges to help align the halves, and then apply clamping pressure across the faces (photo A). To ensure a seamless joint, space the clamps 6 to 8″ apart. Glue up all six pairs, and let the assembled post blanks dry.

Use a threaded rod to trowel glue evenly across the face of the post, ensuring a good, clean glue-up.

As you rip and flip the hexagonal post, make sure that the glue line stays in contact with the rip fence.

4 Referring to figure 2, step 1, rip the post blanks to 3″ wide. (You may need to rip a little material from the jointed edge to remove the remaining rounded corners.) Next, refer to step 2 and lay out a hexagon on the end of your test piece, and mill all the blanks to the proper thickness.

5 Rip the first face, as shown in step 3. Now flip the blank end for end, and rip the adjacent edge; (When you flip the stock for your second cut, the layout lines will be facing you.)

6 Rotate the blank 180° so that the cut edge rests against the fence, and rip the remaining two edges (photo B). Double-check your cuts against your layout lines; if no adjustments are needed, cut the remaining legs. Finally, crosscut the posts (A) to length. (Note: Save your scrap. You'll use the rippings to prevent tear-out when dadoing the posts and a hexagonal offcut to make the dowelling jig.)

7 Finish the pencil posts (A). To add color but reveal some grain, I used BioShield Stain/Finish, a nontoxic, one-part stain and finish. An acrylic paint would create a more classic No. 2 pencil look, or you could finish the shafts with a clear finish. Whatever you choose, it's important that you finish the posts now in order to achieve the scalloped end when you "sharpen" the tip.

8 Chuck a ½″ straight bit into your table-mounted router, and set the fence for a ½″-wide rabbet. Next, wrap the top end of a post (A) with painter's tape to protect the

Figure 2: Turning a 2×4 into a No. 2 in 3 Steps

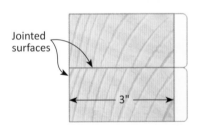

Jointed surfaces

3″

Step 1: Joint one face and edge, and glue up the leg blank. After the glue cures, rip the leg blank to 3″ wide.

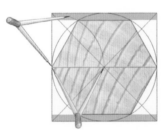

Step 2: Find the centerpoint, and draw a circle. Without adjusting the compass, "walk" it around the circle to find the hexagon's corners. Mill the excess material from the top and bottom faces.

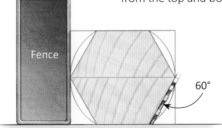

Fence

60°

Step 3: Adjust the fence, and rip along the outside of the layout lines.

Figure 3: Dado Sled

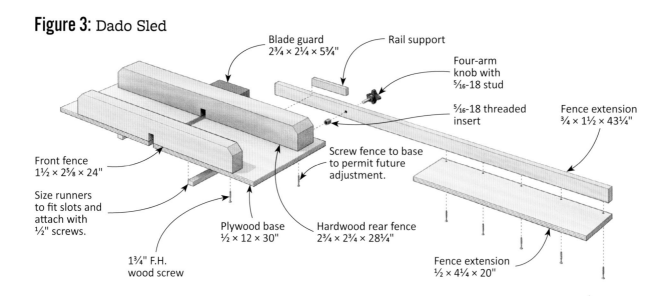

Blade guard
2¾ × 2¼ × 5¾"

Rail support

Four-arm
knob with
5⁄16-18 stud

5⁄16-18 threaded
insert

Fence extension
¾ × 1½ × 43¼"

Front fence
1½ × 2⅝ × 24"

Size runners
to fit slots and
attach with
½" screws.

Screw fence to base
to permit future
adjustment.

1¾" F.H.
wood screw

Plywood base
½ × 12 × 30"

Hardwood rear fence
2¾ × 2¾ × 28¼"

Fence extension
½ × 4¼ × 20"

finish, and slide it into a 12″-long piece of 3″ PVC. Guiding the pipe against a block of wood (or miter fence), feed the post into the bit, and then slowly turn the post/pipe clockwise, as shown in photo C. Gradually raise the bit until the tenon fits inside the 2 ½″ thick-walled conduit. Repeat with the remaining posts.

9 Build the dado sled shown in figure 3. Next, set up your dado cutter to the width of your shelf material, and adjust the cutter for a 1″-deep dado. Tape a strip of wood (left over from ripping the hexagonal post) to the back face of the pencil to control tear-out, and cut the dadoes, as shown in figure 1 leg detail and photo D.

10 At the drill press, drill counterbores and through holes for the connector bolts through the posts (A), where shown in figure 1, leg detail.

Turn the pencil parts

1 From 4×4 cedar stock, create three turning blanks for the erasers (B), each approximately 3 × 3 × 8″. Next, cut four 4½″-long pieces of 2½″-diameter thick-walled conduit for the ferrules (C).

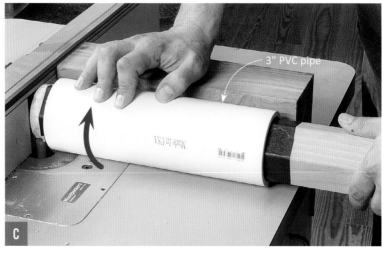

Sliding the hexagonal post into a PVC pipe allows you to rout a round tenon. Painter's tape protects the finish and packs the post in the pipe.

Use a sled with stops to ensure that the shelf dadoes line up. Cut the corresponding dadoes in each leg before readjusting the stop.

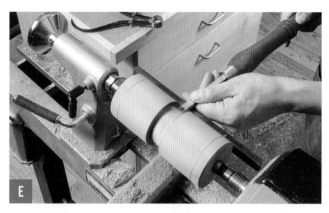

Using calipers to check your progress, turn the eraser blank and tenon to match the conduit's outside and inside diameters.

Groove positioning guide

Jamb chucks

Use the corner of the square-edged carbide cutter to create the V-grooves, then use the flat edge to reduce the diameter between the coves.

2 Using a tablesaw, chamfer about ½″ from the corners of the eraser blanks to facilitate turning, and then mount the blank between your headstock and tail centers. Set the lathe to slow speed (around 1,500 rpm), and use a carbide cutter or roughing gouge to rough out a cylinder. Next, reposition the rest closer to the blank, and adjust the speed to around 1,800 rpm. Using a light touch, turn the cylinder to match the outside diameter of the conduit (approximately 2⅞″).

3 Using a parting tool or square-edged carbide cutter, turn a 1⅛″-long tenon in the center of the cylinder, as shown in photo E. (Note: To obtain a snug-fitting tenon, use calipers rather than relying on dimensions.) Measuring up from the tenon's shoulders, cut the erasers (B) to the sizes listed in the cut list using a saw or parting tool, and then cut through the tenon to separate the pair. Repeat the procedure with the remaining two blanks. Cut the final blank in half but do not trim the ends; you'll use these pieces as jamb chucks to turn the ferrules (C).

4 Using the jamb chucks made in step 3, mount the conduit. Leaving the speed at 1,800 rpm, lightly run a round carbide cutter against the conduit to smooth and true the cylinder. Now, locate the ferrule V-grooves, where shown in figure 1 leg detail, and cut the grooves as shown in photo F. Next, turn the center section. Complete the remaining ferrules (C), and then put the erasers (B) and ferrules aside for now. (Note: This is a good time to spray-finish the ferrules.)

5 With a mitersaw or tablesaw and crosscut sled, equipped with your best crosscut blade, trim 7″ from the bottom end of each post (A). Mount one of the pieces into your lathe with the intended tip against the tailstock. Now, adjust the speed to 1,500 rpm. Staying 1″ away from the headstock end, lightly rough out a cylinder. Stop the lathe to inspect the scalloped edge.

6 Using a parting tool or square-edged carbide cutter, establish the tip's final dimension, as shown in figure 1, leg detail. Now, working downhill from right to left, "sharpen the pencil." Finally, establish a "lead tip" line about 1¼″ in from the tailstock end, as shown in photo G. Repeat with the remaining pencil tips.

7 Using a post offcut, make a doweling jig, as shown in figure 4. Now, using the jig, drill ¾ × 1″ holes in each pencil post end (photo H). Reassemble the tips to the posts using glue and ¾″-diameter × 2″-long dowels (D).

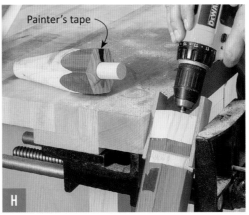

Lay out the lead line with a pencil. Note the wavy edge at the top of the sharpened tip.

Drill matching holes in the posts and tips with a shop-made doweling jig. Use painter's tape to keep track of matching faces.

Dipping the pencil tips into rubberized paint creates non-slip, non-marring footpads.

8 Touch up the pencils' finish where needed. Finally, dip the pencil tips into an air-dry rubber coating, like Plasti Dip, to create a nonslip tip, as shown in photo I.

Make the shelves and attach the legs

1 From ¾″ Baltic birch plywood, cut four shelves (E) to the sizes in the cut list.
2 Sand the faces, knock off any sharp edges, and then finish the shelves with two to three coats of water-based polyurethane.
3 With a helper, fit the shelves (E) into the posts (A). Using the pre-drilled holes as guides, drill ¼ × 3¼″-deep holes into the ends of the shelves.
4 Remove the shelves, and drill 11mm holes through the face of each shelf for the cross dowels, where shown in figure 5.
5 Insert the cross dowels into the shelves, and then attach the posts to the shelves with connector bolts.
6 Attach the erasers (C) to the ferrules (B) and the ferrules to the posts (A). (To join the wood to the PVC, epoxy works). Consider leaving one ferrule unglued since kids appreciate a secret hiding spot for small treasures.

Figure 4: Doweling Jig

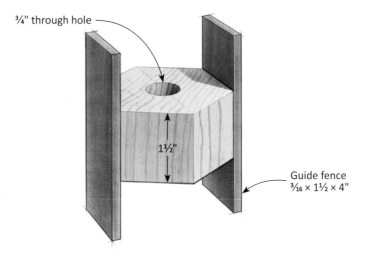

¾″ through hole

1½″

Guide fence
³⁄₁₆ × 1½ × 4″

Figure 5: Leg-to-Shelf Detail

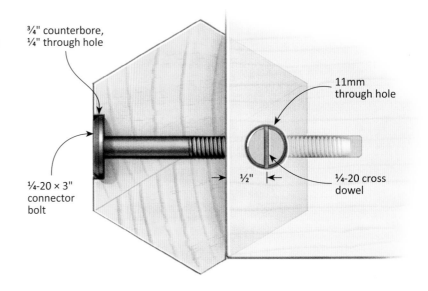

¾″ counterbore,
¼″ through hole

11mm through hole

¼-20 × 3″ connector bolt

½″

¼-20 cross dowel

Overall dimensions: 13¼" w × 3¾" d × 6⅜" h

TURNED BOOKENDS

In the Art Deco style

DESIGNERS/TURNERS/WRITERS:
KIP CHRISTENSEN & REX BURNINGHAM

This unconventional woodturning lets you expand your repertoire of projects while creating an attractive gift item or functional piece for the home in the Art Deco style. We used tiger maple for the base and upright pieces and ebonized the rims and beads for an eye-catching touch of class. A 6 × 25″ piece of kiln-dried 4/4 stock is all you need, while glue and screws hold the bookend assemblies together.

Turning the bookends blank

1 Joint the face and edge of a 1 × 6 × 25″ board, and then crosscut it into two equal lengths. Next, glue the two halves together edge to edge. After the glue dries, sand or plane the back face smooth and flat.

2 Locate the center of the glue-up panel, and use a compass or dividers to draw a circle of maximum diameter on the face. (Ours measured 11″ in diameter.)

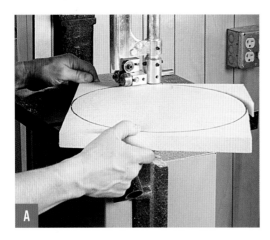

Tool: ½" bowl gouge
Speed: 400 to 500 rpm

Tool: ½" bowl gouge
Speed: 400 to 500 rpm

Tool: ⅜" spindle gouge
Speed: 700 to 800 rpm

Then cut it into a round disc on the bandsaw (photo A).

3 Mount the disc on the lathe by first drilling the pilot holes for the faceplate screws, locating them away from where saw cuts will be made when the disc is divided into quarters later. (Pay attention to the grain orientation as shown.) Center the faceplate on the sanded side of the blank and secure it in place with screws. Now mount the assembly on the lathe.

4 Bring the tailstock into position against the blank for additional support until the roughing-out process is complete. Next, position the bowl gouge so the bevel is parallel to the lathe bed and true up the blank's edge, making push cuts from the back corner to the center, and from the front corner to the center (photo B).

5 Position the tool rest parallel to the face of the blank. Now rough-shape the face by

holding the bowl gouge's tool handle low and making light shear-scrape cuts while pulling the tool toward your body (photo C).

6 Remove the tailstock and switch to a ⅜" spindle gouge to continue making light shear-scrape pull cuts as you form the half-beads at the rim of the blank (photo D), following the bookend profile in figure 1. Use the tip of the tool to make well-defined beads with small V-grooves at the bottom. The half-bead along the rim will later form a full bead after the disc is cut and reassembled.

7 Turn the center bead by using a push cut with the bevel rubbing behind the cutting edge. Start from the top of the bead and work down each side. Make sure that the bottom of each side of the bead is crisp and clean (photo E).

8 Sand the completed face of the bead thoroughly. Begin with 120 grit and

Tool: ³⁄₈" spindle gouge
Speed: 700 to 800 rpm

Figure 1:
Turning Half Profile
(Full-Sized pattern)

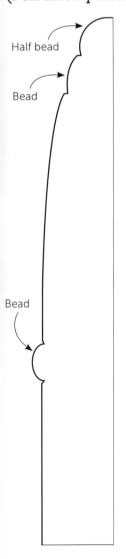

Half bead

Bead

Bead

progress to 400 or 600. To keep the details clean and well formed, tear and fold your sandpaper into small pieces and use the corners to sand around the beads and into the V-grooves.

9 Apply friction burn lines in each of the V-grooves with a scrap piece of plastic laminate that has been sanded into a teardrop shape (like an oversized guitar pick) and taper-sanded on each face to create a sharp edge. With the blank spinning at 1,000 rpm, firmly press the edge of the plastic laminate into the V-grooves and hold it in place until the black line appears (photo F). The lines help define the beads by adding a color contrast to the piece. They also seal the pores of the wood at the bottom of the bead where you'll apply the ebonizing stain, reducing the chance of having the stain bleed into areas where you don't want it to go.

10 Using a black stain or dye, ebonize the half-bead at the rim and the center bead. To do this, bring the tool rest into position and turn the lathe to a very slow speed (about 25 rpm). Dip the cotton swab into the stain and, while supporting your hands on the tool rest, carefully apply the stain to the rotating blank (photo G). Since the tip of the cotton swab is rather blunt, apply stain to the center portion of the bead only. Be careful to not apply stain to the bottom of the V (where the beads intersect the flat surfaces).

11 Use a black permanent marker to ebonize the areas near the bottom of the vees. A marker with a very fine tip may be needed to keep the ink confined as needed. Here it is best to turn the lathe off and to rotate the spindle by hand while carefully adding the color (photo H).

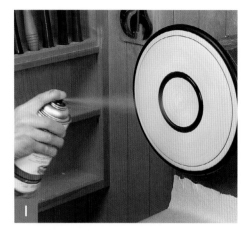

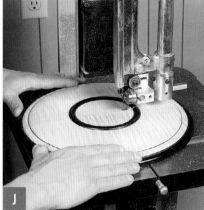

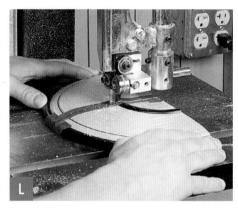

12 Place paper or cloth on the lathe to prevent getting finish on the bed and headstock. With the lathe turning at about 30 rpm, apply a light coat of spray lacquer (photo I). Avoid putting the lacquer on too heavily, because any lacquer runs will likely cause the stain to run as well. Apply three or four thin coats of finish. Lightly sand with 400 grit before applying the final coat.

Cut the blank into bookend shapes and assemble

1 After the finish has cured, remove the turned blank from the faceplate and bandsaw it into equal halves along the glue line (photo J). Then, with the flat face down, carefully sand the cut clean using a disc sander or a sanding block. To make it easier to realign the grain when gluing the parts together, draw grain reference lines across the line of cut on the back of the disc.

2 Find the center of each sawn edge and use a tri-square to transfer a line across the back of the blank. Lay down a length of tape on the face of the blank, and then use a flexible straightedge (here we are using a piece of plastic laminate) to draw a centerline across the face, bisecting each half into quarters (photo K).

3 Return to the bandsaw and cut along the layout lines on each half, creating four quarters (photo L). Use a belt or disc sander to smooth the sawn edges. To provide stability and prevent blow-out, the disc should be positioned with the finished face up while cutting and sanding.

4 Glue the two quarters together, using the grain lines you made previously to book-match the grain at the ends. Apply a modest amount of yellow glue to the back of the mating pieces, align the edges, and hold them firmly by hand until the glue begins to

QUICK TIP

When making layout lines on a finished surface, use painter's tape to protect the finish and make the lines easier to see.

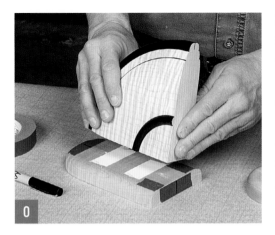

O

tack. Then secure the glue-up in place with masking tape and hand screw. Let it cure for at least 30 minutes (photo M).

5 After the glue dries, disc-sand the edges and ends flush and square (photo N). Be careful to remove as little material as possible and to keep the corners square.

Making and adding the base

1 Cut a 1″ (4/4) piece of kiln-dried matching wood to 4 × 15″. (We used tiger maple.) Joint one face and edge and plane the piece to ¾″ thick. Rip and joint the piece to a finished width of 3¾″. Lightly draw a centerline from end to end and use a compass to lay out the half circle on each end.

2 Bandsaw the half-circle ends of the workpiece, cutting just outside the line. Disc-sand the bandsaw cuts to the line, removing saw marks.

3 Chuck a ⅜″ round-over bit in your table-mounted router, and rout along the top edge of the base piece. Then sand and finish.

4 Set the turned bookend uprights in position on the base piece and visually judge what length to cut each half. (Our base pieces measured 6¾″.) Mark and then crosscut each base section to length.

5 Center the turned bookends on the base, flushing the cut ends. Apply painter's

masking tape to the base to protect the finished surfaces. Then draw centerlines on the tape for alignment. Temporarily adhere double-faced tape to secure the bookends on the base pieces as shown (photo O).

6 Mark and drill countersunk pilot holes through the base pieces and into the bookends where shown in figure 2. (Note that the drill holes are positioned off-center so they are not in line with the face joint of the bookends. Also, we used a manual countersink for depth control.) Test the holes by fully installing the screws. Then remove the screws and the tape and permanently drive the screws in place. Spray two coats of lacquer onto the base and allow it to dry overnight. The next day, lightly sand the base with 400-grit sandpaper to remove nibs or drips, and then spray one final coat on the ends and bases to blend the parts together.

Figure 2:
Bookend
Exploded View

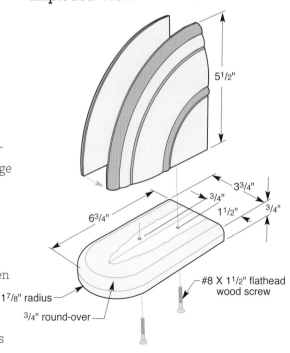

5½″

3¾″

¾″

1½″

¾″

6¾″

#8 X 1½″ flathead wood screw

1⅞″ radius

¾″ round-over

BAMBOO-STYLE STOOL

Try your hand at chairmaking with this small scale project

BY CURTIS BUCHANAN

At first glance, it's easy to see that this stool is a handsome and useful project, but what makes it really special is how it introduces woodworkers to some of the challenges of chairmaking.

Unlike a full-blown Windsor chair, this stool requires only a few board feet of material plus a basic assortment of turning and hand tools and involves no carving or bending. Despite this modest investment, the project lets you try your hand at kiln-drying and cutting tapered tenons to make joints that will stay tight through years of rugged use. In addition, you'll begin to think like a chairmaker and know when to put down the plans and rely on the project to measure parts and check angles so that everything fits like it should.

Before you start building this stool, you need to consider the finish. For first-timers, I recommend using readily available, less expensive woods, and then topping it off with milk paint. Here, I used maple for the legs and stretchers (but any strong hardwood will do) and poplar for the seat, because it's easy to work, takes paint well, and is available in 8/4 (2″) thickness. For a

Overall dimensions:
20" w × 20" d × 26" h

Figure 1: Stool Exploded View

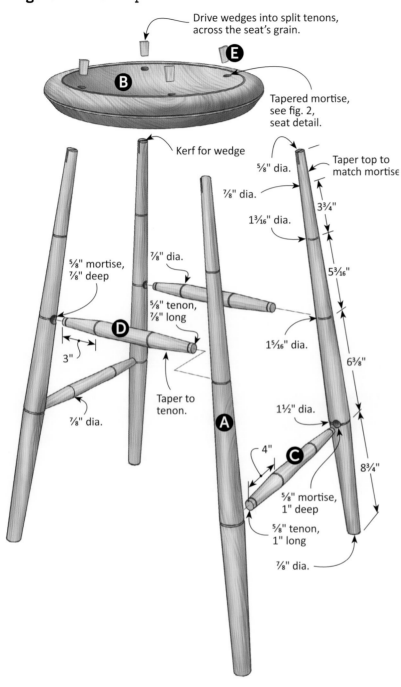

Drive wedges into split tenons, across the seat's grain.

E

B

Tapered mortise, see fig. 2, seat detail.

Kerf for wedge

⅝" dia.

Taper top to match mortise

⅞" dia.

1³⁄₁₆" dia.

3¾"

⅝" mortise, ⅞" deep

⅞" dia.

5³⁄₁₆"

⅝" tenon, ⅞" long

D

3"

1⁵⁄₁₆" dia.

Taper to tenon.

⅞" dia.

6⅜"

A

1½" dia.

4"

C

8¾"

⅝" mortise, 1" deep

⅝" tenon, 1" long

⅞" dia.

Stretcher/Leg Close-Up

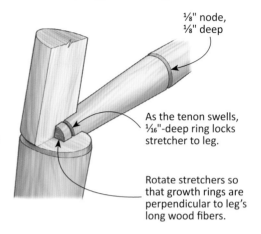

⅛" node, ⅛" deep

As the tenon swells, ¹⁄₁₆"-deep ring locks stretcher to leg.

Rotate stretchers so that growth rings are perpendicular to leg's long wood fibers.

completely different look, you can step up to nicer hardwoods. Curly maple and walnut (see inset on opposite page) is one of my favorite two-tone combinations.

Turn the legs

1 I prefer to split the leg (A) and stretcher (C, D) blanks from a short log, or bolt, that's a few inches longer than the needed length. In addition to being quicker than sawing, splitting ensures straight-grained blanks. If you don't have access to suitable logs, feel free to bandsaw the blanks from 8/4 stock. As you lay out your blanks, follow the long wood fibers as closely as possible for maximum strength.

2 Cut the leg blanks to 27″. Next, mount each leg blank on the lathe between centers and round to 1½″ diameter. For this, I use a 1¾″ roughing gouge and a custom tool rest. (See Leg- and Stretcher-Making Accessories, page 121.)

3 Refer to the leg dimensions on the exploded view, upper right, and photo A, and make a leg story stick. Now remount the blank, set the tool rest about ¹⁄₁₆″ away from the turning, and lay out the node locations with a pencil. Use a parting tool

Tapered Reamer: Build (or Buy) This First

Tapered mortises are essential for chairmaking. Besides the obvious mechanical advantage, the flared end of the mortise offers the clearance needed to install the assembled undercarriage into the seat. In order to make this joint, you'll need to make or purchase a tapered reamer. Plans for making your own reamer are available online at greenwoodworking.com. You can purchase a ready-made 6° reamer from handtoolwoodworking.com. If you own a reamer with a different taper angle, adjust your leg tapering guide accordingly.

Use a story stick to lay out the locations of the nodes. Jot down the desired diameters alongside your tick marks.

Shape the leg with a gouge, using the parting tool cuts as reference points. The leg-sized rest eliminates the hassle of repositioning a shorter rest.

Keep your eyes on the guide and the leg as you turn the taper on the top end. Stop when the angles match.

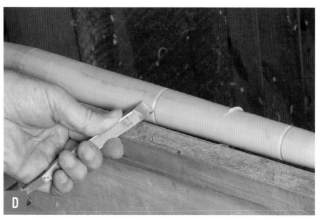

Using the skew's tip, mark the node's center, and then cut the V-groove from both sides of the line.

and calipers to gauge the diameters, turn the node locations to size, and then switch to a ¾″ gouge and finish shaping the leg (photo B), including the taper at the bottom of the leg, but not at the top.

4 Create a tapering guide like the one shown opposite. Using a parting tool, turn the tip of the leg's top end to ⅝″. Locate the guide on the lathe bed so that its narrow end aligns with the upper end of the leg. Now, sight across the leg, and turn its taper to match the the guide (photo C).

5 To finish turning the leg, I prefer using a skew, but if you're not practiced at this you can use sandpaper. Sand the leg through 150 grit for a painted finish, or 400 grit

for a natural finish. Re-mark the leg nodes using your story stick, and then use a skew chisel to cut ⅛″-deep V-grooves, or nodes, about ⅛″-wide, as shown in photo D. (Note: The nodes provide a useful reference for adjusting leg height and locating stretchers.) Now finish turning the remaining three legs.

6 Build the super-simple kiln (page 121). Insert the top of the legs into the box; let the tenons bake while you make the seat (B). If the legs are at equilibrium moisture content (EMC)—here in the Southern Appalachians EMC is 12 to 18%—they should be super dry in 24 hours. (Note: Plan on baking the legs the day before test-fitting them into the seat, and again a day before final assembly.)

Leg- and Stretcher-Making Accessories

Making chairs and stools doesn't require an elaborate setup, but you will need a few accessories. I recommend building these three items before you start your stool.

Custom tool rest

To eliminate the bother of repositioning a shorter tool rest, I built a hardwood rest to match the length of my legs. (I also recommend making a shorter 14"-long version rest for the stretchers.) Use this sketch as a guide. Adjust the base to fit your lathe and the rest height so that the top edge is about ⅛" below the lathe centers.

Tapering guide

For turning the tapered tenons, I use a tapering guide. Unlike a gauge block (a block that's drilled with a tapered hole and then sawn in half) this guide enables me to match the tenon at a glance, without pause.

Super-simple kiln

Here's a simple, but perfectly functional, kiln you can make from rigid insulation, duct tape, bamboo skewers, and a shop light. The heat produced by a 45-watt lightbulb (around 140°) will dry and shrink the tenons on the legs and stretchers. After assembly, the tenons will return to EMC by absorbing moisture, thus swelling and making the joints a little tighter.

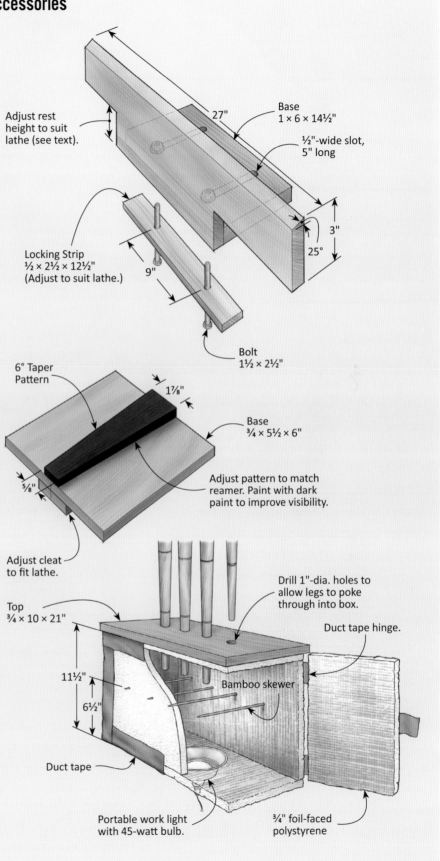

Adjust rest height to suit lathe (see text).

27"

Base
1 × 6 × 14½"

½"-wide slot, 5" long

Locking Strip
½ × 2½ × 12½"
(Adjust to suit lathe.)

9"

3"

25°

Bolt
1½ × 2½"

6° Taper Pattern

1⅞"

Base
¾ × 5½ × 6"

5⅝"

Adjust pattern to match reamer. Paint with dark paint to improve visibility.

Adjust cleat to fit lathe.

Top
¾ × 10 × 21"

Drill 1"-dia. holes to allow legs to poke through into box.

Duct tape hinge.

11½"

6½"

Bamboo skewer

Duct tape

Portable work light with 45-watt bulb.

¾" foil-faced polystyrene

Use a scraper to refine the seat at the edge and create the concave top.

Set the bevel gauge parallel with the seat's layout lines. Keep the bit parallel with the gauge's blade as you bore into the seat.

Turn the seat

1 If you can't find a 14″-wide board, glue up the seat (B) blank from narrower stock. Flatten the bottom face with a plane, bandsaw the blank round, and then attach a faceplate to the bottom face and mount it to your lathe.

2 True the edge of the blank with a roundnose scraper or bowl gouge, and then work the face-grain from the edge to the center. Referring to figure 2 and photo E, dish out the top of the seat with a scraper or gouge. Next, cut the chamfer under the seat with a scraper or gouge. Sand the seat as needed, and then turn the decorative grooves with a small round scraper or gouge, and sand the grooves. Remove the seat from your lathe.

3 Draw two intersecting lines at 90° to each other through the center of the seat's top face; lay out locations of the leg mortises. (Making the lines perpendicular to each other and parallel with the long wood fibers might be a little stronger, but I think positioning the lines at 45° is more visually pleasing if using a natural finish.)

Figure 2: Seat Detail

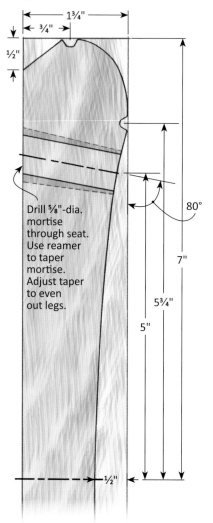

Drill ⁵⁄₈″-dia. mortise through seat. Use reamer to taper mortise. Adjust taper to even out legs.

1¾″
¾″
½″
80°
7″
5¾″
5″
½″

4 Clamp the seat to your bench on top of a piece of scrap. Set a bevel gauge to 80°, and position it alongside the intended mortise parallel with a layout line, as shown in photo F. Sight the angle on the gauge and bore a ⅝″-diameter through-hole. (I prefer the control of brace and auger bit, but you can use a drill and a brad-point bit.) Drill the remaining three holes the same way.

5 Flip the seat (B) top face down and position it so one mortise extends over the edge of your bench. Re-mark the layout line. Insert the reamer into the hole, and adjust the bevel gauge so that its blade is parallel to the front of the reamer. (To do this, subtract half the taper angle. With a 6° reamer, the gauge should be set to 83°.) Next, set a square on the layout line, as shown in photo G, to serve as a guide against tipping the reamer to one side. Now taper the mortise so that the leg extends about ½″ through the top face of the seat. Repeat the process for the remaining leg (A) holes.

6 Insert all four legs (A), and measure the distance from the seat to the middle node, as shown in photo H. Widen the tapers as needed so that the seat-to-node distance is the same with all four legs. While the legs are still set in the seat, mark the kerfs for the wedges, orienting them parallel to the legs' growth rings. Then rotate the legs so that the kerf lines run perpendicular to the seat's long wood fibers. Mark the legs so that they can be fitted and properly rotated in their corresponding holes throughout the assembly process.

Add the stretchers

1 Set the seat (B) upside down on top of blocks so that the tenons will not hit your bench, and insert the legs (A). Stretch a rubber band between the nodes corresponding to a lower stretcher (C). Using the band as a guide, make starting hole marks between the band (photo I). To obtain the length of the lower stretcher (C), measure the distance from mark to

Insert the reamer, apply light pressure, and turn. Set a square and a bevel gauge as shown to help maintain the correct angle.

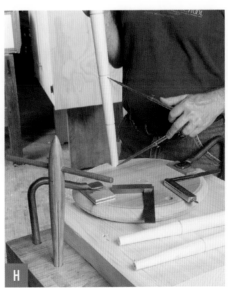

Measure the seat-to-node distance and adjust the tapers until the legs are the same.

Stretching a rubber band between the legs can help you gauge the centerpoint for the lower stretcher.

Leg-Drilling Duo

This clamping jig requires the help of a pair of pistol-grip clamps, but it ranks as the simplest solution for securing cylindrical parts such as legs and spindles. To use, clamp it to your bench so that the beam is parallel with your benchtop, and then clamp the part to the support arms.

   The mirror stand allows you to check the distance between the bit and bevel gauge from another vantage point. This will help you maintain your desired drilling angle.

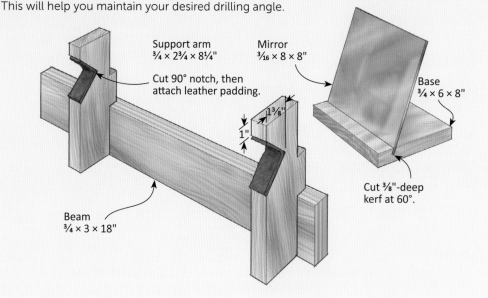

Support arm
¾ × 2¾ × 8¼"

Cut 90° notch, then attach leather padding.

Mirror
³⁄₁₆ × 8 × 8"

Base
¾ × 6 × 8"

1³⁄₈"

1"

Cut ⅜"-deep kerf at 60°.

Beam
¾ × 3 × 18"

mark (photo J), and add 2″ to account for the length of the 1″-long tenons. Reposition the band to the other leg pair and mark the hole locations for the other lower stretcher. Finally, measure the node-to-node distance for the upper stretchers (D) and add 1¾″ to allow for the ⅞″-long tenons.

2 Cut the lower stretcher (C) and upper stretcher (D) blanks to length, turn them to 1″ diameter, and then let the blanks bake in the kiln for at least 24 hours. Next, remount them on your lathe and turn them all down to ⅞″. (Note: While you're waiting for the blanks to dry, build the leg-drilling duo, above.)

3 Now remount the lower stretcher (C) blank, set the tool rest about ¹⁄₁₆″ away, and lay out the node locations with the toe of a skew (refer to figure 1 for the node locations). To size the tenons, I use a ⅝″ open-end wrench as a caliper (photo K).

(Whatever caliper you use, accuracy is important. When you pull the tenon from its mortise, you want to hear a "pop," like when pulling a cork from a bottle.) Taper the ends of the stretcher down to the tenons, and then clean up the stretcher with a skew or sandpaper. Finally cut the ⅛″-deep nodes and ¹⁄₁₆″-deep locking ring with the toe of the skew. Finish turning the remaining lower stretcher, then the two upper stretchers (D), in this same manner.

4 To determine the exact stretcher drilling angle, set a protractor against the seat bottom, as shown in photo L, or you can set your bevel right off the leg.

5 Secure the clamping jig to your bench, and clamp a leg (A) to the support arms. Now drill a ⅝″-diameter × 1″-deep mortise for the lower stretcher (C) (photo M). After drilling the remaining legs, brush glue in the mortises and on the ends of the lower

Extend a folding rule's extension arm between the nodes to find the exact stretcher length.

Using an open-end wrench as a guide, carefully pare down the stretcher ends to fit the mortises.

QUICK TIP

To double-check your mortise location, set a 1¼" spade bit on the leg, and set the tip on your mortise location. When sighted from above the assembly, the bit's spurs should align with the leg's outside edges. If they don't, it means that your mark is not top dead center.

Measure the angle of the leg, and then adjust your bevel gauge to match before drilling the legs for the lower stretchers.

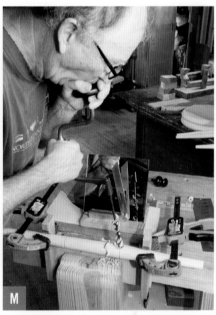

Align the bit with the bevel gauge, and drill the lower stretcher mortises. Use a mirror to check the bit's angle.

stretchers. Rotate the stretcher (as shown in figure 1 inset) so that the growth rings are perpendicular with the long fibers on the legs, and rotate the legs so that the leg assemblies (A, C) lie flat on your bench.

6 Insert the leg and lower stretcher assemblies (A, C) into the seat (A). Next, mark the location of each upper stretcher (D) hole on its corresponding node. (Note: In order to use the "rubber band trick" first employed when marking out the lower stretchers [C], you'll need to cut the band

in order to work past the stretchers that are already in place.) Wrap the band between two opposing legs on the middle nodes, pinch the band's ends together, and mark the centerpoints. Repeat for the remaining pair of stretcher holes.

7 Using the clamping jig, secure a leg assembly (A, C) to your bench. Rotate the assembly so that the lower stretcher runs parallel to your bench. Double-check the mortise location using the tip above. Now set the bevel gauge and mirror alongside the

Clamp the stretcher parallel to the top of your bench, and drill the angled hole for the upper stretcher (E).

Shim the legs as needed to steady the stool and level the seat, and then scribe a cut line around the legs.

leg assembly, and drill a ⅞"-deep hole in the leg for the upper stretcher, as shown in photo N. Position the opposite leg in the jig, drill it, and then repeat with other leg assembly.

8 Lay a leg assembly (A, C) on your benchtop. Apply glue to the mortises and tenons, and then drive in both upper stretchers (D). Next, place the remaining leg assembly on the bench, apply glue, and insert the stretchers. Allow time for the glue to dry.

Attaching the seat

1 Dry-fit the undercarriage (A, C, D) into the seat (B), and mark where the legs meet the bottom of the seat. Remove the seat, and saw the wedge kerfs just shy of your marks. Cut a few wedges (E) from a scrap of dry hardwood.

2 Brush glue on the leg tenons and in the seat mortises, and then fit the undercarriage

back into the seat. Using a mallet, pound the ends of the legs until they are seated firmly. Wipe off any excess glue, and then flip the stool right-side up. Brush a little glue onto one side of each wedge (E), and then tap them into the tops of the legs.

3 Set the stool on a flat, level surface. Insert shims under the legs so that the stool is steady and the seat is level. Mark around each leg, as shown in photo O, and then trim the legs with a backsaw. If you need to make additional minor adjustments, see tip, above right. Finally, chamfer the bottom edges with a knife to prevent chipping.

4 Once the glue is dry, trim the wedged tenons flush with the seat using a wide-sweep gouge, and then follow up with 150 grit (or 400 grit for a natural finish). Finally, inspect and correct any dents, dried glue, or pencil marks, and then apply a finish of your choice.

QUICK TIP

To make minor leg height adjustments, you can turn your workbench into a serviceable jointer by setting a block plane into your vise. Run the long leg over the plane's sole until the wobbling stops.

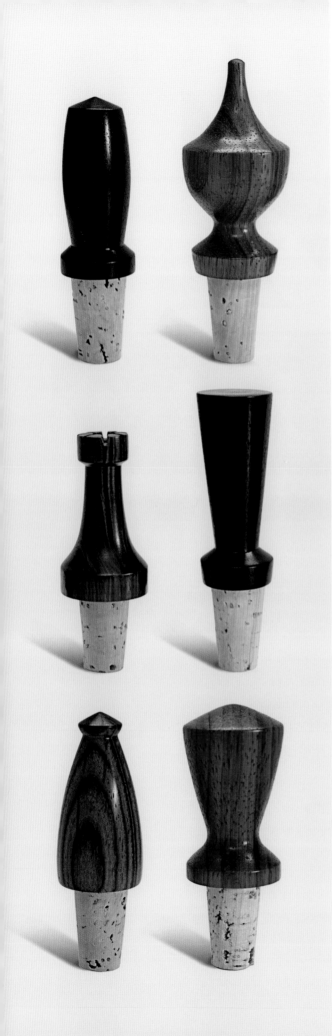

TURNED BOTTLE STOPPERS

They're the perfect, personal token of an evening spent with friends

BY A.J. HAMLER

Weekend projects come in a variety of flavors: Some are easy to make, and some can be made quite inexpensively. Others can be completed quickly, using only a few supplies or materials. Still others can be quite beautiful, even when you have only a minimal amount of time to spend in the shop. And then there are those that are just perfect for gift-giving.

From time to time, however, there comes along a project that is all of these things. Fast, easy projects that are true crowd-pleasers, bottle stoppers turned on your lathe require a minimum of materials (much of which can come from your scrap barrel), but allow maximum use of your creativity. You can make several stoppers in a style or profile you prefer, or make each stopper one-of-a-kind. If you're taking advantage of some of the scrap and offcuts that have been piling up in your shop, you can even match the stopper profiles to the materials you have on hand. The possibilities are endless.

Getting started

Bottle stoppers can be made from any kind of hardwood, but look for something with an interesting grain pattern or a brilliant color, or both. And while you might shy away from using a beautiful but expensive exotic species for a larger project, even a minimal amount of material can turn out several stoppers for only a small investment. However, the dust of some exotics can be irritants, so be sure you have adequate dust collection near your lathe. It's also a good idea to wear a dust mask while turning exotic wood, especially when you create fine dust when sanding.

Each stopper consists of only three parts: the turning blank, a hardwood dowel centered in one end, and a stopper cork with a ⅜″ hole through the center.

As with materials, you'll only need a minimum of tools and equipment for turning bottle stoppers.

Stoppers can be turned between centers, but if you're fortunate enough to have a lathe chuck you'll find the process faster and less wasteful of materials. (I'll describe both methods in a few moments.) Besides your lathe, a basic set of turning tools will do fine—a gouge, skew, and parting tool are about all you need. If you plan to copy a specific profile from a drawing or photo,

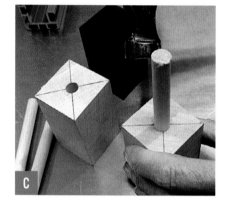

a pair of calipers will come in handy. Have sandpaper in an increasing variety of grit sizes, and some type of final finish. A simple oiled finish works well, as does a light coat of paste wax, but if you're looking for a nice shine the easiest to use is a friction polish—a small amount goes a long way, and it dries in a matter of moments.

You'll also need a ⅜″ drill bit and glue. You can use a waterproof glue if you prefer, but regular shop glue does just fine.

Stock preparation

Each stopper starts as a small turning blank (photo A). These can be purchased already cut or you can simply cut blanks from a larger piece of stock, sizing them to match the profile you're looking for. I've found that a blank measuring 2 x 2 x 2¾″ will work for just about any profile. Of course, if you have a quantity of odd-sized scraps, you can just make your profiles match them. Likewise, if you're looking for a heftier stopper, feel free to cut a larger blank.

There are two ways to prepare your turning blanks, depending on whether you'll use a lathe chuck or turn your stoppers between centers.

Lathe chuck: Cut your blank to just a hair longer than the exact size of stopper you want. You'll use the lathe's tailstock for part of the turning, so you'll need just a bit of waste on the tailstock end.

With the blanks cut, mark the center on each end (photo B), then drill a ⅜" hole, ¾" deep in one end of each blank. A drill press works best for this, as it can ensure that your holes are at 90° angles.

Each bottle stopper uses a hardwood dowel cut to a final length of 2" to accommodate the ¾"-deep hole and the 1 ¼" length of the cork stoppers, but make the dowel as long as needed to fit the chuck securely, and still leave 1 ¼" exposed—this way, the chuck jaws won't mar the dowel where the cork stopper will go. We'll trim the dowel to its finished length when the stopper's done.

Put some glue into the hole and tap the dowel home with a hammer or mallet (photo C). Then, holding a stopper cork in place, mark the dowel the length of the cork to use as a stopping guide when mounting it in your chuck (photo D).

Slip the dowelled blank into the lathe chuck only up to the mark you just made (this will prevent chuck damage to the surface of the dowel) and tighten it securely. Bring the tailstock up to the center of the other end of the blank, and tighten it into place.

Turning between centers: Make the blank ½ to ¾" longer to allow for waste created when mounting on a spur center. As before, mark both ends of the blanks and drill a center hole in one end of each. On the opposite end, cut shallow grooves along your lines with a handsaw for seating the lathe's spur center.

For turning between centers, an extra ¼" for the dowel will work fine. Cut the dowel and glue it into place, then mark the cork length.

Place your spur center into one side of the blank—you can tap it into place with a mallet—and slip it into the headstock (photo E). Bring the tailstock up and center it on the tip of the dowel, then tighten it into place. Note in this photo that I cut off the corners of the blank before mounting. This makes it easier to rough out a cylinder, and creates a lot fewer chips and less dust. You can ease the corners of the blank on a bandsaw or belt sander, or you can trim them off with a bench chisel after you've mounted it on the lathe.

Shaping up

From this point, turning is pretty much the same whether using a chuck or turning between centers. There are a few small differences, but I'll point them out where appropriate.

Start by creating a simple cylinder (photos F and G), followed by roughing out your profile (photo H). Note that I created a waste nib to support the workpiece as I worked the profile. For chuck-turning, use a parting tool to create the nib on the tailstock end; for turning between centers, your waste nib will be at the headstock on your spur center. Both will be removed later.

Take your time when turning your profile, and be sure your chisels are sharp. Failure to do this may result in losing a perfectly good workpiece, especially when chuck-turning. If your chisel "catches" the workpiece, the dowel can snap, not only leaving you with a worthless piece of scrap (photo I), but also creating a dangerous situation when the workpiece flies loose from the lathe.

When your profile is complete, sand through a progression of grits. I started with 100-grit, then moved through 150, 220 and 320. Some exotics, like Macassar ebony, can become quite glossy without a finish, so you may want to sand these up to 600-grit or higher. Again, be sure to wear a dust mask when sanding.

The biggest difference between turning methods comes when sanding is complete and you're ready to apply your finish. For chuck-turning, reduce the size of the waste nib as far as possible with your parting tool. Then back off the tailstock and, with the workpiece spinning at a lower speed, sand the nib off, progressing through grits as before until the top of the stopper is smoothly sanded.

For center-turning, leave the waste nib the way it is for now.

Finishing up

The most amazing part of turning bottle stoppers is the finishing process. I especially like using a friction finish because you can do everything right on the lathe. I used HUT Crystal Coat for the stoppers in this article, but whatever type you use, be sure to follow the manufacturer's specific directions.

With the stopper turning at a low speed, apply a few drops of finish to a clean scrap of cloth, then touch the finish to the spinning stopper until it's thoroughly coated. Increase the lathe speed and rub the cloth over the spinning surface, keeping the cloth in motion at all times. As the friction warms the surface, the finish will cure, developing a glossy shine right before your eyes (photo J). Repeat finish application until you get the look you prefer, and then

follow up by buffing with a clean cloth as the workpiece spins.

If you're chuck-turning, your stopper is done. For turning between centers, you have one more step. With the lathe on a slower speed, use your parting tool to cut your waste nib until you can easily free the stopper from the waste. By hand, sand away any marks left by the nib. Apply a bit of friction polish to the top, and buff it vigorously against a clean cloth until shiny.

You can also sand the nib and apply finish to the top of the stopper by chucking it into a drill press. Wrap the dowel in some stiff paper before putting it in the chuck jaws to avoid marking the dowel.

Popping the cork

Using the mark you made earlier as a guide, trim the dowel to just slightly more than cork length. Apply a small amount of glue to the wider base of the cork and to the inside of the hole, and slide it in place over the dowel until it's snug against the bottom of the stopper. (Do this quickly in one smooth motion so you don't end up with a cork stuck halfway onto the dowel.) Wipe off any squeeze-out with a damp cloth. When the glue has dried completely, touching the end of the dowel gently to a belt, disc, or random orbit sander will true it up to the end of the cork.

You'll find that you can make quite a few bottle stoppers in a short time, so be sure you keep some finished stoppers on hand. When dinner guests admire one sitting handsomely atop a wine bottle, surprise them by letting them take a finished stopper home as a memento of the evening.

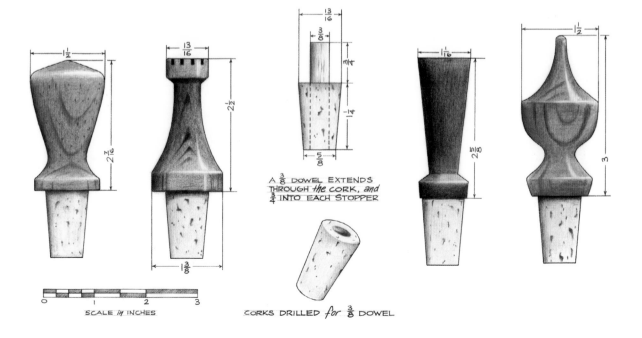

A $\frac{3}{8}$ DOWEL EXTENDS THROUGH *the* CORK, *and* $\frac{3}{4}$ INTO EACH STOPPER

CORKS DRILLED *for* $\frac{3}{8}$ DOWEL

SCALE *in* INCHES

PEPPER GRINDER & SALT CELLAR

Step up your turning repertoire with this spicy combo in contrasting woods

BY LEWIS KAUFFMAN

A couple of years ago, I began making pepper grinders to give as Christmas presents. The grinders were glued up from small pieces of maple and walnut, which was a great way to use up all the offcuts I had saved. But instead of laminating them straight and vertical, I devised a way to glue them together at an angle.

I found that by making a few jigs, I could produce a number of these grinders at one time, and easily duplicate my process later. The following year, I made salt cellars to match. Many of the procedures for the salt cellars are similar to those used for the grinders, with the added challenge of turning a separate fitted lid with a small knob.

The grinders were made using a 6″ pepper grinder mechanism. By adjusting the length of the turning blank, any different-length mechanism could be used. Most mechanisms come with thorough installation instructions.

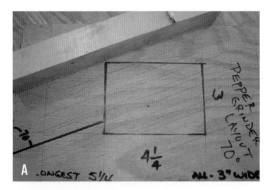

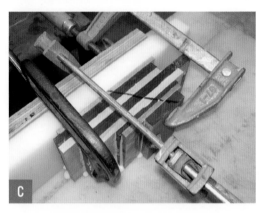

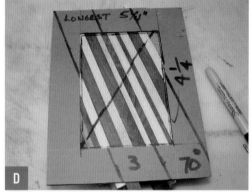

Stock preparation

The first step is to create a blank for the body of your grinder. To get the pieces spaced correctly and to reduce waste, I made a layout jig to position the small pieces of stock (photo A). The final dimensions of the body blank (4¼ x 3″) are drawn onto the jig to aid in placing the stock. The cleat is positioned at about 70°.

I used walnut and maple stock in thicknesses of ¼ to ⅜″ and lengths of 2 to 5¼″. All of the stock is 3″ wide. Because the pieces are positioned at an angle, shorter pieces can be used to start and finish the blank. Also, stock defects can be oriented in areas that will be removed later. Once all of the pieces are in place, make a witness mark across the blank to ensure the pieces maintain their positions when you glue them together (photo B).

To make the glue-up easier, split the blank roughly in half. Wrap a rubber band around each half until you're ready to glue it. The glue-up is done with a simple clamping jig consisting of a 90° plywood fence clamped to an old restaurant-grade plastic cutting board. I used a floor tapping block against the fence to prevent any glue from sticking to the plywood (photo C).

Glue the stock together, using the witness mark to align the pieces. Once the glue dries, repeat the process for the other half of the blank. Then glue and clamp the halves together.

Squaring the blank

Once the glue has dried, lay out the blank's 3 x 4¼″ perimeter with a template, which can also help align the 70° angle of the pieces (photo D). The body of the pepper grinder will be cut from the blank, using these lines as a guide. I constructed the simple jig in photo E to hold the blank while trimming the first long side. It is designed to capture and ride over the rip fence. A clamp holds the blank securely to the jig with the perimeter

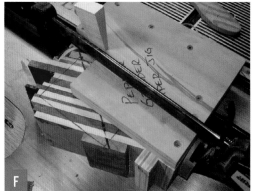

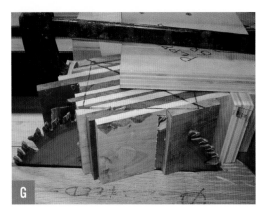

line you drew parallel with the edge of the jig (photo F). I used a wedge to help with alignment and a firm grip on the workpiece. Trim the blank to create a flat, straight side (photo G).

Using the rip fence and miter gauge, finish trimming the blank to its final dimensions of 4¼ x 3 x 3".

The remaining pieces of the blank are a collar (3 x 3 x ⅜" maple) and a top (3 x 3 x 1⅞" walnut). Glue and clamp both the collar and top to the body of the grinder. Finally, glue a 3 x 3 x ¾" waste block to the top of the blank (photo H).

Turning the grinder

Locate the center of the blank on both ends and lay out the diameter of the grinder. Knock off the corners of the blank before mounting it in the lathe (see sidebar).

Mount the blank in the lathe with the waste block toward the drive spur end.

Turn the waste block to fit in your lathe chuck (photo I). Remove the drive spur and replace it with a chuck (photo J). Check the directions for your grinding mechanism to choose the proper size bits and then drill through the grinder body as instructed (photo K). The holes can also be drilled on a drill press and the blank returned to the lathe for finishing. Put a reference mark on the blank to ensure accurate repositioning of the blank after drilling for the mechanism.

I used a jig (photo L) to provide support for the grinder throughout the remaining turning, sanding, and finishing steps (see sidebar on page 140). It fits into the bored-out blank and provides support at the tailstock end. It also holds the grinder together after the top is parted off.

Photo M shows the chuck end of the grinder blank with the jig installed. Re-chuck the blank in the lathe (photo N). Part off the grinder top

A Time When You'll Want to Cut Corners

When turning projects on the lathe, you can save time by knocking the corners off square blanks. This is usually done by tilting the tablesaw blade to 45° or tilting the bandsaw table. In both cases, the saw must be realigned back to 90°, which of course takes time. When cutting small pieces, these methods can bring your fingers dangerously close to the tablesaw blade. To solve both problems, I created this jig (photos 1 and 2) to hold my pepper grinder blanks while knocking off the corners. It consists of a sled with a 90° V-notch cut along its length. The notch holds the work like a round-stock–drilling clamp on a drill press. The clamp holds the work in the notch.

The sled provides a secure base for the stock and slides freely. Meanwhile, your fingers are a safe distance from the blade and the blade stays set at 90° to the table. On the last cut, I add a scrap to make up for the short travel of the clamp (photo 3). Note the stop at the back of the jig to prevent the work from sliding.

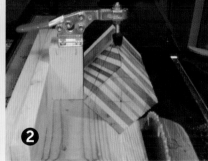

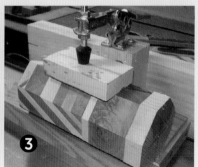

by turning the tenon to the size specified in the grinder mechanism instructions.

Remove the jig and lower portion of the grinder body. Re-chuck the top of the grinder and clean up the tenon (photo O).

Reinsert the jig and tighten securely (photo P). The jig will align the top and body during shaping and sanding.

With the blank re-chucked in the lathe, lay out the transition points according to the illustration on page 141 or to your own specifications. Turn the grinder and sand through 320-grit (photo Q). Part off the grinder from the chuck and touch up the top. Finish with several coats of gloss water-based polyurethane.

Don't forget the salt

Turned pepper grinders always make interesting gifts. By laminating contrasting woods, it's possible to produce a swirled pattern that's eye-catching and looks great in most kitchens and dining rooms. I have delighted many a friend and family member with the gift of a one-of-a-kind grinder outfitted with a quality mechanism and finished to a deep shine.

But what about the salt? One obvious option is to turn a matching shaker. Snap-in, stainless steel shaker tops are available (with plastic plugs for the bottoms). But I decided to make salt cellars instead, small lidded vessels perfect for storing the chunky sea salts and kosher salts that are popular with cooks these days.

The salt cellar doesn't fulfill exactly the same function as a shaker, although you can use it for table salt during a meal with a small spoon if you like. Centuries ago, when salt was an expensive commodity available only to the upper classes, it was displayed in ornate gold, crystal, or porcelain cellars on the dining table. People really wanted to show off their valuable salt! These days, you'll more commonly find a salt cellar right by the stove, where its coarse contents can

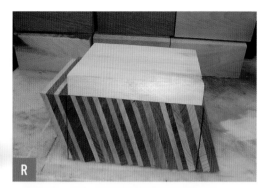

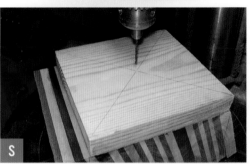

easily be measured out or pinched. A cellar is a handy way to store any frequently used seasoning, such as a savory spice mix.

Preparing the blank

The blank for the bowl will be much shorter and wider than the one for the pepper grinder. I used several pieces of uniform size (about 3 x 5″) but with alternating thicknesses. You can create another jig using a 3 x 5″ perimeter and proceed as earlier, or push the pieces into a sort of parallelogram (as I did) and devise a way to clamp them tightly. The result is shown in photo R. Either way, you will find it easier to glue the pieces in two sets.

Square the blank on one of the large surfaces and an adjoining side before proceeding.

A piece of ¾″ scrap forms a glue block for the lathe work that will follow (photo R). The block is sized to the blank's width and the distance between the lines, which should come out to about 5 x 5″. Glue and clamp the scrap block in place on the jointed, flat bottom of the blank.

After the block dries, locate the center and drill a pivot hole for a circle-cutting jig (photo S). I also returned to the jointer and flattened the "top" of the blank—the end opposite the glue block that will be the top of the cellar—slightly so it would be easier to locate the center point for the lathe's live center.

Cut the blank into a cylinder on the bandsaw. At this point, you can start to see the swirl design that will emerge as you turn the salt cellar (photo T).

Turning the cellar body

Remove the blank from the bandsaw and locate the center of the top of the blank. Finally, we're ready for the lathe. Set the lathe's drive spur into the glue block and mount the piece on the lathe. For reference, I marked the location of the drive spur on the workpiece.

Turn the glue block to a diameter that will fit into your lathe chuck and remount the blank in the chuck. Again, place a reference mark locating the work in the chuck.

Draw reference lines at the various transition points, referring to the illustration on page 141 (photo U). Of course, you can create your own silhouette if you like.

Because I planned on making a number of these, I made a measurement jig to quickly set the calipers for the diameters of all the transition points (photo V). Using a parting tool and calipers, turn the transition points to the proper diameters (photo W).

Now form the outside of the salt cellar (photo X). Move right along to the inside. The wall thickness follows the outer contour and is about ¼″ thick (photo Y).

Sand the inside and outside of the cellar through 320 grit. Part off the vessel from the glue block (photo Z). The overall finished size is about 4½″ in diameter and 2½″ tall.

Making the lid

I prepared the ¾″ maple stock for several lids at once. Start with a 4½″ circle; the finished diameter will depend on the dimension of each lid's mating salt cellar. The glue blocks, as before, are ¾″ scrap pine. Glue and clamp the lid blank to the glue block (photo AA).

Locate the center of the lid blank and drill a ¹⁄₃₂″ pivot hole ⅛″ deep into the maple lid. The same hole will be used later to locate the lid's knob. Cut the lid blank and glue block on the bandsaw with a circle-cutting jig. Next, locate the center of the glue block side of the blank, which will be used for the lathe's drive spur.

With the blank mounted in the lathe, I turned the glue block to the correct diameter for my chuck. Remove the blank from the drive spur and mount it in the chuck, make another reference mark, then begin forming the lid. Match the dimensions of each lid to its salt cellar mate. The bottom of the lid is tapered, which helps center it on the salt cellar.

I gave the lid a dome shape. At the tallest

point it is about ⅝″ thick. The tapered section is about ¼″ thick and the diameters are sized to fit. Once you're satisfied with the lid's shape, sand the top through 320-grit with the lid still in the chuck. I used my random orbit sander. Part off the lid (photo BB).

The final piece of lathe work is turning the small knob for the lid. I turned a ¾ x ¾″ piece of walnut into a dowel and shaped the knob freehand. Size the tenon with a ¼″ open-end wrench (photo CC). The finished knob should be about ⅝″ in diameter and ¾″ tall with a ¼″-long tenon.

Finishing up

Sand the knob through 320-grit, burnish it with shavings (photo DD) and part it off. I waited until after finishing the lid's underside to glue the knob to the lid.

With a ¼″ Forstner bit, drill the hole for the knob slightly deeper than ¼″ (photo EE). The pivot hole used to cut the lid is the pilot hole for this operation.

I made a jig to hold the lid and salt cellar when sanding the rough areas left by the parting tool. The top is slightly scooped-out and a ¼″ dowel protrudes about ³⁄₁₆″ from the center (photo FF). The sides are tapered

Y

Z

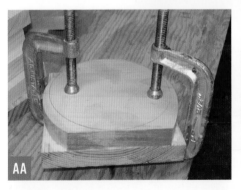

AA

BB

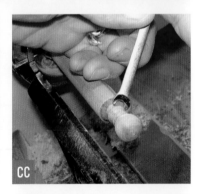

CC

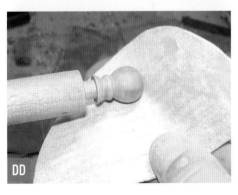

DD

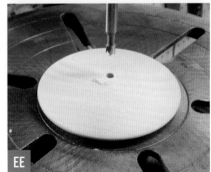

EE

FF

GG

HH

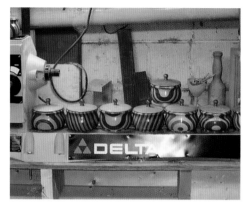

and the diameter at the top is slightly smaller than the inside diameter of the salt cellars. To sand the bottom of the lid, place it on the jig with the hole for the knob over the pin (photo GG).

To sand the body of the salt cellar, I placed a rubber jar opener over the jig and placed the cellar upside down on the jig (photo HH). The combination of the taper and the thin rubber held the workpiece while I sanded the bottom.

A little touch-up sanding and several coats of water-based polyurethane later, my Christmas shopping was done!

Support When You Need It

This simple jig is invaluable for supporting your pepper mill as you turn and sand the outer silhouette. To make it yourself, you just need a little time and a few pieces of hardware.

Cut two pieces of a hardwood such as maple into 2" squares. Piece A should be ¾" thick and B at least 1⅛" thick. Clamp the pieces together, locate the center of the blanks and drill a ³⁄₃₂" hole through both pieces. This hole will help align the pieces during final glue-up and assembly. Unclamp the pieces and drill a ⅞"

hole ⅛" deep in piece B, using the ³⁄₃₂" hole as the center. Drill further with a ⁹⁄₃₂" bit to accommodate the threaded sleeve of a ¼" x 20 T-nut fastener. It's important to drill only deep enough for the fastener, not all the way through B. Install the T-nut fastener, making sure the its flange is below the surface of the wood.

Glue and clamp the two pieces of wood together. Place a ³⁄₃₂" bit or heavy piece of wire through the holes you drilled earlier to align the two pieces. After the glue dries, turn the blank to the dimensions shown.

During the turning process, piece A should be toward the tailstock. This will prevent the enlargement of the original ³⁄₃₂" hole.

After turning and sanding, remove the piece from the lathe and finish drilling the ⁹⁄₃₂" hole. Drill in from the end of B, taking care not to drill into the T-nut fastener threads. Thread a ¼" x 20 threaded rod into the small end of the jig until it just bottoms out on piece A. Use two ¼" x 20 nuts, a lock washer and a flat washer to hold the jig securely in the turning blank.

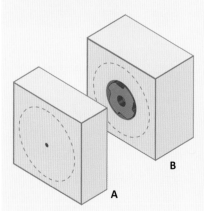
A
B

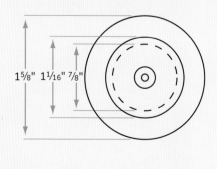
1⅝" 1¹⁄₁₆" ⅞"

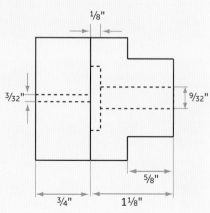
⅛"
³⁄₃₂"
⁹⁄₃₂"
⅝"
¾" 1⅛"

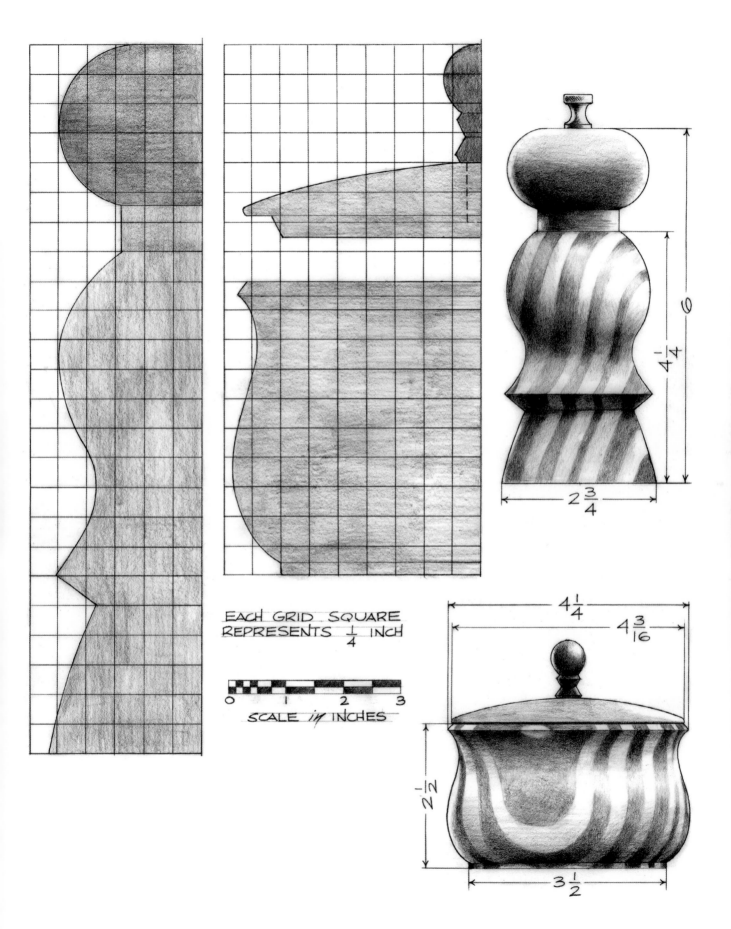

EACH GRID SQUARE
REPRESENTS $\frac{1}{4}$ INCH

0   1   2   3
SCALE in INCHES

WOODTURNER'S TRAVEL MUG

Here's a great way to show off your lathe talents and give shape to a few last-minute holiday gifts

BY JIM HARROLD WITH WOODTURNER TOM SCHOTTLE

Turner Tom Schottle liked this project so much he made six right off the bat, using a variety of woods and wood laminations. Of course, you'll need a lathe ("The bigger, the better," says Tom; although we had success with a Jet mini lathe), a stainless steel mug kit (which can be found online or at your local woodworking store), a hardwood blank (which you could buy or find in your firewood pile), two common chucks, and a few turning tools.

Let's start turning

1 Mount the blank between centers as shown in photo A. Then, using a roughing gouge and a slow lathe speed, round the blank to 3½" in diameter. Next, turn a tenon on one end to fit your chuck (see the tip) and mount the blank in your chuck.

2 To begin hollowing the rough-turned blank, mount a keyed drill chuck (often called a Jacob's chuck) in the tailstock and chuck in a 2⅛" Forstner bit. (This is the first of a two-part process that Tom uses to drill into end grain.) Now, drill a shallow (1") hole to establish a centered registration mark as shown in photo B. Switch to a 1½" Forstner bit and bore in as deeply as possible into the blank, withdrawing the bit as needed to clear out the chips. Return to the larger Forstner bit and drill to the depth reached by the smaller

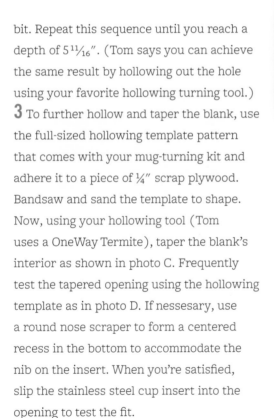

bit. Repeat this sequence until you reach a depth of 5¹¹⁄₁₆″. (Tom says you can achieve the same result by hollowing out the hole using your favorite hollowing turning tool.)

3 To further hollow and taper the blank, use the full-sized hollowing template pattern that comes with your mug-turning kit and adhere it to a piece of ¼″ scrap plywood. Bandsaw and sand the template to shape. Now, using your hollowing tool (Tom uses a OneWay Termite), taper the blank's interior as shown in photo C. Frequently test the tapered opening using the hollowing template as in photo D. If nessesary, use a round nose scraper to form a centered recess in the bottom to accommodate the nib on the insert. When you're satisfied, slip the stainless steel cup insert into the opening to test the fit.

4 Adhere the outside face template that comes with your kit to a piece of ¼″ scrap plywood to use as a reference while further hollowing and tapering the blank. Make it oversized at first. Next, trial-fit the cup insert's flange over the rim. Take care it does not get stuck. Says Tom, "It can

happen and can be almost impossible to remove." Remove a little more material until the rim of the cup bottoms out in the flange recess.

5 With the cup insert temporarily fitted in the blank, mark the bottom edge of the rabbet and use a skew to establish the

QUICK TIP

When making several such turnings, Tom cuts an H-shaped "go-or-no-go sizing gauge" from ³⁄₁₆″ scrap plywood to quickly and easily determine the needed tenon diameter to match his chuck's jaws. He spray-painted the gauge bright orange to locate it in a jiffy.

What You Need to Get Started

While you may have everything but the travel mug kit, here's a look at the items used in this turning.

1) Travel mug kit, 2) Epoxy, syringe, 3) Hollowing tool, 4) 1" oval skew, 5) Woodturning chuck, 6) Lathe drill chuck, 7) 1½" Forstner bit, 8) 2⅛" Forstner bit, 9) Seasoned hardwood blank

Design options & pointers:

Ideally, a solid, dried hardwood blank measuring at least 3¾ × 3¾ × 8" makes a great cup, but it may not be that easy to get your hands on, unless you resaw a piece that size yourself or find a source. An attractive alternative is to laminate contrasting woods to make a blank, or use stave construction, which is explained in the mug kit instructions. Consider also the finished dimensions. Tom recommends a maximum 3" diameter for the turned wood sleeve and a length of 6" tall. The lower half of the sleeve needs to taper to under 2¾" so it fits in your vehicle's cup holder. Most importantly, however, is that the finished cup feels comfortable in your hand.

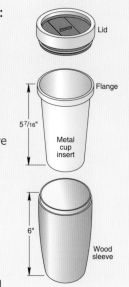

Lid

Flange

5⁷⁄₁₆"

Metal cup insert

6"

Wood sleeve

top outside diameter of the wood sleeve (formerly the blank) as shown in photo E. It should be slightly proud of the outside face of the flange to allow for sanding later.

6 Remove the cup insert and measure 6" down from the rim of the sleeve and mark a line. With a parting tool, turn to a 2¾" diameter at the outside edge of the line. Switch to a 1" skew or ½" gouge and taper the outside edge of the cup, moving from the top outside sleeve diameter to the established bottom outside diameter as shown in photo F.

7 Frequently check the outside taper with either the hollowing template (photo G), or by making the outside face template from ¼" scrap and using it. Use a caliper to gauge the wall thickness of the sleeve, being careful not to go thinner than ³⁄₁₆". Fine-tune the shape and test-fit the cup insert.

8 Smooth the sleeve using 100-, 150-, 180-, and 220-grit sandpaper as shown in

F

G

photo H. Finally, part the sleeve from the blank end.

9 Now, using a parting tool, form a jamb chuck (tenon) on the blank's waste wood, sizing it to the inside diameter of the sleeve's opening as in photo I.

10 Fit the sleeve opening onto the jamb chuck and slide up the tailstock with a ball bearing center to clamp the sleeve in place. Now, using a skew, form a concave bottom as shown in photo J so the travel mug sits upright.

11 Remove the sleeve from the lathe and apply tape around the rabbet. Now finish it as desired. We used five coats of spray lacquer as shown in photo K, sanding and buffing the finish between coats. When choosing a finish, consider that the mug will occasionally be exposed to moisture during cleaning.

12 Mix up a small batch of 5-minute epoxy and carefully daub it around the rabbet and on the upper inside surface of the sleeve (photo L). Avoid applying so much that the epoxy is forced out under the insert and onto the outside of the mug. Now, slide in the cup insert, tapping it gently with a block of wood and mallet until the bottom edge of the flange seats against the outside face of the sleeve. Let dry; then, with mug in hand, find a pot of coffee and fill'er up.

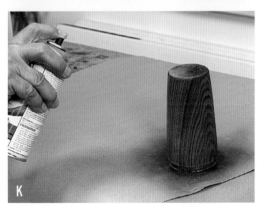

Overall dimensions: 2 ½" d

GRACEFUL PEPPER & SALT MILLS

Pleasing looks meet functionality in this tabletop duo

BY BYRON YOUNG

Few woodturnings see as much everyday use in the home as salt and pepper mills. Aesthetically, you want a pair that features graceful lines and feels good in the hand. My design incorporates smooth flowing curves, V-grooves that hide the base/top seam, and a rounded top that's easy to grasp and twist. Here, because the stainless steel mechanism for the pepper mill and the ceramic mechanism for the sea salt mills are similar, you can follow the same turning instructions and tapered design to shape both. To differentiate between the two, I chose contrasting woods: African mahogany for the pepper mill and lighter colored figured maple for the salt mill.

While mill grinding mechanisms come in several sizes up to 14″, I decided on the ones suited for 6″-high turnings. You'll need a 3 × 3 × 6¾″ blank for each mill. I advise ordering the mechanisms in advance to have on hand during the turning process. Consider ordering extras if you're in the gift-giving spirit. Now, gather up the needed tools and boring bits and let's get turning. It should take 3 to 4 hours to make and finish one mill.

Prepare the mill base and top

Note: Unless otherwise indicated, run the lathe at 1,800 to 2,000 rpm for all turning operations.

1 Strike diagonal lines from the corners on the ends of a 3 × 3 × 6¾″ blank to locate the centers, and then mount the blank onto the lathe using a spur drive and live center.

2 With a 1″ roughing gouge, round the blank to just over the largest diameter of the design in figure 1. Now, referring to the drawing, mark your cylinder for the tenons, V-grooves, and top/base parting location, as shown in photo A. Turn on the lathe, and continue the marks around the cylinder, as shown in photo A inset. I make the parting line wider and darker.

Live center

Spur drive

Top end of mill

A

3 With a ³⁄₁₆″ parting tool, turn the tenon for the mill base and top, where shown in figure 1, to fit into a four-jaw scroll chuck. Switch to a ¹⁄₁₆″ parting tool, and part off the top end of the blank in two operations for safety. First, part down to ½″ diameter where marked on the cylinder. Next, stop the lathe and finish the parting with a handsaw (photo B). Slide the tailstock out of the way, and remove both parts.

Bore the mill base and top blanks

1 Install a four-jaw scroll chuck, and tighten the jaws on the base blank tenon. (Make sure it is secure as there will be significant pressure applied during the drilling process.) Move the tool rest around to the end of the blank and just below its center. Clean up the bottom end of the base blank with a ¼″ gouge. Now, with the toe of a ½″ skew, divot the end, as shown in photo C, to establish its center and prepare the blank for drilling.

Figure 1: Pepper and Salt Mill Elevations

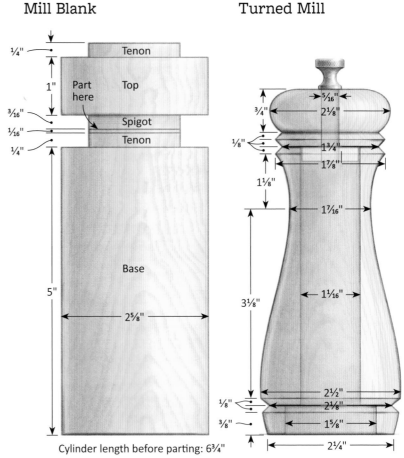

Mill Blank

Turned Mill

Cylinder length before parting: 6¾″

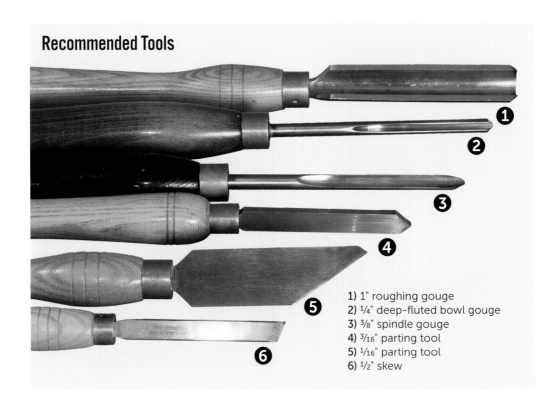

Recommended Tools

1) 1″ roughing gouge
2) ¼″ deep-fluted bowl gouge
3) ³⁄₈″ spindle gouge
4) ³⁄₁₆″ parting tool
5) ¹⁄₁₆″ parting tool
6) ½″ skew

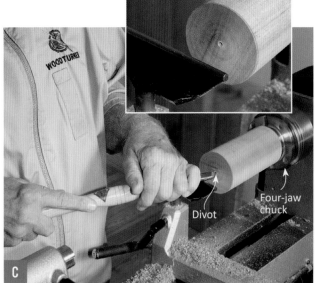

Divot

Four-jaw chuck

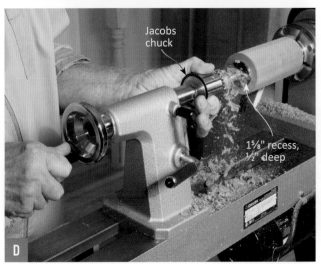

Jacobs chuck

1⅝" recess, ½" deep

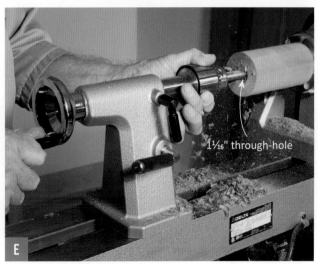

1¹⁄₁₆" through-hole

2 Outfit your tailstock with a Jacobs chuck and 1⅝" Forstner bit. With the bit's spur centered in the dimple, and using a speed of around 1,200 rpm, advance the bit into the spinning base and bore a ½"-deep recess, as shown in photo D.

3 Install a ¹¹⁄₁₆" bit in the Jacobs chuck. Now, bore a little beyond halfway through the base blank at 1,200 rpm, using quick, short cuts to avoid overheating the bit and burning the wood. Rid the hole of debris often by backing the bit out. Stop drilling once the hole exceeds the halfway point in the base blank. (I made a mark on the bit's shaft to help me determine when I had

bored more than halfway in the cylinder.)

4 To complete the through-hole, swap the ends of the base blank. To secure it, switch to 35mm bowl jaws and expand them inside the ½"-deep × 1⅝" recess. Reduce the speed to 700 rpm, and remove the tenon at the top end of the base with a ¼" bowl gouge. Dimple the end with a ½" skew, and then continue drilling the through-hole in the mill base, as shown in photo E.

5 Install the original jaws in your four-jaw chuck, and then mount the top end of the top blank. Install a ⁵⁄₁₆" brad-point bit in the Jacobs chuck, and bore a centered hole through the top blank.

Spigot

Through-hole

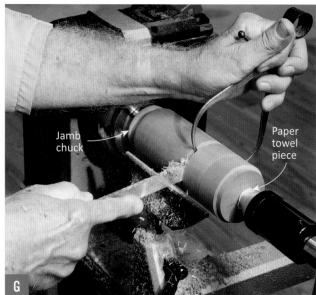

Jamb chuck

Paper towel piece

6 Now, increasing the speed to around 1,800 rpm, turn a spigot to fit snugly in the through-hole in the top end of the base (about $^{11}\!/_{16}$″ diameter), as shown in photo F. (Later, you'll turn the spigot to a 1″ diameter to fit with slight clearance in the through-hole for friction-free twisting of the top when grinding.)

Turn the mill parts to final shape

1 Make a $1^5\!/_8$″-diameter jamb chuck to fit into the $^1\!/_2 × 1^5\!/_8$″ recess at base blank bottom end (see fig. 2). Mount it in the four-jaw chuck. Install a live cone center in the tailstock. Now, fit the cylindrical blanks for the base and top together, and place the assembly between centers on the lathe.

2 Make a copy of the full-sized template on page 152 and transfer the depth dimensions on it for a ready reference. Now, adhere it to a piece of cardboard, and cut it to shape. Use it as needed to check the shape as you turn your mill. Next, using the dimensions on the template or in figure 1, mark the narrowest diameters on the mill assembly.

3 With the $^3\!/_{16}$″ parting tool and caliper, establish the depth of the large tapered cove,

Figure 2: Jamb Chuck

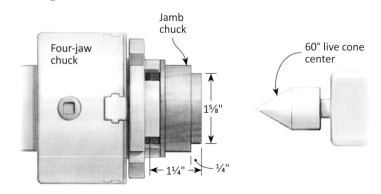

Four-jaw chuck

Jamb chuck

$1^5\!/_8$″

$1^1\!/_4$″

$^1\!/_4$″

60° live cone center

Figure 3: Shop-Made Cone Center

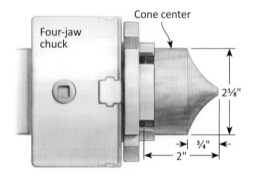

where marked and as shown in photo G.

4 Use a ¼″ deep-fluted gouge to form the tapered shape of the mill, removing the waste between the bead locations. Always move the tool tip downhill during the shaping, as shown in photo H.

5 With a ½″ skew, make the finer cuts to form the V-groovelike coves and beads, as shown in photo I. Here, strive for a depth of between ⅛ to ³⁄₁₆″, keeping the toe of the tool tip down. Lift the handle slowly as you enter the turning, rotating it from left to right or vise-versa, depending on the V-wall you are shaping. Take care to not round over the bead. You want a V shape around the edges as well. Finish-sand from 150 through 800 grit.

6 Switch to a ⅜″ spindle gouge to round the top to shape. Work to establish a 1″ top height from the top/base joint to the top end of the top. Stop the lathe and remove the top.

7 Secure the base with the live cone center at the top end and a jamb chuck at the bottom end. Now, use the ½″ skew to form the V-groovelike cove at the bottom of the base, as described in step 5. Also taper the bottom end of the base to final shape. Now, sand the base from 150-through 800-grit sandpaper. Stop the lathe.

8 With the lathe stopped, apply finish to the base. I wiped on a generous coating of Mylands High Build Friction Polish. Then, with the lathe running at around 1,800 rpm, I pressed a cotton cloth to the surface, raising a long-lasting sheen. Remove the base and chuck.

9 Make the shop-made wood cone center, as shown in figure 3. Now, place the top between cone centers and reduce the spigot's diameter slightly with a ³⁄₁₆″ parting tool, as shown in photo J. Test the fit to ensure that the spigot fits with a slight clearance in the base through-hole.

10 Replace the cone centers with the four-jaw chuck and 35mm jaws. Now secure the top's spigot in the jaws. With a ¼″ bowl gouge, finish shaping the top. Repeat the sanding and finishing processes described in step 8 to complete the top.

11 At the drill press, use a ¹⁄₁₆″ bit to drill the needed ¾″-deep pilot holes for the mechanism screws, where shown in figure 4 and as shown in photo K. Finally, drive the screws and assemble the grinding mill components. Secure the mill top to the base with the knob. Now, fill the mill with peppercorns or sea salt crystals, depending on the mechanism.

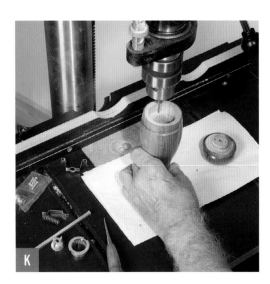

QUICK TIP

Use a piece of paper towel over the cone to prevent it from discoloring the wood.

Figure 4: Mill Exploded View

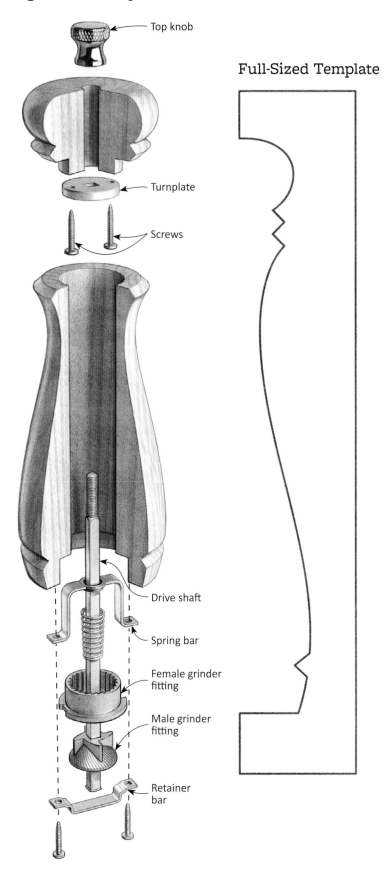

Top knob

Turnplate

Screws

Drive shaft

Spring bar

Female grinder fitting

Male grinder fitting

Retainer bar

Full-Sized Template

ROCKIN' ROLLING PIN

Lay down the dough with this kitchenware essential

BY NICK COOK

Rolling pins have been around for thousands of years. They're used to flatten and shape dough in making cookies, pastas, pizzas, specialty breads, and pie crusts. They come in a variety of shapes and sizes and can be made of wood, metal, clay, and glass. They can be long and skinny or short and fat, with and without handles. I have been turning rolling pins for more than 25 years. My father always referred to them

as a HAT, or Husband Alignment Tool. Indeed, in early cartoons, rolling pins were shown as weapons wielded by angry housewives.

I began making handled rolling pins when I started working with master turner Rude Osolnik. He made laminated pins with short round handles. While I served as his assistant in many demonstrations, he would frequently turn most of the pin and then ask

Figure 1: Rolling Pin Exploded View

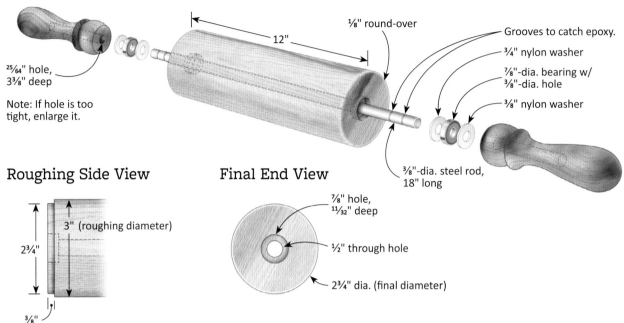

$^{25}/_{64}$" hole,
$3^{3}/_{8}$" deep

Note: If hole is too tight, enlarge it.

$^{1}/_{8}$" round-over

12"

Grooves to catch epoxy.

$^{3}/_{4}$" nylon washer

$^{7}/_{8}$"-dia. bearing w/ $^{3}/_{8}$"-dia. hole

$^{3}/_{8}$" nylon washer

$^{3}/_{8}$"-dia. steel rod, 18" long

Roughing Side View

3" (roughing diameter)

$2^{3}/_{4}$"

$^{3}/_{8}$"

Final End View

$^{7}/_{8}$" hole, $^{11}/_{32}$" deep

$^{1}/_{2}$" through hole

$2^{3}/_{4}$" dia. (final diameter)

me to duplicate the handle on the opposite end. Most of the time it worked out.

There are two basic types of rolling pins: rod-style rolling pins, which are long, thin, and usually made of wood; then there is the roller style. These are shorter, fatter, and with thinner handles. In the next few pages, I'll show you how to make the latter, employing a kit for the rolling mechanism and attaching the handles. (See "What You Need to Get Started" at right.) You'll learn the basics for turning a perfect cylinder and duplicate handles.

Prep the rolling pin cylinder

1 Before drilling the holes in the blanks for the roller pin and handles at the lathe (my preferred method, since this approach centers the holes and makes them straight and true), properly square up the blank material. Now, locate the centers on each end of the blanks (I used a center finder), and mark them with an awl or punch. Set the handle blanks aside.

What You Need to Get Started

For the roller-style rolling pin shown, you need three separate pieces of wood. The first is a 3"-square × 12"-long tight-grained hardwood blank for the roller. The other two blanks should be of a contrasting hardwood and measure 1$^{1}/_{2}$" square × 6" long for the handles.

If you want to skip drilling through the long roller cylinder, buy a predrilled rolling pin blank as seen above (walnut; maple; cherry; curly maple). These blanks include both the through-hole and $^{7}/_{8}$" recess, allowing you to skip steps 1, 5, and 6 under "Prep the rolling pin cylinder." Regardless of which way you go, you'll also need a rolling pin hardware kit, as seen below. For these items, visit a local craft store or Internet retailer.

Note: When turning the rolling pin blank, use a 12″-long tool rest. You can buy one and a post that matches your lathe's rest assembly.

2 Mount the roller blank between a spur center and cone center. (For the prepared blank, use the roller jamb chuck in figure 2 and cone center.) Turn it to a 3″ cylinder with a ¾″ roughing gouge at 1,500 rpm.

3 Switch to a parting tool or bedan, and turn a ⅜″-long × 2¾″-diameter tenon at each end of the roller (photo A).

4 Replace the spur center (or jamb chuck) in the headstock with a scroll chuck. Tighten the jaws on the tenon at one end of the cylinder. Adjust the tool rest, and true up the end of the cylinder by shaving it with a spindle gouge.

5 Lower the speed to 500 rpm, and turn off the lathe to prepare for drilling. Install a Jacobs chuck and a ⅞″ Forstner bit in the tailstock. Now, drill a ⅞″ recess, ¹¹⁄₃₂″ deep,

in one end, checking with a depth gauge (photo B).

6 Switch to a ½″ brad-point bit, and drill into the roller end for the through-hole. (I start the through-hole with a short bit because it flexes less than the longer bit.) Then install a longer bit to achieve the needed depth, as shown in photo C. A piece of tape 6½″ from the end of the bit establishes the needed depth. Turn the blank end for end and repeat steps 5 and 6. The holes should meet in the center.

Figure 2: Jamb Chucks

Roller Jamb Chuck

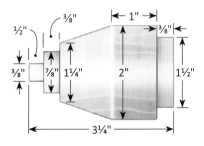

Handle Jamb Chuck

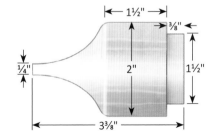

Turn and finish the roller

1 Turn a roller jamb chuck to drive the roller blank. To do this, mount a 2 × 2 × 2" block in the four-jaw scroll chuck, and turn the exposed end round at 1,500 rpm, making a tenon that fits your chuck. Reverse the jamb chuck blank in the scroll chuck, and turn this exposed end to match the roller jamb chuck shape in figure 2. You want the stepped tenon to fit snugly in the ⅞ and ⅜" holes in the roller blank (photo D).

2 Fit the tailstock with a conical live center, and mount the roller blank between centers. Start with a parting tool or a bedan, and with the lathe running at 1,500 rpm, make a cut about 1" from each end to establish a 2¾" final diameter. Check the cut depth with either a caliper or a vernier scale (photo E).

3 Position the tool rest parallel to the axis of the lathe and as close as possible to the workpiece. Rotate the material by hand before turning on the lathe to ensure the rest does not contact the turning. Now, with a ¾" spindle roughing gouge at 2,000 rpm, roughly turn the blank to remove the waste and any lumps and bumps. Guide your index finger along the tool rest to accurately turn a true cylinder, one that is the same diameter from end to end. Continually check the diameter along the cylinder with a caliper.

4 Make a light planing cut with the skew, as shown in photo F, to remove any imperfections and leave a surface that requires very little sanding. If uncomfortable using a skew, use a sanding block with 80-grit sandpaper to even out the high areas, or make an extremely light cut with a spindle roughing gouge while riding on the bevel. You want to maximize the length of the bevel to support the

cutting edge and avoid tear-out. Check the diameter with a caliper.

5 Use a straightedge (photo G) to check the end-to-end trueness of the roller. Touch up if needed, recheck, and then cut a ⅛" round-over on the edges with ⅜" spindle gouge.

6 Next, sand the roller through 220 grit. Wipe it clean, and finish. I use paper towels to apply any finish on the lathe. The finish should be food-safe and easily refreshed. I first apply mineral oil without the lathe running and then turn the machine on at a moderate speed and burnish the oil into the wood with a fresh paper towel. I then use a

QUICK TIP

When drilling deep holes, back the bit out often to cool it and clear the flutes of debris.

block of beeswax and rub the surface with the lathe running at a slow speed, as seen in photo H, followed by a dry paper towel to polish. This creates a satiny smooth finish.

Turn the handles

1 Retrieve the handle blanks, and mount one of them between a spur center and a live cone center. Turn a short tenon at one end to fit into your scroll chuck. Repeat for the remaining handle blank.

2 Fit the tenon for one handle blank into your scroll chuck, and turn the blank to a 1½"-diameter cylinder at 1,000 rpm. Repeat for the other handle blank.

3 With one handle blank still mounted in the chuck, increase the lathe speed to 1,500 rpm, and true up the opposite end with a spindle gouge. Repeat for the remaining handle blank.

4 Using a Jacobs chuck and ²⁵⁄₆₄″ brad-point bit, drill a hole 3⅜″ deep in each handle blank. (A ²⁵⁄₆₄″-diameter hole allows for the epoxy and makes it easier to insert the steel rod.)

5 Make the handle jamb chuck in figure 2 from a 2 × 2″ block to drive the handles at the headstock. Use a live center at the tailstock. Mount a handle blank between centers.

6 Make a full-sized copy of figure 3 and spray-adhere it to a piece of cardboard. Use a craft knife to trim the template to shape.

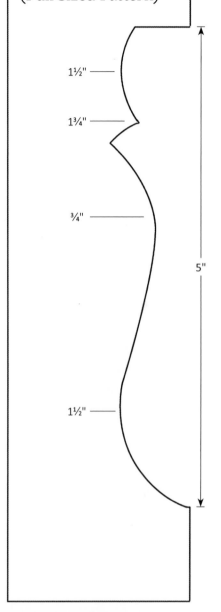

Figure 3: Handle Pattern and Template (Full-Sized Pattern)

1½"

1¾"

¾"

5"

1½"

Rod → Bearing → Block ←

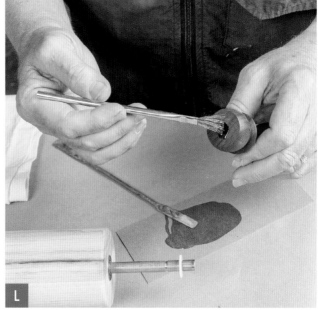

Use the template to lay out the handle shape and a parting tool to establish the depths.

7 Use a spindle roughing gouge to remove waste and a ⅜″ spindle gouge and skew (if comfortable) to shape and detail the handle (photo I). I begin by defining and shaping the large bead at the roller end of the handle and then work on the grip portion.

8 Check the shape against the template (photo J). Repeat the procedure to create an identical handle.

9 Sand the handles through 320 grit and finish. To give the handles a more durable and protective finish than the roller, I apply three coats of a wipe-on polyurethane and then beeswax used in a stick form. Buff the surface. After finishing the handles, part them off with a parting tool. Sand and touch up the unfinished ends.

Assemble your rolling pin

1 Assemble the rolling pin by first making a mark 3″ from each end of the stainless steel rod in the rolling pin kit. This indicates where the outside edge of the bearing will need to stop.

To simplify installation of the steel rod, bearings, and washers, I bored a ⁷⁄₁₆″ hole through a 2 × 2 × 3¾″ wood block and used it, along with a dead-blow hammer, to drive the tight-fitting bearing into place.

2 Referencing figure 1, slide a nylon washer on the steel rod, followed by a bearing. Insert that end of the rod into the wood block with a hole in it, and tap the rod's upper end to drive the bearing into place. Add the roller, a nylon washer, and the second bearing. Tap this bearing in place (photo K). The bearings and washers should bottom out in the ⅞″ holes. The rod ends should protrude 3″ beyond the roller ends. Slide a nylon washer onto each end of the rod.

3 Mix a batch of 5-minute epoxy, and work it into the handle holes (photo L). Fit the handles onto the steel rod, and tap them into place, snug to the outside nylon washers. Let the epoxy cure before use.

BIG-WHEEL PIZZA CUTTER

Get a handle on an all-business blade

BY MARLEN KEMMET

All pizza cutters are not created equal. The unique kitchen tool shown here features a multi-colored SpectraPly handle and wide 4″-diameter chrome-plated cutter that makes short work of slicing up a thick meat-lover's pizza, a party-sized cookie, or even quesadillas. A threaded insert in the handle lets you unscrew the cutter for cleaning in the dishwasher.

Turn the handle to shape

1 Using either multi-colored laminated wood stock or figured stock, cut a handle blank that measures 2 × 2 × 6″. (Handle length can vary depending on your handle's design, but you'll need to allow an extra ½″ in order to part off the handle.)

2 Mark diagonals on both ends of the blank to find the centers. Using a small handsaw, cut ¹⁄₁₆″-deep kerfs on one end for mounting on the spur drive at the headstock as shown in figure 1.

3 Build a simple right-angle work support with screws, and position it on your drill-

Figure 1: Lathe Setup

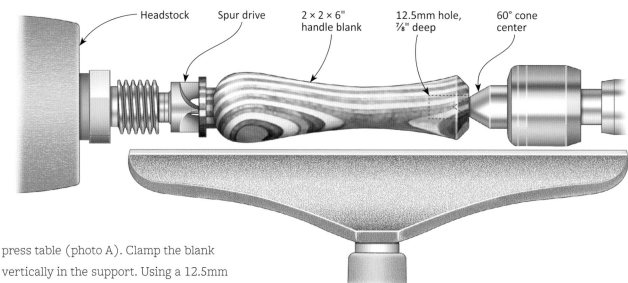

Headstock   Spur drive   2 × 2 × 6" handle blank   12.5mm hole, ⅞" deep   60° cone center

press table (photo A). Clamp the blank vertically in the support. Using a 12.5mm bit, bore a centered ⅞"-deep hole into the unkerfed end of the blank for housing the threaded insert and mounting the blank on your cone center. (I wrapped painter's tape around the bit ⅞" from the bit's end to serve as a depth stop.)

4 Mount the handle blank between centers, fitting the end with the hole for the threaded insert onto your cone center. With a roughing gouge, turn the blank round at around 1,200 rpm.

5 Measure and mark the handle diameters on the cylinder, where shown in the handle template. Also, for additional help, make a copy of the full-sized handle template, adhere it to a piece of cardboard or hardboard, and scrollsaw out just the colored portion to serve as a template.

6 Using a ¼" or ⅜" gouge, turn the handle to shape, as shown in photo B, at around 1,500 rpm. Guide off your layout marks, and check the diameters with a caliper. Maintain a ⅞" hole at the end of the turning that will receive the pizza cutter insert. Also, leave at least ½" of waste material at the butt end for parting later.

7 As you near completion, check the turning against your template, as shown in photo C.

A Use a simple right-angle support to drill a perpendicular hole in the handle for the threaded insert.

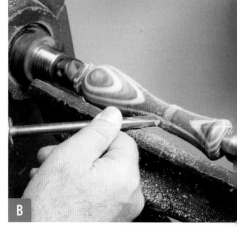

B Turn the handle to shape, running the tip of the gouge downhill from each end to form the cove.

C Use the template to ensure your turning matches the shape of the handle featured here. This particular design provides a rest for your thumb.

D

Separate the handle from the tenon by rounding the butt end with a parting tool.

E

Use a T-wrench to drive the threaded insert squarely into the hole, flushing its top end.

8 Sand the handle through 320 grit, and apply a finish of your choice. (I used General Finishes Salad Bowl Finish.)

9 Part off the waste tenon using either a parting tool, as shown in photo D, or a small handsaw. Sand this end to shape, being careful to maintain a rounded profile. Now finish the sanded butt end.

Assemble the parts

1 Mix and apply 5-minute epoxy on the outside surface of the threaded insert, being careful not to get any on the inside threaded surface. Wrap a clean cloth around the handle so as not to mar the finish, and clamp it securely in your bench vise.

2 Drive the threaded insert into the handle's hole, using a broad-bladed screwdriver or T-wrench for a $5/16$-18 insert, as shown in photo E, flushing it with the end of the handle.

3 Finally, thread the cutter onto the handle and slice away. When cleaning the pizza cutter, wipe the handle with a damp soapy cloth only. Unscrew the cutter for washing it in the dishwasher.

Handle Template 100% Size

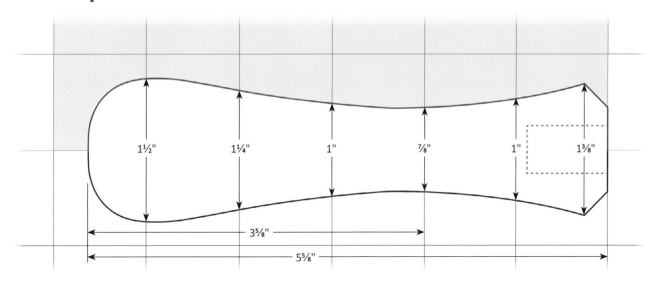

1½" 1¼" 1" ⅞" 1" 1⅜"

3⅝"

5⅝"

CLASSIC CAKE STAND

A turning that's guaranteed to take the cake

BY MICHAEL KEHS

Dimensions: 12" dia. × 7" high

Any artist who premiers his or her work in public will tell you that it's all about the presentation. A magnificent painting mounted in a crummy frame is going to lose some allure; that's just the way it is. And we all know that a birthday gift somehow seems more valuable when it's wrapped with a bow.

Likewise, any chef knows that presentation is as important as taste, which is where this lovely pedestal comes in. It elevates your baked goods to high style

while keeping them fresh under a classy glass dome. When you set this piece on the dessert table, woodworking aficionados in the vicinity are likely to start salivating over the shapely turning as much as they may drool over the edible offerings it presents.

Part of the beauty of this project is that it's easy to make, doesn't cost a lot in the way of materials, and offers a great exercise in both spindle turning and faceplate turning. I made this from cherry, but any other close-pored hardwood like maple, birch, or beech will finish up as nicely. That said, an open-pored wood will work, but you may want to use grain filler to ensure a smooth finished surface.

Note: I bought my 11¼″-diameter glass dome from williams-sonoma.com. If you choose something different, get it before starting work, so you can modify the plate to suit, adding about ¾″ to the dome diameter.

Turn the base and plate

1 Make a jamb chuck, as described in the sidebar on page 167.

2 Lay out the blanks for the plate and base on 1½″-thick stock. Using a compass, lay out the center and 12″ diameter on what will be the top of the plate. Similarly, mark out the center and 6″-diameter on what will be the bottom face of the base. Then bandsaw the blanks to shape, cutting slightly outside your lines.

3 Draw a circle about 2¾″ in diameter on the bottom of the base and the top of the plate to establish the tenon shoulders, and then another circle at about 3½″ in diameter to designate the width of the groove that will create the tenon.

4 Mount the plate blank between the chuck you made in step 1 and a live center in the tailstock, with the top face of the plate toward the tailstock. Working at about 800 rpm, turn a ¼″-long tenon using a parting tool (photo A). Repeat for the base, turning the tenon in the bottom face.

5 Mount the base tenon in your four jaw chuck. True up the edge at about 800 rpm using a ½″ bowl gouge. Put a mark on the edge at 1¼″ from the top of the base and another at ⅞″. Mark out a 2 ¾″-diameter circle, which defines the contact area with the bottom of the post. Then, at 400 rpm, drill a 1 ½″-diameter hole ¾″ deep (photo B).

6 Using a bowl gouge, shape the top of the base at about 1,100 rpm, cutting from the 2¾″-diameter circle out to the ⅞″ mark on the edge (photo C). If it helps you, create

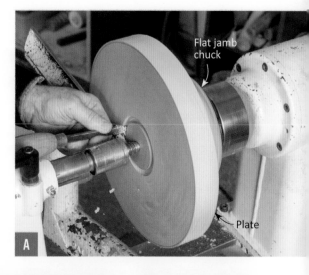

Flat jamb chuck

Plate

A

1½″ Forstner bit

Base

B

C

Figure 1: Baked Goods Pedestal

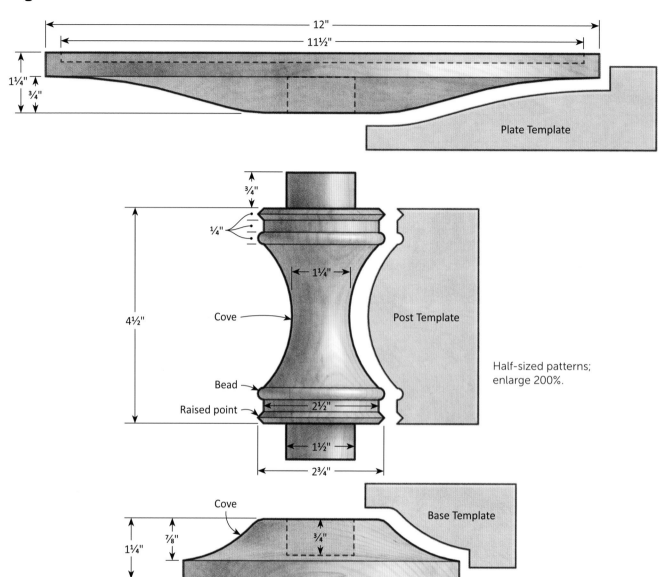

a template as shown in figure 1, and use it to check your progress. Sand the cut area through 220 grit, and ease the sharp edge where the inner flat meets the cove. Avoid the blank perimeter in order to retain the pencil line. Apply grain filler if desired.

7 Mount the plate tenon in your four-jaw chuck, and true up the edge with a bowl gouge at about 600 rpm. Put a mark on the edge at 1¼" from the bottom of the plate and another at ¾". Mark out a 2¾"-diameter circle on the bottom of the plate, which

defines the contact area with the top of the post. Then drill a 1½"-diameter hole ¾" deep at the center of the underside of the plate, again at about 400 rpm.

8 At about 900 rpm, shape the plate in the same manner as the base, cutting from the 2¾" circle out to the ¾" mark on the edge. Sand as before, and apply grain filler if desired.

9 Mount the base on a chuck with #1 jaws, spreading them inside the hole drilled in the top of the base. Now, at about 1,100 rpm,

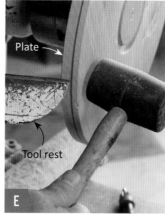

Using Grain Filler

If you choose to use an open-grained wood like walnut, oak, ash, or mahogany, you may want to fill the pores before applying a finish to ensure a mirror smoothness. Wood grain filler is available in "clear," "natural," and colored forms. (I prefer Old Masters brand, available at many hardware stores or online). Natural is typically used on lighter colored woods, but can also be tinted with colorants to suit your chosen wood.

For turnings, first use a paper towel to scrub filler into the surface, working in the direction of the grain with the lathe turned off. While the filler is still damp, turn on the lathe (at 400 to 600 rpm for smaller diameter pieces, and 200 to 300 rpm for larger pieces), and use a soft cotton cloth to wipe off all the excess. Follow up with a thorough wiping with a clean cloth with the lathe still running. Let the filler dry overnight, and then sand along the grain with the finest previous grit used. After wiping the surface clean, you're ready to apply finish.

turn down to the 1¼" mark, creating a ⅛" or so deep recess across the bottom of the base at the same time (photo D). Sand and fill the grain if desired.

10 Similarly mount the plate onto the #1 jaws, but leave the chuck just shy of tight for the moment. Next, to minimize wobble, align the tip of your tool rest with the pencil line on the edge, and rotate the plate by hand to inspect for alignment, tapping it where necessary to adjust it (photo E). Now, tighten the chuck, adjust your lathe speed to about 900 rpm, and turn the surface down to the 1¼" mark using a bowl gouge. No need to fuss the flatness at this point; just make sure it's not bellied outward.

11 Measure the outside diameter of your glass dome, add ⅛", and mark half of that as the radius of your plate recess.

12 Using a parting tool at about 900 rpm, cut three depth-reference grooves, insetting the outermost groove about ¼" from your recess line. Aim for a groove depth that's just shy of ⅛", as measured from a straightedge spanning the top (photo F).

13 Working at 900 rpm, use a ½" bowl gouge to cut the ⅛"-deep recess, swooping inward toward the center in short, ever-increasing diameters (photo G). Switch to a ¼" bowl gouge to round the transition from the inner edge of the rim to the flat section of the recess. Keep the tool bevel oriented parallel to the outer edge of the plate throughout the cut (photo H). (Note: In the photo, I'm gently pressing the tip of the gouge against the raised lip using my thumb. This prevents the tool from being pushed backward and affords great control for the cut.) Check your results with a wooden straightedge, mark any high spots, and then use a flat scraper with slightly rounded corners to finesse the surface (photo I).

14 Sand with 80- and then 100-grit paper attached to a straight board that's about ½″ shorter than the width of the recess (photo J), working the sanding stick side-to-side. (Note that the sanding stick in the photo is being held away from the piece simply for better visibility. In use, the stick rides on the tool rest.) Finish-sand using a power sander with a 3″ disc. Hand-sand the radius at the lip, and then the plate edge. Apply grain filler if desired.

Turn the post

1 Mount a 3 × 3 × 6″-long post blank between a cup center in the headstock and a live cup center in the tailstock. Set your lathe speed to about 1,500 rpm, and use a bowl gouge to turn the square blank to a rough cylinder. Next, use a parting tool to cut a few 2¾″-diameter reference grooves, and then use a spindle roughing gouge to create a 2¾″-diameter cylinder.

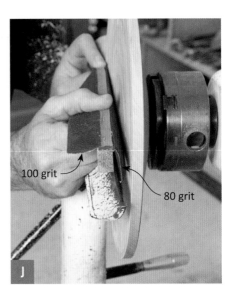

A Simple Jamb Chuck for Flat Work

I did the initial turning of this plate and base using a shop-made flat jamb chuck, which can be employed for any flat workpiece. The chuck is simply a 6"-diameter MDF disc with a facing of ⅛"-thick neoprene rubber, which provides the necessary friction. In use, the workpiece is pressed between the chuck in the headstock and a live center in the tailstock.

To make one, begin by bandsawing a disc of ¾" (or thicker) MDF to an appropriate diameter; the bigger the disk, the better the grip. Then use spray adhesive to attach ⅛"-thick neoprene rubber to the disc. Computer mouse pads with only one slick face are a good source of neoprene; just make sure to glue the slick face to the disk. Alternatively, you can use nonslip pad, although it's not as durable as neoprene. Screw the disc to a lathe faceplate, and turn the edges for balanced concentricity. Now you're ready to work.

2 Mark off a ¾"-long tenon on each end of the post blank. Use a parting tool to cut the tenons, slightly undercutting each shoulder to ensure intimate contact with the base and plate (photo K). I finesse the fit of one tenon before moving on to the other, removing the piece to test the fit in the mortise to ensure that it's snug.

3 Mark off the post details, where shown in figure 1. On each end, use a parting tool to cut a 2½"-diameter depth-reference groove on the centermost side of the bead and a 2 ½"-diameter flat between the raised point and bead (photo L).

4 Shape the raised points with a ⅜" spindle gouge (photo M), and then round over the beads with the same gouge (photo N).

5 Mark the center of the cove, and use a parting tool to cut a 1⅜"-diameter depth-reference groove. Then use a ½" spindle gouge to shape the cove to a final diameter of 1¼" (photo O).

6 Sand the piece through 220 grit, and fill the grain if desired.

Assemble and finish

1 Glue up the pedestal. If the post tenons fit their mortises as they should, just tap the parts together; there's no need for clamps. If the fit is wobbly, I suggest gluing them together with epoxy mixed with some sanding dust to serve as filler.

2 Apply the finish of your choice. I wiped on one coat of WATCO Danish Oil, reapplying it over the course of 15 minutes to make sure it stayed wet. I then let it stand for 15 more minutes before wiping off the excess. After it cured for a couple of days, I vigorously buffed it to a shine.

3 Have your cake and eat it too.

SHOP-MADE BASEBALL BAT

Turn back the clock with this vintage design

BY KEN WEAVER

In the early years of baseball, around 1845, bats were homemade, rough-cut with an axe and finished on a shaving horse using a drawknife. With no official regulations on their construction, bats were made in all sizes and shapes. Some were as short as 24″, while others were as long as 48″ (allowing an unbelievable 8′ swinging arc!).

Early bat makers experimented with curved bats, bats with a narrow slit cut down the center, and even flat bats. If you didn't have the means to turn a bat back then, players weren't picky—a cut handle from a rake or a pitchfork would do just fine. In short, a player could use just about anything he wanted.

Early regulations entered the scene in 1859, but even they weren't that strict: Barrels were limited to 2½″ in diameter, but players could still use any length they desired. Ten years later the bat length was limited to 42″, and in 1895 the maximum barrel diameter was increased to 2¾″. Bats weighed in the 24 to 48 oz. range (today's bats weigh about 33 oz.), and cost around

25 to 40 cents for an unfinished bat and up to 85 cents finished.

While regulations were beginning to govern bat size, they didn't limit creativity. Some bats were adorned with decorative shapes on the bat knob, such as a mushroom, a carved baseball, or an acorn. One of the most unique bats that appeared in the early 1900s was the double-knob, also known as the double-ring handle, that had a standard knob at the end and second knob 6″ above that. This bat was favored by such greats as Ty Cobb, Nap Lajoie, and Honus Wagner. This is the bat we'll make for this project.

In the years of the transition from the horse and buggy to the automobile, tongues from wagon wheels were a perfect source of bat blanks and it was not uncommon to see ads soliciting the public to make bats. The first bat patent was issued in 1864, while the first manufactured bat came 20 years later in 1884. The first baseball bat factory and trademarked bat were established in 1887.

Getting on deck

Bats have been made from many types of wood, including ash, oak, maple, and hickory. As the years went by, the players found that a bat made of ash would hit the ball best. Ash makes a medium-weight bat which allows a batter to swing at the advancing ball quickly. This became important as the speed of the pitch increased.

As you plan your bat, first determine whether you want to make one for actual use, or for display purposes; this will help you decide what species of wood to turn. We'll be turning ash in this project, but if you plan to display your finished bat, you can use just about any wood at all that would make for a handsome showpiece.

Start with a turning blank in your chosen wood (photo A). Ready-made blanks are available from a number of sources in both square and rounded stock, or you could have one cut to order at your local lumber supplier.

Find and mark the center of each end of the blank (photo B). Then set your lathe's spur center on your marks and tap it firmly into place with a mallet (photo C). (You could also cut a pair of ⅛"-deep grooves following the centerlines you marked, for easier mounting with your spur center already in place on the lathe.) With the blank now mounted on the lathe, check that it's secure between centers (photo D).

(Note: For easier turning, you might want to remove the four corners of the square blank and create a roughly octagonal shape before mounting on the lathe. You can use a bandsaw or handsaw before mounting.)

A

B

C

D

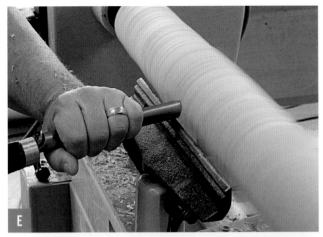

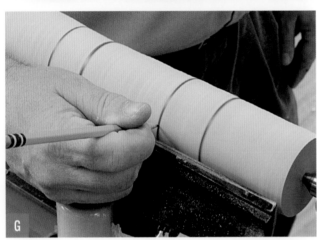

Roughing into first

At this point, you can move the tool rest into place and begin roughing the blank into a cylinder using a gouge. I usually run my lathe between 600 to 1,000 rpm for this step (photo E). For the double-knob bat we're making, the cylinder will be a maximum of 2⅜″ at the barrel end, so rough your entire blank to about ⅛″ above that. Using a caliper, check frequently to be sure you don't remove too much waste (photo F). While it's generally best to keep the thickest portion of your turning—the barrel end of the bat, in this case—near the headstock, if you should inadvertently take off too much from the headstock end, you can simply plan to make that end of the blank your handle instead.

Keep working the blank until it has been turned to a uniform diameter.

Shaping into second

The next step is to decide on what style or profile bat you want to produce. Here's where you can be creative or follow a certain era's specifications as mentioned at the beginning of the article.

You can enlarge and cut out either of the profiles pictured on page 173 to make a turning template, or come up with a similar profile of your own. If making your own, draw a sketch with dimensions at key transition points or even better, make a profile cutout to follow.

As already stated, the double-knob bat we're making here measures 2⅜″ in diameter at its widest point; overall length is 35″. Starting from the barrel end, our bat tapers very slightly—only ⅛″—over the first 8″. From that point it tapers a bit more

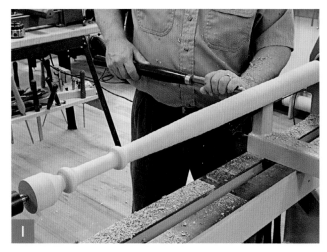

steeply to a diameter of 2″ at the 12″ mark, 1⅜″ at 18″, down to 1¹⁄₁₆″ at the 25″ point. From there to the front of the first knob the shaft remains a uniform 1¹⁄₁₆″. The handle portion between the two knobs flares very slightly from 1¹⁄₁₆″ just behind the first knob, to 1⅛″ just in front of the second. The front knob is 1¹¹⁄₁₆″ in diameter at its widest point, while the end knob is 1¾″.

Remember to start and end your profile about 1″ from the blank ends (if you have a very long blank, it's all right to leave more than 1″). Using a caliper and pencil, transfer your key transition points that will define the shape of your bat to the blank, as in photo G. Now you're ready to start making your own piece of baseball history come to life.

Turning into third

Using a caliper to check progress, cut on these lines to the diameter, plus about ⅛″. As the double-knob handle is the most intricate part of this bat, we've elected to start on the handle end (photo H).

Begin to shape your profile between the handle and the rest of the barrel using the roughing gouge (photo I). I run my lathe between 1,000 to 1,800 rpm for this step.

Once you've completely roughed the shape of the bat profile, increase the lathe speed and use a skew along with the calipers to finish turning the bat. I usually run my lathe up to 2,600 rpm for this step.

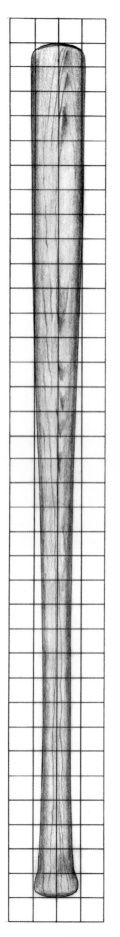

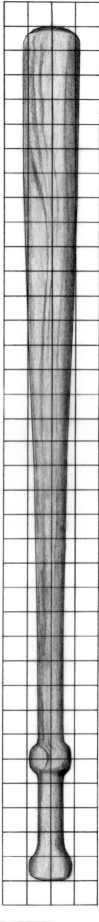

EACH GRID SQUARE
REPRESENTS 1 INCH

Finishing into home

When you're satisfied with shaping, proceed through increasing grits of sandpaper to arrive at a nice, smooth surface (photo J). The last step before removing your bat is to burnish the surface. Do this by gently but firmly rubbing several handfuls of shavings across the spinning surface as in photo K. You'll actually be able to see a shine developing on the wood.

Using your parting tool, turn the waste at each end of the spindle to ¼″ or so as in photo L, then remove the bat from the lathe. Cut off the waste tips at the ends, and hand-sand and smooth the cutoff nubs from the ends.

I like to stain my bats and seal them with a coat of paste wax. But with historical reproductions, you can arrive at a final finished look and still be true to the originals. In the case of your new bat, you can top it off with a plain linseed oil, tung oil, or Danish oil finish. You can stain it if you like, or even paint it. Of course, you can always just leave it natural.

PICNIC-PERFECT CROQUET SET

Turn the mallets and stakes; then build the bonus storage box

DESIGNED AND BUILT BY TOM WHALLEY
WRITTEN BY MARLEN KEMMET

Overall dimensions: Mallet 2 ¾" dia. × 9" w × 37" l;
Stake 1 ⅜" dia. × 18" long; Box 14 ⁵⁄₁₆" w × 16" h × 47 ⅝" l

It's unclear if the lawn game paille-maille or pall mall, which evolved into croquet, originated in France or Ireland, or stemmed from related games dating back to Roman times. Regardless, in the 1860s, the game as we know it took England by storm and later spread overseas. Today, whether played for fun or competition, croquet has become a welcomed friends and family activity.

While mass-produced croquet sets are available, it's not likely you'll find a deluxe set on par with this one. Lathe-turned mallet heads, held fast to the handles with wedge-pin joinery, include alignment strips for aiming ball strikes. And, like the mallet heads, shaping the simple stakes serves as an exercise in duplicate turning. I did both using a roughing gouge and Easy Wood Tools, which have carbide cutters that don't require sharpening. I purchased the hard plastic colored balls and metal wickets that complement the set. And as a bonus, I offer plans for a croquet set storage box. Its handle and wheels let you cart the set around the yard or from a vehicle to the playing field.

Note: For the court setup and rules for nine-wicket croquet, search the Internet for the United States Croquet Association.

Figure 1: Mallet Exploded View

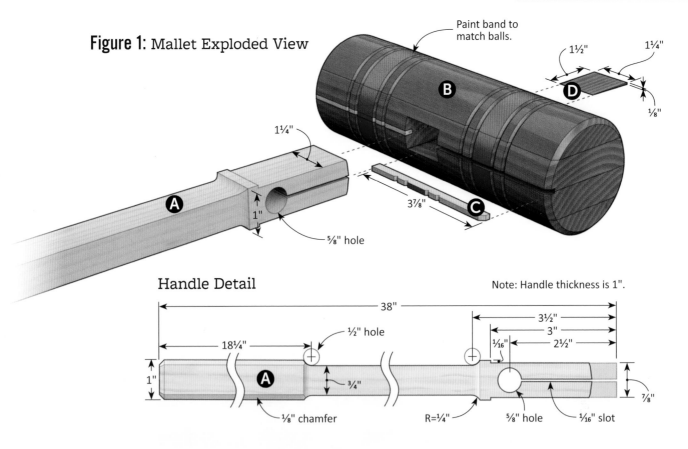

Paint band to match balls.

B

D — 1½" 1¼" ⅛"

1¼"

A

1" — ⅝" hole

3⅞" C

Handle Detail

Note: Handle thickness is 1".

38"

3½"
3"
2½"
1/16"

½" hole

18¼"

1"

A

¾"

⅛" chamfer

R=¼" ⅝" hole 1/16" slot

7/8"

Start with the mallet handles

1 From milled ¾″-thick white ash, cut two 1½ × 38″ pieces for each handle blank (A). The croquet set includes six mallets, so we cut 12 pieces. Glue and clamp six sets of two pieces together face-to-face with the ends and edges flush. (You also can go with thicker stock and cut and plane it to the needed square size in step 2.)

2 Square each handle blank lamination to 1¼″, taking an equal amount from each surface to keep the joint line centered.

3 To create ¼″ radii where shown on figure 1, start by clamping two handles together, and mark centerlines for the ½″ hole centerpoints down from the ends of the laminations. Using a Forstner bit at the drill press, drill the holes where marked, centering the point of the bit over the joint line. After drilling a hole, unclamp the handles (A), rotate them against each other, and drill another hole to create the next

pair of mating radii, as shown in photo A. Repeat until all eight radii on each handle have been drilled. Repeat for the remaining paired handle blanks. Widen the resulting radius cuts below the shoulders at the scrollsaw to accommodate the bandsaw blade used in step 4.

4 Make a simple right-angle carrier jig to fully support an entire handle (A) when sawing. (My jig measures 65″ long with a

A

With the paired handle blanks aligned and clamped in place, drill ½" holes to form the ¼" radii.

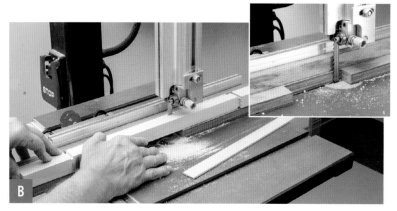

Bandsaw between the radii on each handle edge by moving the jig and handle along the saw's fence to remove the waste.

Use a miter gauge for support when cutting the kerfs on opposite surfaces of the bottom ends of the handles for the mallet heads to seat against.

centered 4"-long notch that is ⅛" shy of the vertical member.) Cut a notch on the outside edge of the jig's base (see photo B inset) to accommodate a ½" bandsaw blade. Now, place a handle blank in the jig, fitting the blade into a radius cut. With the bandsaw's fence adjusted and the jig against the fence, move the jig and handle to cut between the top and bottom radii, as shown in photo B, to form the ¾"-thick portion of the handle. This requires cutting all four edges of the handles in the same manner.

5 At the tablesaw, rip ⅛" off opposite surfaces for a handle (A) with a final thickness of 1" and width of 1¼". (See fig. 1.) Sand the handles smooth.

6 At the router table, cut a ⅛" chamfer along the four corners and around the top ends of the handles (A), where shown in the handle detail in figure 1.

7 At the tablesaw, crosscut a ¹⁄₁₆"-deep kerf 3" from the bottom ends on two opposite surfaces of the handle bottoms, where shown in figure 1, to create shoulders for the mallet heads to seat against later (photo C).

8 Set the fence, and then bandsaw a ¹⁄₁₆" centered slot 2¾" long into the bottom end of each handle (A) for housing the wedge (D) later.

9 Mark a pair of cutlines ¹⁄₁₆" in from the edges, adjust the fence, and then bandsaw

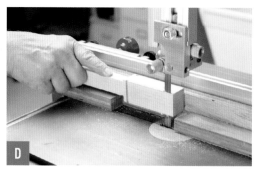

Cut shoulders on the handle bottom, guiding off the fence and marked cutlines. Stop at the kerfs.

the shoulders on the bottom ends (photo D). Feed the stock slowly through the blade so as not to cut off the shoulder. The dimensions of the handle tenon at this point should measure ⅞ × 1¼ × 3" for a snug fit into the mallet head mortise later.

10 Using a ⅝" Forstner bit, drill a hole in the tenoned end of each handle (A), centered on the slot where shown in figure 1. This allows you to flex the tenons slightly for fitting tightly into the mallet head's mortises. Finish-sand each handle, removing any saw marks.

Create the laminated mallet heads

1 Cut four pieces of ¾"-thick walnut (or two 1½"-thick pieces) to 3 × 10" for each mallet head blank (B). Measure the width of the handle tenons, and cut a pair of centered mating dadoes ⁷⁄₁₆"-deep on two

Figure 2: Mallet Head Details

Mallet Head Blank Top View

Head Blank End View

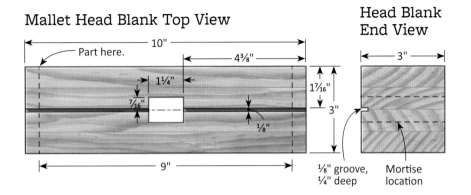

¹⁄₈" groove, ¼" deep

Mortise location

Mallet Head with V-Grooves

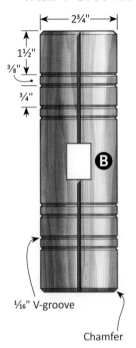

B

¹⁄₁₆" V-groove

Chamfer

mating walnut pieces to fit snugly around a tenon (see fig. 1). (The mallet heads in the set shown required ¹⁄₁₄"-wide dadoes in the mating pieces.) Now, clamp the head blank pieces for each mallet head together, and dry-fit the handle tenons in the mortises. Adjust if needed.

2 Glue and clamp the four pieces for each head blank (B) together, making sure the dadoes align to receive the handle tenons. To keep the mortised edges flush, use a piece of wood to align the mortise edges. Remove any glue squeeze-out from the mortises.

3 Cut a ¹⁄₈" groove, ¼" deep, centered on the mortise and along the length of each head blank (B), where shown in figures 1 and 2. Cut two pieces of maple to ¹⁄₈ × ¼ × 4⅜" for each head to fit into the grooves and serve as alignment strips (C). Glue the strips in place, flushing the inside ends with the mortise. Later, when attaching the handles (A), the strips in the mallet head should face up to help with aiming and striking the ball squarely.

4 Mark the centers of the mallet head blanks (B/C), and mount a blank onto the lathe using a spur drive and live center. With the lathe running at 1,000 rpm, round a mallet head blank (B/C) with a roughing gouge, working the bevel back and forth along the tool rest. Maintain even light cuts, being careful to not catch the tool's cutting edge on the mortise.

Finish-turn to 2 ¾" diameter (photo E). (Here, I switched to an Easy Wood Rougher for a smooth, sandable cylinder.)

5 Referencing figure 2, make a cardboard storyboard, and mark on it the locations for the V-grooves and parting cuts on the mallet head (B/C). This ensures that the mallet heads will be alike. Now, turn the V-grooves in the head (photo F). We used the Easy Tool Detailer with its V-shaped carbide cutter.

6 Using a parting tool, start cuts to eventually take ½" off both ends of the mallet head (B/C), where previously marked. Turn a slight chamfer on the ends of the head.

7 Finish-sand the mallet head (B/C) through 150 grit. Buy six small containers of outdoor acrylic paints that match the colors of the six croquet balls. (I purchased two-ounce bottles at a local crafts store.) Use a stiff bristle brush and one of the colors to carefully paint two stripes on the mallet head. If paint gets in the grooves, sand them with a bit of folded sandpaper to remove it. Let dry.

8 At 1,500 rpm, use a parting tool to turn both ends of the mallet head (B/C) to the 9″ finished length until the tenon at each end of the head measures ½″ in diameter. Stop the lathe and finish the parting cuts with a handsaw. Repeat steps 4 to 8 to complete the remaining five mallet heads, using a different color for each.

With the tool rest parallel to the cylinder, guide off your index finger to keep the cutter at the same depth while reducing the diameter.

Press the V-shaped cutter straight into the mallet head to cut ¹⁄₁₆" deep and back it straight out.

Join the handles to the heads

1 Fit the tenoned end of each handle (A) through a colored head (B/C), and mark the extended portion of the tenon. Mark and trim the waste at the bandsaw, making the handle end replicate the curvature of the mallet head.

2 Cut the walnut wedge blank (D) to the size in the cut list. Shape each individual wedge, as shown in figure 1 at the bandsaw and sander.

3 Apply exterior glue to all four sides of the bottom end of a handle. (I used Titebond III.) Insert the handle into the mallet head until the shoulder of the handle makes contact with the head.

4 Apply glue to the walnut wedge, and insert it into the split bottom end of the handle. Use a small hammer to tap the wedge firmly into place. Allow the glue to dry, and saw off the excess. Sand the handle and wedge flush with curvature of the head.

5 Apply an exterior-grade finish to the handles and heads. (I applied three coats of spar urethane, sanding lightly with 320-grit sandpaper between coats.)

Turn the stakes

1 Cut four pieces of ¾"-thick white ash to 1 ½" wide x 20" long for the two stake blanks (E). Glue and clamp two pieces together face-to-face with the ends and edges flush for each stake blank. If you have thicker 6/4 (1½") stock, use it to save time.

2 Mark diagonal lines on the ends of the stake blanks to find the centers. Mount a blank onto the lathe using a spur drive and live center. (Transferring the dimensions to a cardboard storyboard can ensure accuracy here as well.)

3 Round the stake blank using a roughing gouge, and finish-turn it to 1 ⅜" diameter. Referencing figure 3, mark the V-grooves and turn them to shape. Turn a ⅛" chamfer at the top end of the stake. Finally, mark and turn the tapered end. Sand the stake smooth, and paint between the grooves. Remove the stake from the lathe, and repeat for the second stake. Add an exterior finish to the stakes.

Build the mobile storage box

1 From ¾" plywood (I used Baltic birch), cut the box front end (F), back end (G), and sides (H) to size. Cut a ¾" rabbet ⅜" deep along the bottom inside edge of (F), (G), and (H) to house the box bottom (I) later, where shown on figures 4 and 5. Cut the same size rabbets along the ends of each side piece. Cut a ¾" groove ⅛" deep and ⅞" from the top edge of the two side pieces.

2 Drill the countersunk screw holes in the end pieces (F, G), where shown in figure 5.

QUICK TIP

Before cutting the rabbets and dadoes in the box parts, measure the exact thickness of the plywood you'll be using. Adjust the width of the rabbets and dadoes to snugly fit the mating plywood pieces.

Figure 3:
Stake Detail

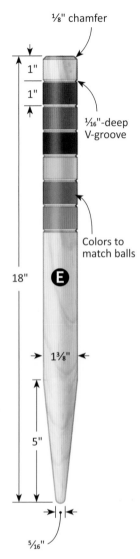

⅛" chamfer

1"

1"

¹⁄₁₆"-deep
V-groove

Colors to
match balls

18"

E

1³⁄₈"

5"

⁵⁄₁₆"

3 Dry-clamp the plywood pieces to check the fit, and then glue the ends (F, G) to both side pieces (H), as shown in photo G, checking for alignment of the pieces along the bottom rabbeted edge. Elevate the box on blocks to provide clearance for the clamps. Later, remove the clamps and sand the box smooth.

4 Measure the rabbeted opening, and cut the box bottom (I) to fit. Mark the locations for the pair of dadoes on the inside face of the bottom, where shown in figure 4. Cut the dadoes where marked.

5 Mark the locations and drill the 12 countersunk screw holes through the bottom face of the bottom (I). Be sure to center the four holes drilled in the dadoes.

6 From ¾" plywood, cut the ball divider (J), mallets support (K), and wickets support (L) to size. Mark the location and cut the slot in the wickets support. Rout a ⅛" round-over along the top edges of the ball divider, mallets support, and wickets support. Glue the mallets support to the wickets support with the bottom edges offset ⅛", allowing for the mallets support to seat in the ⅛" dado. Now, screw the parts to the inside face of the box bottom (I), centering them between the bottom's edges.

7 Cut the wickets lock (M) to size. Drill a pivot hole through it, and drill a mating hole into the top edge of the wicket support (L). Screw the piece in place.

8 Cut the box front support (N) to shape, and screw it to the box bottom.

9 Cut the two pieces making up the wheels support (O) to size. Cut a ⅜" groove, ³⁄₁₆" deep, 1⅞" from one edge of each piece, where shown in figure 5, for creating a starting channel for the lag screw pilot holes. Glue and clamp the pieces together face-to-face, aligning the grooves.

10 Drill a ²⁷⁄₆₄" hole, 3" deep, centered in each end of the channel of the support (O). Using a socket set, tap the holes with a ½" lag screw, as shown in photo H.

11 Center, glue, and screw the laminated wheel support (O) to the box bottom 1" from the end.

12 Finish-sand and apply finish to the assemblies (F to O). Do not apply finish to the edges of box bottom (I). Glue and clamp the bottom assembly into the rabbeted opening in the box assembly (F/G/H), as shown in photo I.

13 Cut the end trim (P) and side trim (Q) to size from ¾" maple. Cut a ¾" groove, ⅛" deep, centered along the bottom side of the trim pieces so they fit snugly onto the plywood back end (G) and sides (H). Notch the trim pieces as shown in figures 4 and 5.

14 Glue and clamp the trim pieces (P, Q) to the box top.

15 Cut the two top track pieces (R) to size. Sand them smooth, and glue them in place. Apply finish where needed.

Add the box handles and top

1 Referring to figure 5, mark the outline of four handle brackets (S) on a piece of ¾" stock 1½" wide. Mark a center point on each piece, and drill a ⅝" hole where marked. Cut the four brackets to shape.

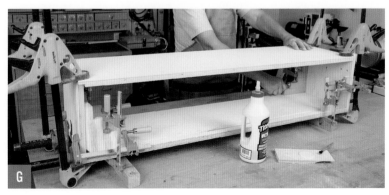

Clamp square angle braces in the box corners when gluing and assembling the box ends and sides.

Figure 4: Box Exploded View

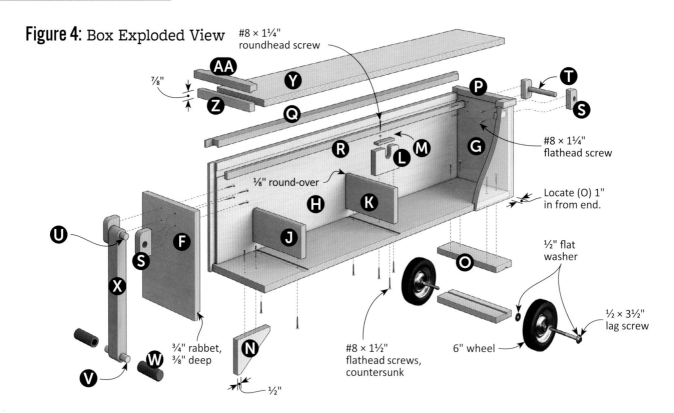

#8 × 1¼"
roundhead screw

⅞"

AA

Z

Y

Q

T

P

S

R

M

L

G

#8 × 1¼"
flathead screw

⅛" round-over

H

K

Locate (O) 1"
in from end.

U

F

S

X

J

½" flat
washer

O

¾" rabbet,
⅜" deep

N

W

V

½"

#8 × 1½"
flathead screws,
countersunk

6" wheel

½ × 3½"
lag screw

H

Tap the holes in the laminated support for the lag screws that will hold the wheels in place.

I

Apply glue, and then fit the box bottom assembly into the rabbeted opening in the box. Clamp the assembly all around for a good bond.

2 Cut the back handle (T), pivot pin (U), and handle connector (V) to length from ⅝″ dowel stock. Cut the handle ends (W) to length from 1″ dowel stock.

3 Drill a ⅝″ hole, 1⅛″ deep, centered in one end of each handle (W). To do this, I used a handscrew to secure the pieces vertically and then drilled the centered holes.

4 Laminate two pieces of ¾″ maple. From this lamination, cut the arm (X) to size. Radius the ends, and then drill the ⅝″ holes (see fig. 5).

5 Sand the parts smooth and finish. Assemble the handle assemblies (S to X) in the configuration shown (see fig. 4). Screw the handle brackets to the box ends (F, G).

6 Cut the plywood top (Y) to slide smoothly in the box top grooves.

7 Cut the top end (Z) and handle top trim (AA) to size. With the top (Y) inserted into the box, fit, clamp and glue Z and AA in place. Remove the lid assembly, and then sand and finish it.

Figure 5: Box Parts Detail

Note: See the **cut list** below for overall dimensions.

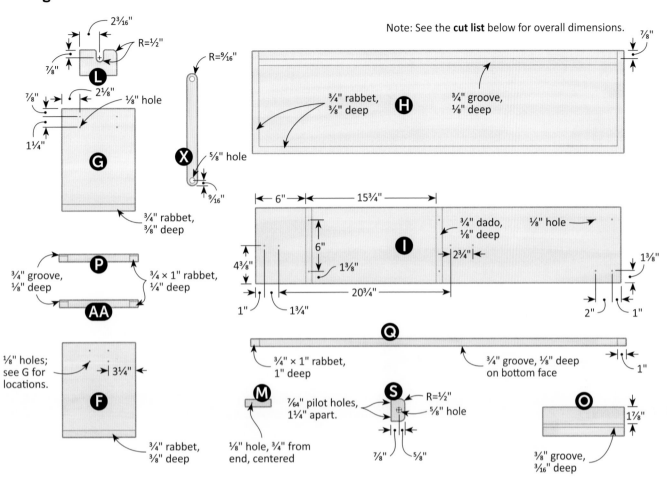

Croquet Set Cut List

	Part	Thickness	Width	Length	Qty.	Mat'l
A*	Handle blanks	1½"	1½"	38"	6	LA
B*	Mallet head blanks	3"	3"	10"	6	LW
C*	Alignment strips	⅛"	¼"	1⅜"	12	M
D*	Wedge blank	⅛"	1¼"	12"	1	W
E*	Stake blanks	1½"	1½"	20"	2	LA
STORAGE BOX CUT LIST						
F	Front end	¾"	10 ¹⁵⁄₁₆"	8¾"	1	BP
G	Back end	¾"	11⅞"	8¾"	1	BP
H	Sides	¾"	11⅞"	45"	2	BP
I	Bottom	¾"	8¾"	44¼"	1	BP
J	Ball divider	¾"	3⅝"	8"	1	M
K	Mallets support	¾"	4⅛"	8"	1	M
L	Wickets support	¾"	2⅞"	4⅜"	1	M
M	Wickets lock	¼"	¾"	3"	1	M
N	Box front support	¾"	3¾"	5"	1	M

	Part	Thickness	Width	Length	Qty.	Mat'l
STORAGE BOX CUT LIST, *continued*						
O	Wheel support	1½"	3¼"	9¾"	1	M
P	End trim	¾"	1¼"	9½"	1	M
Q	Side trim	¾"	1¼"	45½"	2	M
R	Top tracks	¾"	½"	43½"	2	M
S	Handle brackets	¾"	1½"	2½"	4	M
T	Back handle	⅝" dia.	dowel	5¼"	1	M
U	Pivot pin	⅝" dia.	dowel	3"	1	M
V	Handle connector	⅝" dia.	dowel	3½"	1	M
W	Handle ends	1" dia.	dowel	3"	2	W
X	Arm	1⅛"	1½"	13"	1	LM
Y	Top	¾"	7⅞"	43⅜"	1	BP
Z	Top end	¾"	⅞"	8¾"	1	M
AA	Handle top trim	¾"	1¼"	9⁷⁄₁₆"	1	M

*Indicates parts that are initially cut oversized. See instructions.

Materials: LA=Laminated Ash, LW=Laminated Walnut, M=Maple, W=Walnut, BP=Birch Plywood, LM=Laminated Maple

Hardware/Supplies: (2) 1½ × 6"-diameter steel wheels; (2) ½" lag screws 3½" long; (4) ½" flat washers; (8) #8 × 1¼" flathead wood screws; (12) #8 × 1½" flathead wood screws; (1) #8 × 1¼" roundhead wood screw; exterior acrylic craft paints to match colors of balls (2 oz. bottles).

QUICK & EASY DUCK CALL

Turn a barrel, add the kit parts, and get quacking

BY BYRON YOUNG

Luring ducks to close shooting range has been a centuries-old quest for wildfowl hunters everywhere. For lathe-owning duck hunters, that quest has just gotten a bit easier (and more fun) with the call insert kit parts shown at right. Designed for close-in calling, the assembled call (insert and barrel) creates a raspy duck sound that mallards can't refuse. The insert slips into the barrel—either wood or acrylic—that you turn at the lathe. Two accessories you can add are a metal accent band to prevent the barrel from cracking and a lanyard for hanging the call from your neck.

Note: To make quick work of the barrel turning, use a pen-turning mandrel and the duck call tooling kit.

Banded acrylic call

Form the barrel

1 Prepare or buy a 1½ × 1½ × 3″ hardwood or acrylic blank. Mark the center at one end of the blank, and drill a ⅝″ through-hole (photo A). (I clamped a drill press vise to the table for this.) If using acrylic, drill the hole at a slow speed to avoid melting. Back out the bit to clear the debris.

2 Mount the blank on the mandrel using the duck call tooling kit (figure 1). Snug up the components. Ensure that the tailstock's live center is firm against the mandrel before turning on the lathe. (I cut the center tube of the kit to ½″ long to accommodate the blank length.)

3 With the lathe running at approximately 2,000 rpm, use a roughing gouge to round the blank. Work the cutting edge from end to end, turning the cylinder to the widest diameter of 1⅜″ (figure 2).

4 Trace or make a copy of the barrel template in figure 2 on a piece of cardboard. Cut the template to shape. Now, at 2,500 rpm, round the insert end of the blank with a spindle gouge in keeping with the template (photo B).

Kit Components and Accessories

The call kit consists of a **1)** polycarbonate insert, **2)** short reed, **3)** long reed, and **4)** rubber wedge. Accessories include a **5)** lanyard and **6)** metal band. Inserts and bands are available in several colors and finishes.

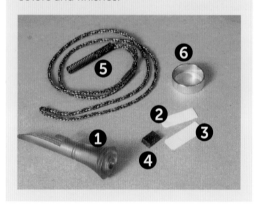

Figure 1: Lathe Setup

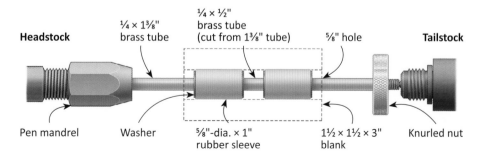

Headstock — ¼ × 1⅜″ brass tube — ¼ × ½″ brass tube (cut from 1⅜″ tube) — ⅝″ hole — **Tailstock**

Pen mandrel — Washer — ⅝″-dia. × 1″ rubber sleeve — 1½ × 1½ × 3″ blank — Knurled nut

Note: The duck call tooling kit we used contains (3) ¼ × 1 ⅜″ brass tubes, (4) washers, and (2) ⅝″-dia. × 1″ rubber sleeves.

5 Measure ½″ in from the cylinder's insert end, and, with the lathe running, use a pencil to mark the location of the lanyard slot. Make the second mark ⅛″ in from the first (photo C).

6 Use a spindle gouge to establish where the barrel's taper begins beyond the slot (photo D).

7 Now, rough-shape the tapered portion of the barrel with a roughing gouge, moving the tool's cutting edge "downhill" from the widest to the narrowest portion (photo E).

8 Round over the mouthpiece end of the barrel with the spindle gouge (photo F), and use the same tool to final-shape and smooth the barrel.

9 Double-check the barrel's shape against the template (photo G).

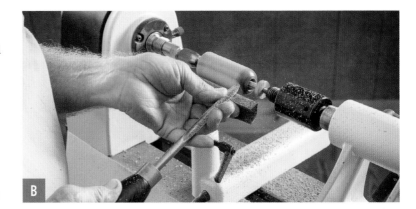

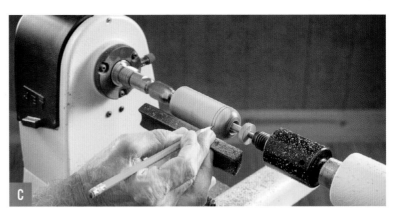

Figure 2: Full-Sized Barrel Template and Specs

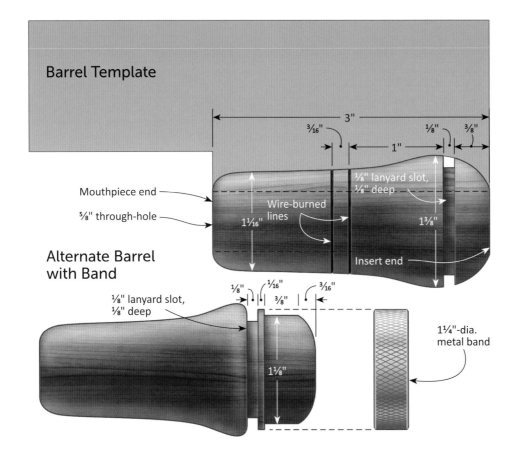

Barrel Template

Mouthpiece end
⅝″ through-hole

3″
³⁄₁₆″
⅛″ ⅜″
1″
⅛″ lanyard slot, ⅛″ deep
1¹⁄₁₆″
Wire-burned lines
1³⁄₈″
Insert end

Alternate Barrel with Band

⅛″ lanyard slot, ⅛″ deep
⅛″ ¹⁄₁₆″ ³⁄₈″ ³⁄₁₆″
1⅛″
1¼″-dia. metal band

Turning the Tenon for the Band

If you intend to add a metal accent band, refer to the alternate barrel with band in figure 2 for the dimensions. Note that the lanyard slot is located further in from the end if the band is added. Use a bedan or parting tool to form the tenon. With the lathe stopped, check the tenon's diameter with a caliper. It needs to match the inside diameter of the band. Test-fit the band on the tenon.

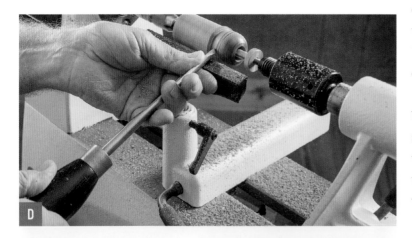

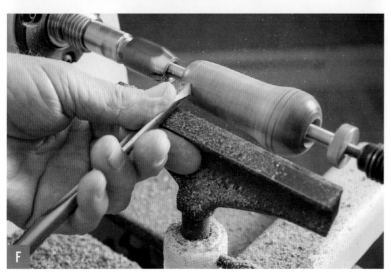

10 Cut the ⅛" lanyard slot ⅛" deep using a parting tool (photo H). With the lathe stopped, test-fit the lanyard in the slot. It should be flush with the surrounding wood.

11 Sand the barrel. For American hardwoods—such as maple, cherry, or walnut—sand through 320 grit. For oily exotic woods such as cocobolo, sand through 800 grit. For acrylic, sand through 1,200 grit, using wet-dry Micro-Mesh cushioned abrasives.

12 To add decorative burn lines, mark the barrel where shown in figure 2. Using a skew, score a fine (⅟₃₂") crease in the wood to guide the burn wire (photo I). Increase the lathe speed to 3,000 rpm, and hold a wire to each crease to help the wire track (photo J). (I made a simple wood wire holder to avoid being burned when the wire heats up. In lieu of that, you could hold the wire with vise grips.)

13 Finish the wood. (I applied a clear, soft paste wax with my fingers and buffed with a paper towel at 1,000 rpm. I followed this with a harder coat of carnauba wax (photo K) and buffed it with a paper towel to a pleasing shine. Remove the barrel from the mandrel.

Assemble the duck call

1 If installing a band, apply CA glue to unwaxed barrel tenon and fit the band on it, carefully wiping away any excess to avoid marring the polished finish.

2 Place the longer bottom reed on the flat of the insert. Set the shorter reed on top of the longer reed, dimpled face down. Flush the square ends and press the reeds and rubber wedge into the insert's slot until it bottoms out. The tapered edges of the wedge should conform to the sides of the insert.

3 Fit the insert in the barrel, and press them together.

4 Finally, loop the lanyard onto the call, fitting it in the slot. Snug it up with the sleeve. Make a test "quack." I do this by cupping my fingers over the insert and blowing in the mouthpiece to create the duck sound.

Overall dimensions (handle only): 1⅞" dia. × 7⅜" l

When spring officially arrives, the urge to dig in the dirt can prove overwhelming. But before you venture outside, have your lathe help you fashion grip-friendly hardwood tool handles for a garden shovel and fork, like those shown above. The secret behind the comfort lies in offset turning, where you intentionally mount the blank off center and remove waste along one quadrant of the cylinder. Combined with bead and cove work, the offset turning results in a handle that nestles in the palm of your hand, while providing purchase for your thumb when thrusting the tool into the soil.

Prepare the stock

1 Label one end of a 2 × 2 × 8″ turning blank as the butt and the other as the ferrule. Also, label one face of the turning blank as the front and the adjacent faces as the sides. Next, make a centered mark 6½″ down from the ferrule end on one side face. At your drill press, bore a ⅜″ tool-hanging hole where marked (see fig. 1).

2 Strike diagonal lines from opposite corners on both ends of the blank to establish the centers. Mark the centers with an awl. Then draw a line that is centered and perpendicular to the hanging hole across the butt end of the blank. On the butt end of the blank, measure ³⁄₁₆″ away from the center hole on this line and mark a secondary point with an awl. The line and awl mark will serve as reference for offset mounting later.

3 Mount the blank between centers, gripping the butt end in a four-jaw chuck. Install a keyed or Jacobs chuck with a ⅜″ bit at the tailstock end. Set your lathe speed at 500 rpm and bore a 2¼″-deep tang hole at the center mark in the ferrule end of the blank as shown in photo A. Crank the bit out as needed to clear debris.

4 Replace the Jacobs chuck with a cone center. Adjust the tailstock to snug the cone center into the ⅜″ tang hole, securing the blank. Locate the tool rest just below the blank's center. At 1,000 to 1,500 rpm, round the blank to 1⅞″ diameter using a 1″ roughing gouge. Work the cutting edge back and forth as shown in photo B. Check the diameter with a caliper.

5 Measure the inside diameter of the brass ferrule, and adjust your caliper accordingly. Align the ferrule with the end of the blank and mark the tenon length as shown in photo C.

6 With the tool rest just below center and the lathe speed at 1,000 rpm, turn the ferrule tenon by moving the square tip of a ⅜″ bedan or parting tool toward the blank's center. As shown in photo D, keep the handle perpendicular to the blank as you shear off the waste. Check the diameter with the caliper setup in step 5. Fit the ferrule on the tenon. You want a tight friction fit. Leave it on the turning for the duration to prevent the cone center from splitting the tenon when securing the work between centers. (We'll epoxy it later on.)

Shape the handle's contours

1 From ¼″ scrap plywood, make the marking and sizing jig in figure 2, locating

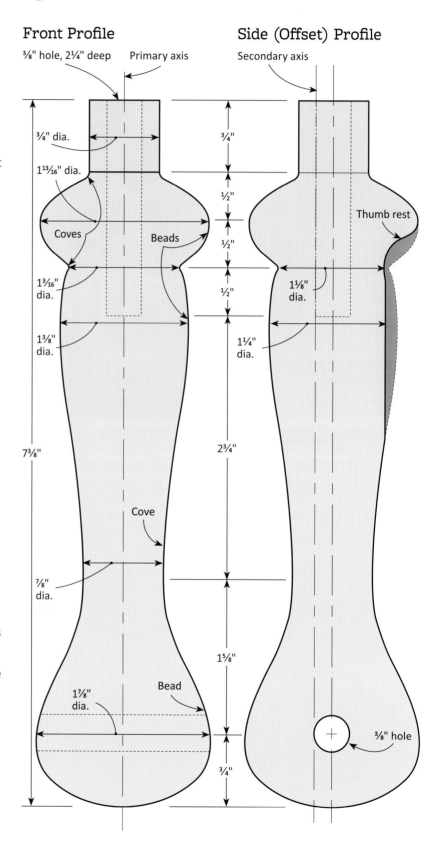

Figure 1: Handle Views

Front Profile

⅜″ hole, 2¼″ deep   Primary axis

¾″ dia.
1¹³⁄₁₆″ dia.
Coves   Beads
1³⁄₁₆″ dia.
1⅜″ dia.
7⅜″
Cove
⅞″ dia.
1⅞″ dia.
Bead

Side (Offset) Profile

Secondary axis

¾″
½″
½″
½″
Thumb rest
1⅛″ dia.
1¼″ dia.
2¾″
1⅝″
⅜″ hole
¾″

Use tape to mark the hole depth on the bit, and then drill in increments, backing the bit out to remove debris.

Remove the waste to transform the turning square into a cylinder with a 1" gouge.

Use the brass ferrule to mark the length of the tenon on the blank.

Employ a ⅜" bedan (shown here) or parting tool for forming the ferrule tenon.

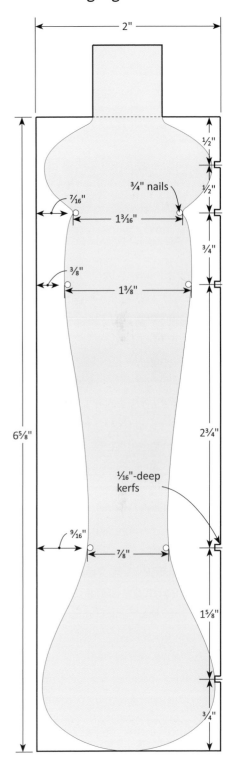

Figure 2: Marking and Sizing Jig

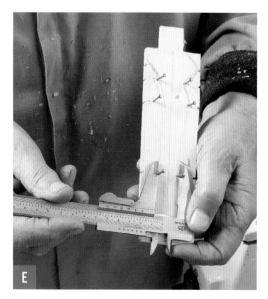

E

Drive brads into the jig where shown to serve as a quick reference when setting up your caliper.

F

Establish the turning diameters along the handle blank's length using a parting tool and caliper.

the nail holes where shown. Using your bandsaw, cut 1/16"-deep kerfs along the jig's edges where marked. (These match the key diameters in figure 1.) Now, drive 3/4"-long brads into the jig where indicated. The spacing of the nails allows you to quickly set up your caliper when establishing your cove and bead diameters as shown in photo E. It also helps with consistency when making more than one handle.

Note: The handle diameters and nail locations shown match up well with a medium-to-large hand grip. If making handles for a small-to-medium hand grip, reduce these dimensions by 3/8" between the nails along the jig's length and across the width.

2 With the blank spinning at minimum rpm, place the jig on the tool rest, aligning its tenon section with the blank's tenon. Fit a pencil point in the kerfs, and mark the critical diameters on the blank.

3 Remove the jig. At 1,000 to 1,500 rpm, slowly drive a parting tool straight into the blank to cut to the diameters shown in the front profile in figure 1. Check the diameters with a caliper as shown in photo F.

4 Adjust the tool rest to just below center.

G

To create graceful curves, move the edge of a 3/8" gouge from the wider diameters to the narrower ones.

With the lathe speed increased to 2,000 rpm, use a 3/8" spindle gouge to form the beads at the wide critical points of the turning where shown in the front profile in figure 1. With the gouge handle dipped lower than the cutting end, allow the bevel to ride the blank as you tip the edge into the wood and move it back and forth along the beaded areas. Check the diameters occasionally as you work.

Figure 3: Offset Jamb Chuck

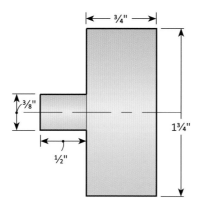

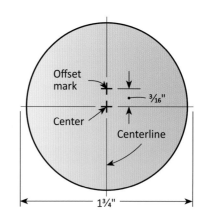

5 Now, using the same cutting motion and speed, form the coves between the 1⅞″ and 1⅜″ beads, and between the 1¹³⁄₁₆″ and 1⅜″ beads with the ⅜″ spindle gouge, removing the waste and moving the cutting edge towards the narrower diameter (photo G).

6 Reduce the lathe speed to 500 rpm and sand the shaped handle blank, moving through a progression of grits from 150 to 400.

Complete the handle with offset turning

To make the finished handle more ergonomic, you need to reduce the front quadrant where shown in the side profile in figure 1. This is done by offsetting the blank ³⁄₁₆″ on each end. You need a jamb chuck to mount the blank to avoid damaging the ⅜″ hole at the ferrule end for the metal tool tang.

1 Remove the cone center from the tailstock's live center and the blank from the four-jaw chuck. Insert a 2 × 2 × 4″ scrap blank into the four-jaw chuck. Now, make the offset jamb chuck dimensioned in figure 3. To do this, adjust the speed to 1,000 rpm, and round the blank to 1¾″ diameter using a 1″ roughing gouge. Mark out the location

for the ⅞ × ½″ tenon ¾″ in from the end. Using the ⅜″ bedan or parting tool, form the tenon, checking its diameter. Then part-off the jamb chuck to its final 1¼″ length.

2 With a center finder tool, mark the center on the end of the jamb chuck with an awl; now continue the line across the chuck's edge. Measure and mark ³⁄₁₆″ away from the center mark on the centerline with an awl where shown in figure 3. This will be your offset mark.

3 Next, replace the four-jaw chuck in the headstock with a spring-loaded safe driver (or spur drive center). Install a live center into the tailstock. Now fit the jamb chuck's tenon into the ⅜″ tang hole in the blank and place the live center into the offset awl hole made previously. Next, place the point of the safe driver into the offset awl point made in step 2 under "Prepare the stock." Now, use the edge of the tool rest as a guide to orient the alignment mark on the edge of the jamb chuck with the line you made earlier on the butt end of the blank. Secure the assembly between centers (see fig. 4).

4 Fix a sheet of white paper behind the turned blank to better see the ghost image of the offset turning. With the lathe running at 2,000 to 2,500 rpm, form the offset handle

Figure 4: Offset Lathe Setup

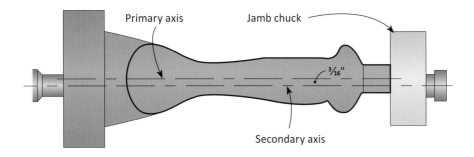

Primary axis

Jamb chuck

³⁄₁₆"

Secondary axis

using your ³⁄₈″ spindle gouge. Create the flat area along the handle by easing the cutting edge into the ghost image of the off-center stock (photo H). You'll want to remove the waste in the offset shape in the side profile in figure 1.

5 Using the same tool and tool rest location, turn the thumb rest on the first bead down from the ferrule end.

6 Turn off the lathe and hand-sand the handle to soften its turned edges. Now, replace the jamb chuck with the cone center at the tailstock end, fitting it in the ferrule hole. Insert the point of the safety center into the true center at the butt end of the blank. Secure the blank by tightening the tailstock in place. Now, at 1,000 rpm, form the rounded end of the butt with your ³⁄₈″ spindle gouge, referring to figure 1. Sand this area and part off the completed handle.

7 Apply a polyurethane or other durable finish to the tool handle. Let dry.

8 Mix up epoxy, pull off the brass ferrule, and apply a thin coat around the tenon. Reinstall the ferrule. Next, spread epoxy in the tang hole with a nail. Now, fit the tang of the stainless steel shovel or fork into the handle (photo I). Add a leather hanging strip and go dig in the dirt.

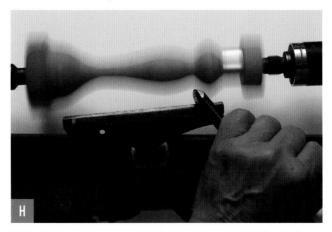

Follow innermost edge of the ghost image with ³⁄₈" spindle gouge to shape the flat areas on the handle.

Install the ferrule and steel tang to the handle with two-part epoxy.

SHOP-MADE COLLET HELPS YOU GET A GRIP

A simple shop-made solution for securing workpieces

BY JON T. HUTCHINSON

Turning bottle stoppers can be both fun and gratifying, whether done for pleasure or profit. However, it can also be frustrating and sometimes even dangerous.

My first experience with turning stoppers was to load a blank between centers, turn the profile, and then attempt to drill a hole squarely in one end for a dowel that would hold a cork. Unless the end result is to intentionally create a stopper that tilts or

sits off-center on the bottle, this is not a preferred method.

So I bought a standard metal chuck for my lathe, drilled the dowel holes in the blanks, glued ⅜″ dowels in the blanks, and then used the chuck and the tailstock to hold the blank while turning. This worked fine as far as holding the blank steady goes, but once the turning was finished I discovered the chuck jaws had bitten into the dowel, deforming it beyond recognition and making it impossible to glue a cork to the maimed surface.

During the period of trial and error on subsequent stoppers, I came up with a better way to hold the dowels attached to my turning blanks. My solution was to turn a wooden chuck sized to hold stopper dowels. This would be a four-jaw chuck—or, more correctly, a collet that could be used with or without the lathe's tailstock. I didn't make any detailed drawings of my concept; I just decided what it should look like, how it should perform, and got down to business using what scrap material I had on hand that would work well.

Getting started

For this project, the basic design of the collet has been refined a bit from my original, and uses materials that most turners generally have on hand. However, there's one required piece of hardware you should find first.

As you'll see a bit later, the jaws of the collet grip the stopper dowel by sliding a metal ring over the jaws and snugging it down tight. Metal rings are easy to come by, but because there's some slight variance in inside diameter depending on the ring supplier—and because you'll be turning your collet to match the size of the ring— it's best to get the ring first.

Most hardware stores carry an assortment of metal rings, usually back where they keep chains and hooks, so you can find one to fit whatever size collet you make. Most stores carry both steel and brass rings (photo A). You'll probably find that brass rings are more consistently smooth around the inside edge—steel rings often have a distinct joint where they've been welded. Try to find a

ring with an inside diameter of 1 ⅛", but if you can't, make your collet to fit the size of the ring that's available.

Before we start cutting wood, it's important to note that you don't have to stick to the exact sizes of stock used here. This project is freeform in size and shape—much like turning bottle stoppers in general—so you can make your collet pretty much any way you like.

Making the blank

To create the turning blank for the collet, the first step is to cut a rough circle of hardwood a bit larger in diameter than your lathe's metal faceplate (photo B). The faceplate

shown here measures 3″, so the hardwood circle is 5″ in diameter, a good working size. Adjust your blank size according to the size of the faceplate you'll be using. You can use just about any wood you like, but you'll find that standard 2 x 6 x 6″ hard maple turning blanks work well.

For the collet neck blank, a 3 x 3 x 3½″ piece of hard maple will work nicely. A solid piece of stock is preferable, but lacking that, you can glue up the neck blank from two thinner pieces. Mark the center of the neck blank (photo C). For easier turning, knock the corners off the blank on the tablesaw or bandsaw to create an octagonal shape.

Drill a pilot hole in the center of the neck blank, and countersink and drill a pilot hole in the round blank. This is a good time to

drill the round blank for screws to attach the faceplate—it'll be more difficult once the blank is glued up.

Apply glue to the neck and attach it to the round blank with a screw (photo D). For the size of stock used here, a 3″ screw worked perfectly.

Time to turn

Attach the faceplate and mount the completed blank on the lathe, checking for clearance on your tool rest (photo E).

Turn the basic shape of the collet any way you like, forming a general taper down to the outer end that matches the size of the inside diameter of your metal ring (photo F). Be careful at this point—you don't want to turn the neck too small, or the ring will slide too far down. Continue turning your taper until you can slide the ring about ¾″ down the neck, but no more.

(If you should accidentally turn the neck too much, you can still fix it. Because the neck is tapered, if you make it too small simply cut a bit of the neck off so that the ring slides down only ¾″.)

Give the turning a good sanding, increasing grit size till the workpiece is nice

and smooth. The ring will probably slide down slightly more than ¾″, so don't be too aggressive when sanding, as you don't want to drastically change the neck diameter.

Creating the jaws

Next, you'll need to drill two ¼″ holes, perpendicular to each other, through the sides of the neck 1½″ from the outer end. If you've used solid stock for the neck, you can drill the holes anywhere around the circumference, but if you glued the neck blank from separate pieces, don't drill along the glue joint, or it may weaken the collet when the saw kerfs are cut a bit later.

You can drill the holes using a hand drill with the workpiece still mounted on the lathe if you've got a steady hand. However, a simple jig mount to hold the workpiece gives you greater control and accuracy by drilling the holes on a drill press (photo G). A jig mount allows you to unscrew the faceplate/collet assembly from the lathe as a unit, and cradle it securely for drilling and cutting the collet jaws.

Pencil a set of 1½″ perpendicular lines down the neck, and drill through the neck and into the jig mount. (This will leave a hole in the jig mount, which we'll use a bit later when cutting the slots for the jaws.)

Return the assembly to the lathe.

Now, here's where I found a real use for the metal chuck I'd bought to turn bottle stoppers. With the chuck in the tailstock, I put in a ⅜″ bit, turned on the lathe and drilled down the center to the perpendicularly drilled ¼″ holes (photo H). Mark the depth on your drill bit with masking tape to avoid drilling too deeply.

Remove the collet assembly from the lathe and return it to the jig mount. Slip a short length of ¼″ dowel through the neck and into the hole drilled earlier into the jig itself.

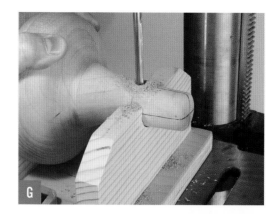

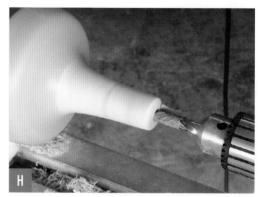

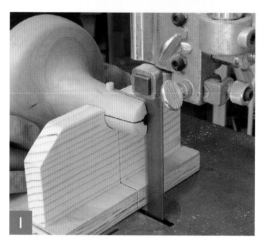

This will align the hole perfectly vertically, making it easy to cut a true kerf on the bandsaw (photo I).

If you chose not to make a mounting jig, you can use a backsaw supported on the tool rest to make perpendicular cuts aligned with the holes through the sides of the wooden collet blank. However, making the jig mount is well worth the time it takes, especially if you plan to make additional collets to accommodate different dowel sizes.

Finishing up

Return the assembly to the lathe once more, and slip a folded piece of sandpaper into the jaw slots to clean them up a bit and remove the sharp outside edges (photo J).

Do a test fit of the metal ring, and slide a short length of dowel into the collet. Pull the ring down the neck to close the jaws and secure the dowel. The ring should slide down to between ¾″ and 1″, roughly halfway between the holes and the end of the neck.

At this point, your bottle stopper collet is complete, but a few coats of finish will not only make it look good, but will help protect it from finishes you might use when making stoppers.

Using the collet

My one metal faceplate is now and forever a dedicated piece of my shop-made collet. I doubt that the collet would ever be exactly centered again should I remove it from the metal faceplate and then re-attach it at a later time. To preserve the accuracy of your collet, I'd suggest buying a metal faceplate that you can leave permanently attached.

While I made my collet to fit the size dowels I use, you can size yours to hold any size. And it's not limited to use in turning bottle stoppers. I use mine to turn finials and other small pieces that require a dowel in one end for attaching to a larger piece.

Turning anything in this collet with the tailstock on the other end for support is extremely safe. The blank butts right up to the end of the neck, and the collet holds the piece firmly after the tailstock is moved back to finish turning the top of the piece.

The best part is that the collet holds a bottle stopper blank securely, but it doesn't lock it rigidly in place. Unlike a metal chuck, which bites deeply into the dowel, the circular wooden collet jaws have a bit of "give" to them. Accidentally catch a chisel or gouge when using a metal chuck, and you'll dig a good-sized divot into your turning at best, or snap the dowel at worst—possibly sending the unfinished stopper flying. Catch a gouge on your workpiece while using this wooden collet, however, and your workpiece stops momentarily, giving you time to pull back on the chisel before ruining the piece.

This collet is also very friendly for applying a finish to a turned piece. Since the dowels I use are about 1″ long, I'm able to loosen the jaws and pull the turning out ¼″, then retighten the jaws. This small space allows me to get to the bottom of the turning with a finish, so all finishing is done on the lathe. Occasionally the turning is not quite centered when pulled out from the collet, but that can be quickly remedied by pushing it in just a hair with the jaws tightened.

From start to finish, this inexpensive shop-made collet has put the fun back in turning bottle stoppers and other small projects—and taken away most of the risks of injury and the frustrations of failure.

MATERIALS

(Note: The collet in this project is made of hard maple, but any hardwood will work.)

2″ hardwood blank, sized slightly larger than lathe faceplate

3 x 3 x 3½″ hardwood blank

3″ screw

Brass or steel ring with 1⅛″ inside diameter

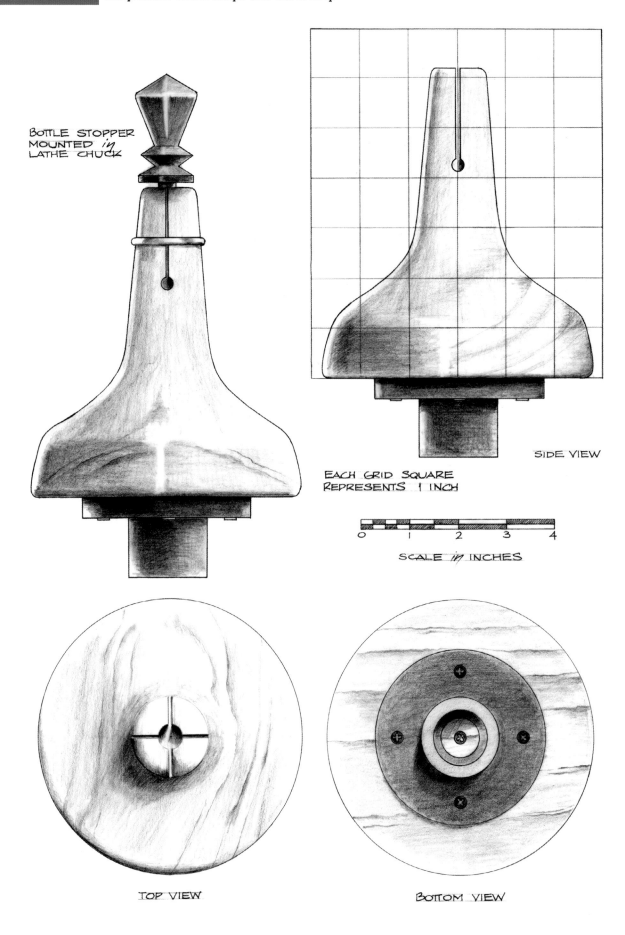

BOTTLE STOPPER
MOUNTED *in*
LATHE CHUCK

SIDE VIEW

EACH GRID SQUARE
REPRESENTS 1 INCH

SCALE *in* INCHES

TOP VIEW

BOTTOM VIEW

SHOP-MADE MALLETS

A trio of tappers for your tool chest

BY KEN BURTON

If you enjoy making your own tools, as I do, you'll find these three mallets to be a great weekend project. They don't use a lot of material, they go together fairly quickly, and the final result yields tools that become a regular part of your shop workforce. The designs include a simple one-piece turned mallet used for striking chisels and carving tools, a cylindrical-head joiner's mallet intended for assembly work, and a square-faced joiner's mallet for both chisel work and assembly purposes.

The first two designs are made primarily on a lathe (a mini lathe works fine), while the third relies heavily on the tablesaw. Note that the 5° taper on the head of the turned mallet and the angled striking faces on the square-faced mallet accommodate the swing of your arm to create a more direct blow in use. In contrast, the faces of the assembly mallet are parallel to the handle to help keep your orientation square when coaxing joints together.

Making these mallets provides a great opportunity to pull into play those precious wood scraps you've been hoarding, while creating tools that should take care of most of your joint-cutting and assembly needs.

Round joiner's mallet

1 Mount the stock for the head between centers on your lathe. Turn the piece round with a spindle gouge. Part it to length, leaving just enough stock at the bottom of the parting cuts to keep the spinning piece intact. Sand the head to 220 grit before removing it from the lathe. Cut the head free, and sand away the saw marks from both faces.

2 Chuck a ⅛"-diameter bit in your drill press, and use it to center a V-block on the drill press table directly below the quill. Clamp the block to the table and swap out the ⅛" bit for a ¾"-diameter Forstner bit.

3 Cradle the mallet head in the V-block and drill a ¾"-diameter hole completely through its center, as shown in photo A. For added stability, you can glue 220-grit sandpaper to the faces of the V.

A

Drill the handle hole by cradling the mallet head in a V-block that was sawn on the tablesaw.

Good Mallet Woods

For good mallet head stock, select heavy, dense material that's resistant to splitting. Many exotic species such as jatoba and bubinga fit the bill nicely. However, there's no shortage of appropriate domestic hardwoods such as beech, hop hornbeam, locust, and dogwood that will work just as well. Many of these aren't widely available commercially, but they're worth searching out, even if it means doing some tree trimming yourself. On the other hand, hard maple will work fine, and it's plentiful from wood suppliers. For mallet handles, use a strong, shock-resistant wood like ash or hickory. In fact, I salvaged a broken hickory axe handle for one of my mallet handles.

Round Joiner's Mallet

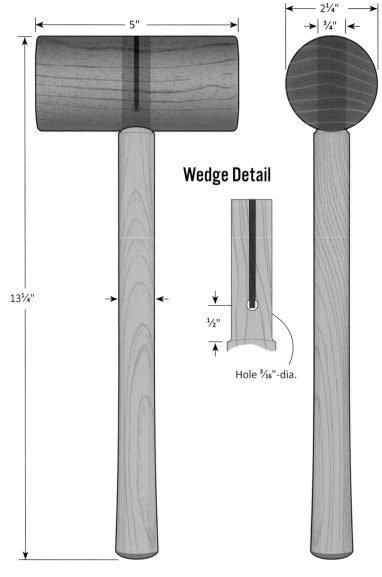

5"

2¼"

¾"

13¼"

Wedge Detail

½"

Hole ³⁄₁₆"-dia.

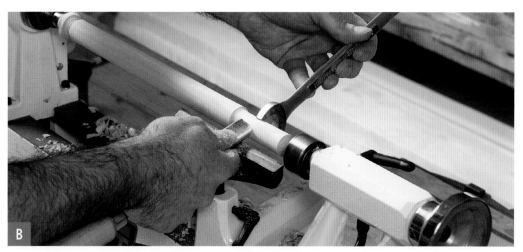

QUICK TIP

An open-end wrench makes a great caliper while turning tenons on a lathe because its wide, fixed jaws are much easier to hold against the spinning workpiece than the skinny jaws on most calipers.

While turning the handle tenon, you can use a ¾" open-end wrench to gauge the final diameter.

Start making the wedge with a strip of ³⁄₁₆"-thick scrap that is long enough to provide a good grip. Sand it to shape, making the thin end about ¹⁄₃₂" thick.

Install the wedge perpendicular to the axis of the head; then trim and sand away the tenon waste.

4 Mount the handle blank on the lathe, and turn it to a 1″ diameter. Sand it, and then turn the ¾″-diameter tenon to about 2¾″ long (photo B). Check the fit of the tenon in the mallet head before cutting the handle to final length.

5 Drill a ³⁄₁₆″-diameter hole through the tenon about ½″ from its shoulder. Cradling the handle in the V-block used earlier, make a bandsaw cut extending from the end of the tenon into the hole. (The hole prevents any possible crack from traveling down the handle when the wedge is inserted later.)

6 Cut a strip of scrap about ³⁄₁₆″ thick, ¾″ wide, and 10″ long to make into the wedge. Create a taper using a stationary sander, as shown in photo C. The finished wedge should taper from about ¹⁄₃₂″ less than the kerf width to a fat ¹⁄₃₂″ more than the kerf width along 2¾″. The idea is that the installed wedge should run nearly the entire length of the slot while compressing the wood fibers and expanding the kerf a bit at the top of the handle.

7 Glue the handle in the head, and drive in the glued wedge to reinforce the joint (photo D). Be sure to orient the slot in the handle perpendicular to the axis of the head so the wedge doesn't want to split the head.

Turned mallet

1 Start with a piece of wood 3 × 3 × 12″ long. (If you can't find a thick enough piece, you can build one up by face-gluing thinner pieces together.) Rip off the corners of the blank on the tablesaw to make the piece roughly octagonal. This will make turning the piece round that much easier.

2 Mount the blank between centers on your lathe, and turn it to a cylinder.

3 Turn the head to the shape shown at right. Use a parting tool to establish the diameter at the smaller end of the head; then switch to a spindle gouge to cut the taper.

4 Turn the handle to the shape shown. Feel free to modify the form to suit your hand. Again, use a parting tool to establish the final diameter at the center of the bulge. Then switch to a spindle gouge to do the shaping, as shown in photo A.

5 Sand the mallet to whatever grit you like while it is still on the lathe. Saw away any excess material from the ends, and sand away the saw marks. Finish the mallet with several coats of penetrating oil.

Turned Mallet

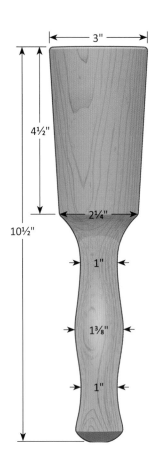

3″

4½″

10½″

2¼″

1″

1⅜″

1″

After turning the mallet head to shape, create a smooth transition from the head to the handle.

A

Cut the handle dado through the center section of the head blank, using stops clamped to an auxiliary miter gauge fence to register the sides of the cut.

B

When sawing the tenon on the mallet handle, you can safely use the rip fence as a stop because there is no waste piece being created that could kick back.

C

To make sure the mallet is well-balanced, keep the dado centered as you cut the angles on either end of the head.

D

Use a wide chisel to pare the handle tenon dead-flush with the interior surface of the mallet head.

Square-faced joiner's mallet

1 Cut two pieces of ⅞"-thick stock and one piece of ¾"-thick stock for the mallet head. Make each squared piece about ⅛" wider and longer than the finished dimensions shown in the side view at right. Also cut the material for the handle to the size shown.

2 Face-glue the ¾"-thick piece to one of the ⅞"-thick pieces. After the glue dries, sand the long edges of the two-piece blank flush, but don't curve the top edge yet.

3 Set up a dado head for a wide cut on your tablesaw. The exact width doesn't matter, as the cut you'll be making is wider than most dado heads can make in a single pass. Lay out a 1"-wide dado, centering it across the length of the blank. Attach a sacrificial fence to your miter gauge that extends 6" or so past the blade. Clamp stops to the fence at either end of the blank to locate the two sides of the cut, as shown in photo A. Then cut the dado, with the ¾"-thick part of the blank against the saw table. Take a series of subsequently deeper cuts, raising the dado head as you approach the perfect depth.

4 Make a 1¼ × 1½ × 14"-long blank for the handle. With the same dado head setup, saw a ¾"-thick × 1"-wide × 3½"-long tenon on the end of the mallet handle (photo B). First cut across the narrower edges to establish the 1" width of the tenon, and then check its fit in the mallet head dado. Adjust the height of the dado head if needed, and then pare the edges with a wide chisel to fine-tune the fit. Reset the height of the dado to cut the tenon to a thickness of about 1/32" fatter than the mallet head dado.

5 Swap the dado head for a regular saw blade, and cut the ends of the mallet head at a 5° angle (photo C). Cut the second ⅞"-thick piece to match. (This operation is also easily done on a chop saw.)

6 Place the handle in the head, and pare the tenon flush to the adjacent surface, as shown in photo D. A good fit here is crucial for a proper glue-up that ensures working strength.

7 Lay out the tapered cuts on one side of the handle, where shown. Make the cuts on the bandsaw, and then plane, scrape, and sand away the saw marks.

8 Chuck a ¼″-radius round-over bit in a table-mounted router, and shape the edges of the handle (photo E). Afterward, sand the handle thoroughly, avoiding the tenon.

9 Glue the handle in place in between the two head pieces (photo F), carefully aligning the bottom edges of the pieces.

10 Drill a ⅜″-diameter hole completely through the head and handle. Then glue a dowel in place to reinforce the connection.

11 Lay out the slight arc at the top of the mallet, as shown above. Cut the curve on the bandsaw, and then sand away the saw marks with a stationary belt or disc sander. Also sand the angled faces to flush them up.

12 Chamfer the edges of the head with a block plane. This makes the mallet a little friendlier to handle and helps keep the head from chipping should you strike something off center.

13 Finish the mallet with penetrating oil.

E

When rounding the handle edges, prevent the bit from throwing the work by beginning the cut while levering against a fulcrum pin.

F

Two stout clamps should be enough to glue on the third mallet head piece.

Square-Faced Joiner's Mallet

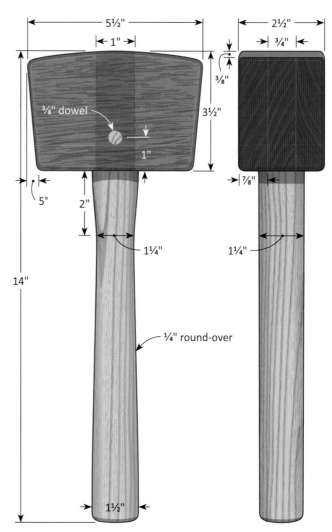

LATHE DUST COLLECTOR

Create a healthy turning station with this simple fixture

BY JIM HARROLD WITH JERRY BOLIN AND BILL SANDS

Reader Jerry Bolin of Prattville, Alabama, sent in this dust-collector idea for mid- and full-size lathes. It attaches to the ways via a pair of shop-made clamps. Convinced of its merit, I had contributing craftsman and turner Bill Sands build Jerry's collector and test it out, hooking it up to a dust collector, and then to a shop vacuum. While it was never meant to draw in large shavings and chips, it effectively sucked in the fine, hazardous dust from scraping and sanding—the stuff that could otherwise end up in your lungs or cover shop surfaces. Of course the dust collector had more pull, but the shop vacuum also performed well.

The collector is simple to make, using ½" Baltic birch plywood, scrap hardwood, jig hardware, and 4" schedule 40 PVC pipe. The perforated collector pipe is secured to a pair of base side assemblies that adjust in and out, depending on the turning's diameter. A trio of PVC sleeves (or shutters) fit and rotate over the collector pipe holes, allowing you to concentrate the suction to just the

Figure 1: Lathe Dust Collector Exploded View

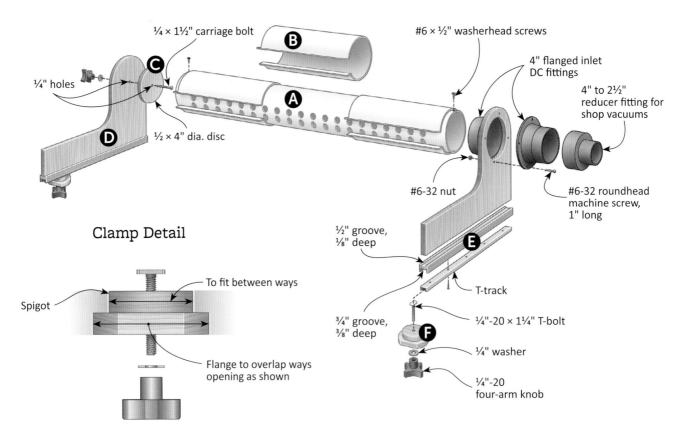

Clamp Detail

Cut the collector pipe and shutters

turning at hand, whether a bowl or long spindle. Before building the dust collector, be sure to size the parts for your particular lathe, using the formulas in the box at right.

Cut the collector pipe and shutters

1 Crosscut the 4"-diameter PVC pipes to length—one for the collector pipe (A), and the three for the shutters (B). (I used my 12" mitersaw. Using a bandsaw, while supporting the PVC pipe with a miter gauge, also works.)

2 Using a metal rule, lay out two rows of ¾" suction holes, starting 3" in from the ends of the collector pipe (A). Space the hole centers 1¼" apart radially and linearly along the pipe. Using a ¾" Forstner bit, drill the holes, as shown in photo A.

3 Using spring clamps to securely hold a shutter pipe (B) to a right-angle jig, raise

Sizing the Parts to Your Lathe

Because the makes and sizes of mid- and full-sized lathes differ, adjust the dimensions of selected parts based on your machine, referring to figure 1 and these formulas:
- **Perforated collector pipe (A) (4" PVC):** Length = maximum center to center distance for your lathe.
- **Shutters (B) (4" PVC, 3 needed):** Length/shutter = (length of collector pipe − 1¾")/3.
- **Base sides (D) (½" plywood; 2 needed):** See base side template; for larger lathes extend length for appropriate clearance, considering the maximum swing of your lathe.
- **Base side rails (E) (hardwood, 2 needed):** Size = ⅞ × 1" × length of base sides (D); for larger lathes, extend lengths to match extended base sides (D). Do the same for the T-track.
- **Turned clamps (F) (1"-thick hardwood, 2 needed):** Outside diameter = gap between ways + overlap; spigot length = thickness of ways; spigot diameter = gap between ways − ¼".

the tablesaw blade to ½", and then safely cut a kerf in the pipe, as shown in photo B. Cut kerfs in the remaining pipes.

4 Make a PVC bending jig by cutting a ½ × 4¼ × 16" piece of hardwood scrap. Cut a

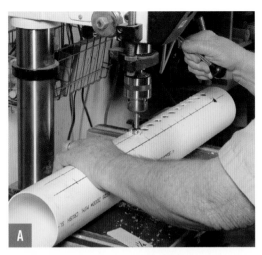

Hold the pipe to the drill press fence as you bore each suction hole at the marked locations.

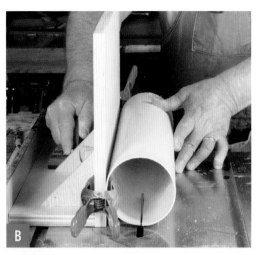

Clamp each shutter pipe to a right-angle jig to hold it firmly and then rip along its length.

Burnishing block

Move the heat gun along the shutter pipe; when the plastic becomes pliable, bottom out the edge in the kerf and roll the pipe over.

centered ⅛″ kerf, ½″ deep along one edge. Clamp the jig in a bench vise. Now, insert one ripped edge of a shutter pipe (B) into the jig's kerf. Using a marking knife, cut along the jig's edge to score a line ½″ up from the ripped edge. (Doing this helps with the bending when heat is applied.) Raise the pipe ¼″ to expose the scored line and use a heat gun to apply heat evenly along the pipe length. Now press the pipe edge fully in the kerf, and bend the pipe flanges, as

shown in photo C. While the pipe remains hot, burnish the heated bend with a block of wood to form a 90° flange. Use only enough heat to soften the PVC for bending. Repeat for all ripped shutter edges.

Make the base sides, end cap, and clamps

1 Lay out the end cap (C) on ½″ plywood. Using a lathe, form the cap to fit snugly in the headstock end of the collection pipe

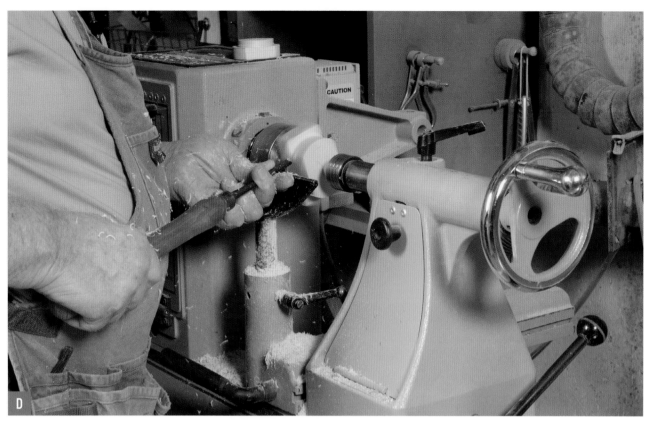

Turn the clamps to shape at the lathe, and then test-fit the clamp parts to your ways.

(A). Test-fit the piece. Remove it and drill a centered ¼" hole in the cap. Insert a ¼ × 1 ¾" carriage bolt in the hole, and fit the cap in the pipe, flush with the end. Drill a pair of opposing pilot holes, where shown in figure 1, and secure the pipe to the cap with #6 × ½" washerhead screws.

2 Referring to the base side template, lay out a side on a piece of ½" plywood, tack or tape a second piece of plywood underneath, and then bandsaw both sides (D) to shape. Drill a ¼" hole in the headstock base side for securing to the end cap (C). Scrollsaw a 4⅛" hole in the opposing (tailstock) base side. Now attach the flanged inlet fittings to the tailstock side with machine screws and nuts. Note that a full-sized lathe may require longer sides.

3 Cut the rails (E) to size, and then, using a dado set, cut the grooves shown in figure 1. Glue the rails to the bottom edges of the base sides, flushing the ends. Cut and screw in the T-track, flushing it with the rail ends.

4 From 1"-thick scrap hardwood, cut and then turn two clamps (F) to size, as shown in photo D. (See the clamp detail in figure 1 for a look at the completed part.) Ensure that the grain, when the clamps are installed, runs perpendicular to the ways. The spigot should fit between the ways. Drill the ¼" hole in the center of each clamp. Add the hardware.

5 Using the hardware and plastic dust-collection fittings shown in figure 1, slip the shutters on the pipe, assemble the base sides to the pipe, and then to the lathe. Give your dust collector a trial run. (Consider adding a blast gate if the connection will be a permanent part of a full-shop dust collection system.) If using a shop vacuum, fit on a 4" quick-connect fitting that reduces to the diameter of your hose.

Base Side Template

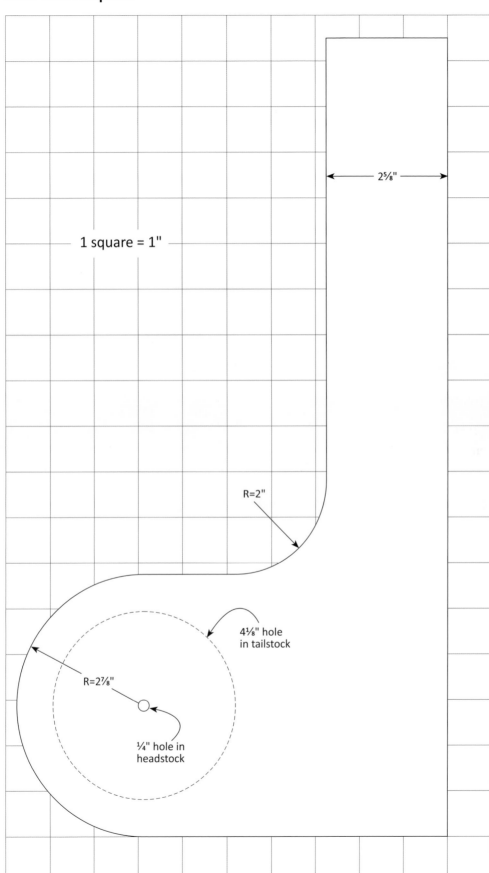

1 square = 1"

2⅝"

R=2"

R=2⅞"

4⅛" hole
in tailstock

¼" hole in
headstock

Note: For full-sized
lathes, lengthen the
sides to accomodate
the maximum swing
of your lathe while
providing clearance for
the dust collector pipe.

10 TIPS FOR TURNING TRICKY WOOD

Imperfections provide the perfect opportunity to create unique vessels

BY PHIL GAUTREAU

My specialty is turned wood bowls and vases made from highly figured, visually interesting wood. I've come to enjoy the challenges presented by blanks with unusual characteristics—bark inclusions, burl, spalting, quilting, voids, birds-eye, and other figured grain conditions. The tips explained here are especially important for turning the "tricky" wood described above. But you'll also find some of them helpful for many other types of turning projects.

I prefer air-dried or kiln-dried wood over green wood because dry wood is more stable. Also, dry stock can be turned from start to finish, without the intermediate drying that green wood requires.

Source wood creatively and carefully

1 Finding figured turning blanks is challenging, especially when you live in a big city like I do. I've purchased many blanks from a handful of trusted sellers on eBay. When I can't physically examine the wood, I have to rely on images supplied by the seller along with a detailed description. So I insist on good photos and accurate details with regard to species, dimensions, moisture content, density, and notable characteristics. It helps greatly when the seller has roughed out the blank so I can see more of the grain.

Catalog and protect your blanks

2 If I'm not planning on turning a blank right away, I label it to keep track of basic information—species, size, seller's name, purchase date, cost, and (in some cases) a client or craft show destination for the finished object. It's important to avoid moisture and temperature extremes when storing wood. The workshop I share in Brooklyn is fairly good in this regard. Green blanks, which I sometimes get from local sources, demand special treatment to avoid checks and cracks as the wood dries out. I saturate green wood with Anchorseal to slow down the drying process, thus minimizing cracks and splits.

Big leaf maple burl bowl, highly figured, with bark inclusions (10 × 7").

Spalted and quilted sugar maple bowl with bark inclusions (13½ × 3").

Yew wood vase with large bark inclusions and knots (4 × 9").

Allow unusual features to inspire the design

3 When ready to turn, I inspect the blank again for figuring, unusual markings, color or texture changes, or features requiring extra consideration. Now is the time to decide whether to accentuate or eliminate. For example, a piece of embedded bark could either be stabilized with adhesive or eliminated by keeping it out of the planned turning. A few of my finished pieces are shown above to illustrate how unusual characteristics can be incorporated into a design.

Work safe

4 I switched from safety goggles to a full face shield after a chunk of spalted maple sent me to the hospital for several stitches above my lip. When I began to turn yew blanks, I invested in a NIOSH-approved, double-cartridge respirator as protection against toxic wood dust. I use the respirator whenever I'm turning certain wood species

and always when I'm sanding any type of wood. It definitely provides more protection than disposable dust masks. I often wear fingerless weightlifter gloves because the padded palms provide cushioning. Having my fingers exposed still gives me plenty of feel when turning or sanding.

Have a good selection of "go-to" tools

5 Since there's no such thing as a "typical" tricky blank, my tool selection depends

1/4" Spindle gouge

3/8" Spindle gouge

3/8" Bowl gouge

1/2" Bowl gouge (conventional grind)

1½" Heavy-duty scraper (rounded bevel)

1½" Heavy-duty scraper (diagonal bevel)

1½" Heavy-duty scraper (flat bevel)

1/2" Skew chisel

1/2" Roundnose scraper

Multi-tip scraper

3/16" Diamond parting tool

Hollow master

(not shown) 3/4" Roughing gouge, 3/8" Bowl finishing scraper

5

on blank characteristics and the desired design. I've come to rely on the gouges, scrapers, and parting tools shown above. If the blank is fairly cylindrical to start, I'm likely to true it up using ½" bowl gouge with a swept-back grind. With odd-shaped blanks I use a parting tool to create relief cuts followed by cleanup with a roughing gouge or bowl gouge. My square end scraper does a good job of lightly cleaning up a bowl's exterior profile.

When hollowing the inside of the vessel I start with a diamond parting tool to a depth of approximately ½" to create the initial interior wall. Using this as a guide, I begin hollowing using a ½" or ¾" bowl gouge with conventional grind, taking scooping cuts. I clean up the interior with a variety of scrapers to blend and smooth the curved surfaces and flat bottom of the vessel. My favorites are a ¾" round/side cut scraper and a ½" roundnose scraper.

6

Watch your speed and feed pressure

6 I'll set speed as low as 300 rpm for imbalanced blanks, but spin to over 1,500 rpm for final true-up. I take care to present the tool to the wood carefully, avoiding aggressive feed pressure until I'm in an area where wood grain and density are consistent. It's important to know where the voids and variations are located in your blank. Areas with bark inclusions and density variations can throw off chunks. I try to minimize this by dropping rpm when turning a vulnerable section.

Stop more frequently

7 Turning tricky wood is the opposite of production lathe work. Every piece is unique, and I get the best results when I don't rush. It's important to stop the lathe frequently to examine the blank and see how it's reacting to the tooling or sanding. With the work stationary, I also see if new figuring or unusual characteristics have been revealed. This is an important rule for beginners as well as seasoned turners.

Stay sharp

8 Sharp tools are essential with any kind of turning, and with tricky wood I find myself spending even more time at the grinder. A sharp cutting edge will help keep a bark inclusion intact and enable me to shape the workpiece with more control and less feed pressure. I make sure my grinder has been dressed with a diamond wheel dresser to ensure a flat surface before setting the

tool bed to suit the proper bevel angle for the desired cut. I use a variety of bevel angles for my tools. I like the crispness of a swept-back grind on my gouges for exterior shaping of highly figured wood but use a more blunted traditional bevel for hollowing.

Improve patching and finishing skills

9 I prefer not to patch or fill, but I sometimes need to stabilize portions of a blank. I stabilize minor cracks or inclusions by applying liquid cyanoacrylate directly to the defect. For larger cracks or bark inclusions that contain voids, I mix gel cyanoacrylate and sawdust to create a fast-drying filler. It often helps to blow adhesive into cracks with an air compressor.

My standard finish involves two steps. First I apply a thin coat of WATCO Butcher Block Oil, wipe off the excess, and leave the piece to dry. After lightly buffing all surfaces with super-fine (0000) steel wool and wiping off any loose metal particles, I apply Boos Block Board Cream. This butcher block finish has the consistency of petroleum jelly, but I prefer applying it in liquid form after heating it. An important note: Prevent the Boos finish from caking up in bark inclusions by first saturating these with mineral oil.

Learn from your mistakes

10 My home is full of turned vessels that provided various lessons in what not to do. These pieces are still unique and beautiful; they just aren't good enough for me to sign and sell. Don't be discouraged if a tricky woodturning project doesn't come out as you had planned. It takes practice and at least a few mistakes to get a feel for this kind of turning.

9

SIX FINISHES FOR WOODTURNERS

Match the products with the projects

BY NICK COOK

There is no one finish suitable for all of your woodturning projects. So where do you start when selecting the right one? The criteria for choosing the most appropriate finish for your turning include the type of wood, the project's size and intended use, durability, drying time, desired sheen (satin or gloss), ease of application, solvent or water-based, cleanup, repairability, and whether the finish can be used with food. While that's a mouthful, I've simplified the selection process by focusing on six finishes that pretty much cover the gamut from small daily-use turnings to furniture parts to purely decorative pieces.

Before you even consider the appropriate finish, however, it's critical that you prepare the turning's surface properly because no finish will cover or hide torn grain, tool marks, or sanding scratches.

Finish 1: Seal the deal with CA

CA (cyanoacrylate) glues have proven ideal for small projects for quite some time. Recent developments have made some CAs more user-friendly and less likely to streak. The thinner viscosity of the Stick Fast CA Wood Finishing Kit makes it easier to apply.

Combined with the abrasive mesh and polishing compound (included in the kit), the multistep application process lets you produce a hard, durable finish quickly. And while the CA dries to a satin finish, it can be buffed to a high gloss. Be sure to heed safety precautions whenever working with CA.

Best uses: CAs are especially good for pens, wine stoppers, game calls, and other small projects.

Downside: Take care when applying CA finish. Use nitrile gloves to keep CA off your skin and to prevent fingers from sticking to paper towels. Wear safety glasses or face shield. Finally, ventilate the area as fumes can irritate. Buy a bottle of super solvent, just in case.

Application: The Stick Fast system contains thin CA finish, medium CA finish, aerosol CA activator, 400-grit sanding mesh, satin polish, and gloss polish. Similar to other CAs (by Satellite and Titebond), the finishing is simple. With the lathe at 300 to 1,000 rpm, apply a few drops of thin CA to your project with a paper towel (photo A). Then spray an aerosol mist of CA activator to cure the finish instantly and seal the wood (photo B). Sand the project

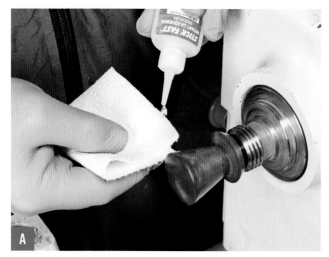

lightly with abrasive mesh before applying medium CA finish (photo C). Using the same technique, apply three to five coats of medium CA finish, misting with CA activator after each application. There's no need to sand between coats of medium CA finish. However, the surface should be sanded with a sanding mesh to a uniform dullness or satin appearance. Then, apply a small amount of satin CA polish with a paper towel (photo D), and buff until dry. Repeat with gloss polish for a gloss finish.

Finish 2: Let it shine with water-based

General Finishes Water-Based Wood Turner's Finish produces a rich amber tone that can be buffed to either a satin sheen or high gloss. It is food-safe, durable, and acid resistant. A water/urethane product, it's safe to work with and can be applied with a paper towel, brush, or sprayer. It applies easily and cleans up with water. More good news: it lets you achieve an attractive surface with only one coat for sealing and successive coats for a deeper luster. It is not seen as a filler for open-grain woods.

Best uses: Use this finish on salad bowls, platters, salt and pepper mills, and other utility items needing a durable finish.

Downside: Longer drying time means that you need to wait a bit to apply multiple coats.

Application: With the lathe off, apply water-based finish with paper towels (photo E) or brush it on with a foam brush. When applying multiple coats, the first application will dry in 30 to 45 minutes. Apply additional coats in 30 minutes. The final finish requires 5 to 7 days to cure to be food-safe. Use a flannel/cotton buffing wheel with carnauba wax to bring out the satin sheen following the final coat (photo F).

Finish 3: 3-step lacquer and wax

Gloss spray lacquer produces a glass-clear coating that goes on quickly. I prefer spraying over brushing. Here, I use Deft Clear Wood Finish. It dries fast and lets you reapply it in 30 minutes, with no sanding in between.

I like gloss lacquer over satin for building depth and because it contains fewer solids. Plus, you can repair it with a wax remover, light sanding, and another coat.

Best uses: Consider lacquer for small and large decorative turnings—vessels and other showy pieces. I don't recommend it for utility ware in contact with food.

Downside: Lacquer is flammable, and its fumes can be a problem. Spray only in well-ventilated areas and away from heat sources.

Application: Sand small hollow forms and similar decorative turnings through 600-grit sandpaper before applying as many as five coats of gloss lacquer. With the lathe turned off, clean the turning, and then hold the can's nozzle about 6 to 8" from the surface and spray (photo G). Rotate the turning for an even coat all around. Once dry, use #0000 steel wool with clear Briwax to level the surface (photo H). Buffing with a buffing wheel and carnauba wax will bring out the shine. For a satin finish, skip the steel wool and wax and apply a final coat of satin lacquer finish.

E

F

G

H

Finish 4: Strike it rich with oil

WATCO Penetrating Danish Oil, Natural, is a blend of boiled linseed oil and varnish that penetrates, seals, and adds a low luster. While it comes in several shades, such as natural, walnut, cherry, and golden oak, I find that natural is the obvious choice for all woods. It applies easily, though it takes time to achieve the desired result. The final finish is relatively soft, somewhat durable, and repairs quickly. And while it dries slowly, it produces a warm amber tone.

Best uses: WATCO Penetrating Danish Oil works well for general turnings and furniture such as the stool legs and seat shown below.

Downside: It dries slowly, typically taking several hours. In fact, I like to wait 24 hours before reapplication. Take care to properly dispose of your oily paper towels to avoid a spontaneous combustion fire. The product results in a satin sheen only.

Application: With the lathe off, wipe on a full wet coat of oil using a paper towel (photo I), and allow it to penetrate into the wood for 15 to 20 minutes. Then wipe off the excess and burnish it into the wood with a dry paper towel. This is not the same as burnishing raw wood with sandpaper. Allow the coat to dry 24 hours or more, and then reapply to build three to five coats over the course of several days or weeks. When the piece is completely cured (again, 24 hours after the final coat), apply a coat of wax using #0000 steel wool (photo J). Finally, buff the wood surfaces to achieve a pleasing satin sheen.

Finish 5: Speedy friction finishes

One popular category includes friction finishes such as HUT Crystal Coat and Mylands High Build Friction Polish. When correctly applied, the end result is a glowing high-gloss, one-coat finish executed in record time.

Best uses: Apply friction finish to pens and other small turnings.

Downside: Because of its alcohol base, oils from your hands can degrade a friction

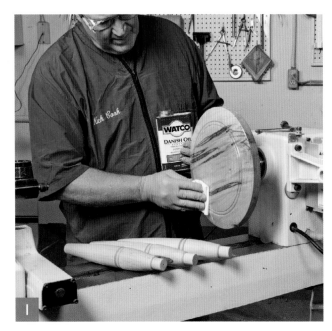

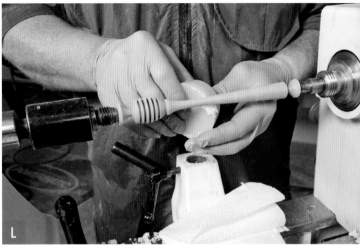

finish over time. Other ingredients include petroleum distillates, shellac, and waxes, making the finish highly flammable. Its fumes can irritate. To be safe, ventilate the work area, and stay away from any heat source.

Application: Sand surfaces to 600 grit or higher. Then, shake the bottle and add a few drops to a paper towel. With the lathe turned off, wipe the friction finish on the turning. Then, with the lathe on, hold a paper towel to the turning with moderate pressure.

Finish 6: Super-simple mineral oil

While mineral oil is a by-product from distilled petroleum, it remains one of the best food-safe finishes for utility items, and it's cheap! (I found a 16 oz. bottle at a local pharmacy for a few bucks.) It is colorless, odorless, tasteless, and totally inert. It goes on easily, can be applied on or off the lathe, and is easy to repair. Add beeswax to it to add more protection and sheen, but not on art objects. It collects dust. Reapply as needed.

Best uses: I use the mineral oil and wax combo for honey dippers, spurtles (stirring sticks), salad bowls, baby rattles, and other utility items.

Downside: This finish offers only low water resistance. It needs regular recoats and can collect dust. Expect a low luster only.

Application: Apply mineral oil with the lathe running at a low speed (photo K). (A plastic pump bottle like the ones used for liquid soap makes a great dispenser for your oil.) Use paper towels to make a pad, and pump a squirt or two of oil on it. Blot the oil to avoid a puddle on the pad as the spinning object will sling the liquid onto you and everything in the shop. As you apply the oil, burnish it into the spinning wood.

The addition of beeswax over the mineral oil adds luster and a little more protection. Then take a block of beeswax and apply it directly (photo L). Use a dry paper towel to buff the surface to a soft, fragrant finish.

CONTRIBUTORS

Small Projects & Gifts

Pen Turning 101
Written by: Joe Hurst-Wajszczuk
Photos by: Jim Osborn
Illustrations by: John Hartman

Pen Presentation Box
Written by: Marlen Kemmet
Photos by: Jim Osborn and
    Doug Hetherington
Illustrations by: Melanie Powell

Spiral Turned Box
Written by: Chris Pouncy
Photos by: Jim Osborn and
    Brian Francis
Illustrations by:
    Frank Rohrbach III

Inside-Out Ornament
Written by: Mike Kehs
Photos by: Larry Hamel-Lambert
    and Paul Anthony
Illustrations by: Mario Ferro

Lady's Purse Mirror
Written by: Jim Harrold
Turned by: Tom Schottle
Photos by: Ken Brady

Tree Ornament
Written by: Don Russell
Photos by: Stan Kaady

Pen Turning Made Easy
Written by: Tom Hintz
Photos by: Tom Hintz

Bowls

Stylish Salad Bowl Set
Written, designed, and turned by:
    Rex Burningham and
    Kip Christensen
Photos by: Chad Mcclung,
    Rex Burningham, and
    Kip Christensen

Turning a Calabash Bowl
Written by: Mike Mahoney
Photos by: Mike Mahoney
Illustrations by: Charles Lockhart

Live-Edge Bowls
Written by: Mike Kehs
Photos by: Paul Anthony
Illustrations by: Mario Ferro

Hollow Turned Vessel
Written by: Mike Kehs
Photos by: Jim Osborn and
    Paul Anthony
Illustrations by: James Provost

Furniture & Home

Classic Candlestick
Written by: Jon Hutchinson
Photos by: Ken Brady and
    Tom Hintz

Shop-Made Shaker Knobs
Written by: Jim Harrold
Photos by: Chad McClung
Illustrations by: Melanie Powell

Turn a Showy Finial
Written by: Jim Harrold
Designed and turned by:
    Craig Bentzley
Photos by: Paul Anthony

Turn & Weave a Shaker Stool
Written by: Kerry Pierce
Photos by: Brian Kellett and
    Kerry Pierce
Illustrations by: Vince Tanassi

Golden-Glow Oil Lamps
Written, designed, and turned by:
    Kip Christensen and
    Rex Burningham
Photos by: Michele Coleman,
    Rex Burningham, and
    Kip Christensen

Pencil-Post Bookshelf
Written by: Joe Hurst-Wajszczuk
Designed by: Andy Rae
Photos by: Larry Hamel-Lambert
Illustrations by: John Hartman

Turned Bookends
Written, designed, and turned by:
    Kip Christensen and
    Rex Burningham
Photos by: Morehead Marketing
    and Rex Burningham

Bamboo-Style Stool
Written by: Curtis Buchanan
Photos by: Morehead Photography
    and Doug Thompson
Illustrations by: Charles Lockhart

Kitchen

Turned Bottle Stoppers
Written by: A.J. Hamler
Illustrations by: Kevin Pierce
Photography by: Ken Brady and
 A.J. Hamler

Pepper Grinder & Salt Cellar
Written by: Lewis Kauffman
Photos by: Lewis Kauffman
Illustrations by: Kevin Pierce

Woodturner's Travel Mug
Written by: Jim Harrold
Turned by: Tom Schottle
Photos by: Ken Brady

Graceful Pepper & Salt Mills
Written by: Byron Young
Photos by: Larry Hamel-Lambert
 and Morehead Photography
Illustrations by: John Hartman

Rockin' Rolling Pin
Written by: Nick Cook
Photos by: Morehead Photography
 and Stan Kaady
Illustrations by: Melanie Powell

Big-Wheel Pizza Cutter
Written by: Marlen Kemmet
Photos by: Jim Osborn and
 Doug Hetherington
Illustrations by: Melanie Powell

Classic Cake Stand
Written by: Michael Kehs
Photos by: Larry Hamel-Lambert
 and Paul Anthony
Illustrations by: John Hartman

Sports & Outdoors

Shop-Made Baseball Bat
Written by: Ken Weaver
Photos by: Jim Osborn and
 A.J. Hamler
Illustrations by: Kevin Pierce

Picnic-Perfect Croquet Set
Written by: Marlen Kemmet
Designed and built by:
 Tom Whalley
Photos by: Larry Hamel-Lambert
 and Caleb Rizzuti
Illustrations by: John Hartman

Quick & Easy Duck Call
Written by: Byron Young
Photos by: Jim Osborn and
 Larry Hamel-Lambert
Illustrations by:
 Frank Rohrbach III

Garden Tool Handles
Written by: Tom Schottle
Photos by: Jim Osborn

Tools & Shop

**Shop-Made Collet
Helps You Get a Grip**
Written by: Jon T. Hutchinson
Photos by: A.J. Hamler
Illustrations by: Kevin Pierce

Shop-Made Mallets
Written by: Ken Burton
Photos by: Jim Osborn and
 Paul Anthony
Illustrations by: Patrick Welsh

Lathe Dust Collector
Written by: Jim Harrold with
 Jerry Bolin and Bill Sands
Photos by: Morehead Photography
Illustrations by:
 Frank Rohrbach III

**10 Tips for Turning
Tricky Wood**
Written by: Phil Gautreau
Photos by: Micah Rubin

Six Finishes for Woodturners
Written by: Nick Cook
Photos by: Brad Newton

INDEX

Note: Page numbers in *italics* indicate projects.

MORE GREAT BOOKS *from*
SPRING HOUSE PRESS

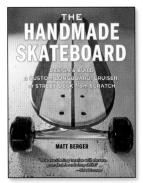

The Handmade Skateboard
ISBN: 978-1-940611-06-8
List Price: $24.95 | 160 Pages

Classic Wooden Toys
ISBN: 978-1-940611-34-1
List Price: $24.95 | 176 Pages

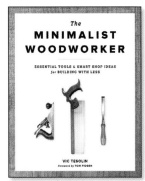

The Minimalist Woodworker
ISBN: 978-1-940611-35-8
List Price: $24.95 | 152 Pages

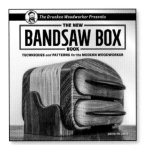

The New Bandsaw Box Book
ISBN: 978-1-940611-32-7
List Price: $19.95 | 120 Pages

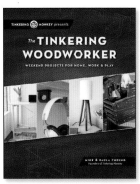

The Tinkering Woodworker
ISBN: 978-1-940611-08-2
List Price: $24.95 | 160 Pages

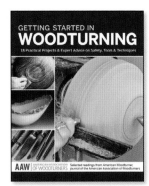

Getting Started in Woodturning
ISBN: 978-1-940611-09-9
List Price: $27.95 | 224 Pages

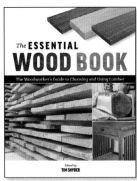

The Essential Wood Book
ISBN: 978-1-940611-37-2
List Price: $27.95 | 216 Pages

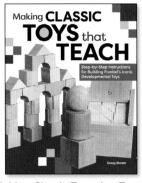

Making Classic Toys that Teach
ISBN: 978-1-940611-33-4
List Price: $24.95 | 144 Pages

Make Your Own Cutting Boards
ISBN: 978-1-940611-45-7
List Price: $24.95 | 168 Pages

SPRING HOUSE PRESS

Look for these Spring House Press titles at your favorite bookstore, specialty retailer, or visit *www.springhousepress.com*.
For more information about Spring House Press, call 717-208-3739 or email us at *info@springhousepress.com*.